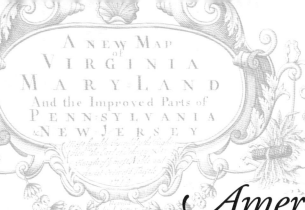

America's First
Factory Town

Ellicotts' Mills in 1854, the eighteenth-century factory town grown into a city.
Ellicotts' Mills, Md., Chromolithograph by E. Sachse & Co.
(*See related image on pages 112–13.*)
Maryland Historical Society.

America's First Factory Town

The Industrial Revolution in Maryland's Patapsco River Valley

Henry K. Sharp

Chesapeake Book Company

BALTIMORE, MARYLAND

2017

Published with the support of

The Howard County Executive and Council
Howard County Historical Society
Patapsco Heritage Greenway, Inc.
Howard Heritage Fund
Charles L. Wagandt

Chesapeake Book Company
112 Elmhurst Road,
Baltimore, MD 21210
© 2017 Henry K. Sharp

Names: Sharp, Henry K., 1959- author.
Title: The first American factory town : the industrial revolution in
   Maryland's Patapsco River Valley / Henry K. Sharp.
Description: Baltimore : Chesapeake Book Company, [2017] | Includes
   bibliographical references and index.
Identifiers: LCCN 2017025033 | ISBN 9780982304969 (pbk. : alk. paper)
Subjects: LCSH: Industrial revolution--Maryland—Patapsco River Valley. |
   Patapsco River Valley (Md.)—Economic conditions. | Patapsco River Valley
   (Md.)—History.
Classification: LCC HC107.M32 P3869 2017 | DDC 330.9752/02—dc23
LC record available at https://lccn.loc.gov/2017025033

Printed in the United States of America
The paper used in this publication meets the minimum requirements of the
American National Standard for Information Sciences Permanence of Paper for
Printed Library Materials ANSI Z39.48-1984

Designed by James F. Brisson

For Hank and Vicky

Blacks

Asquiths

Ellicotts upper u

Saw Mill

N

Ellicotts

Hinton

Mendenhalls

Dr Pues

Cornthwai

Howards

Martins

Dorseys

Wests

Dorseys

Hockle

Owings

Owings

Run

Deen

Spurriers

Though mechanical time can, in a sense, be speeded up or run backward, like the hands of a clock or the images of a moving picture, organic time moves in only one direction—through the cycle of birth, growth, development, decay, and death—and the past that is already dead remains present in the future that has still to be born.

Lewis Mumford

Technics and Civilization

1934

A NEW MAP
of
VIRGINIA
MARY-LAND
And the Improved Parts of
PENNSYLVANIA
& NEW JERSEY

Most humbly Inscrib'd to the Right
Hon.ble the Earl of Orkney &c.
Knight of y.e most Noble and
Ancient order of y.e Thistle
1719

Revis'd by I. Senex

PENNSYLVANIA PARS

CHESTER

BALTEMORE

COUNTY

CÆCIL

COUNTY

TALBOT

COUNTY

M A R Y L A N D

ANN ARUNDEL

COUNTY

KENT CO.

STAFFORD

COUNTY

ANN ARUNDEL M.
PORTLAND M.

CALVERT

CHARLES

CALVERT

COUN

DORCHESTER

COUN

COUNTY

MARY

COUN

C H E S A P E A K

B A Y

V I R G I N I A

WESTMORLAND Co.

RAPPAHANOCK COUN

NORTHUMBERLAND

COUNTY

LANCASTER

Rappahanock River

KING GEORGE

KING & QUEEN

MIDLEX CO.

NEW KENT CO.

HENRICO Co.

CHARLES

CITY CO.

SURRY CO.

ISLE OF WIGHT CO.

Cape Charles

Bay of Chesapeake

TABLE OF CONTENTS

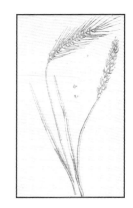

Hooks

Ellicotts upper   Stoney Hill

Saw Mill

Ellicotts

Menderihalls   Balt? C?

Cornthwaits

Dorseys

artins   Ridgely

Dorseys

Hockley

Deep Run

America's First Factory Town

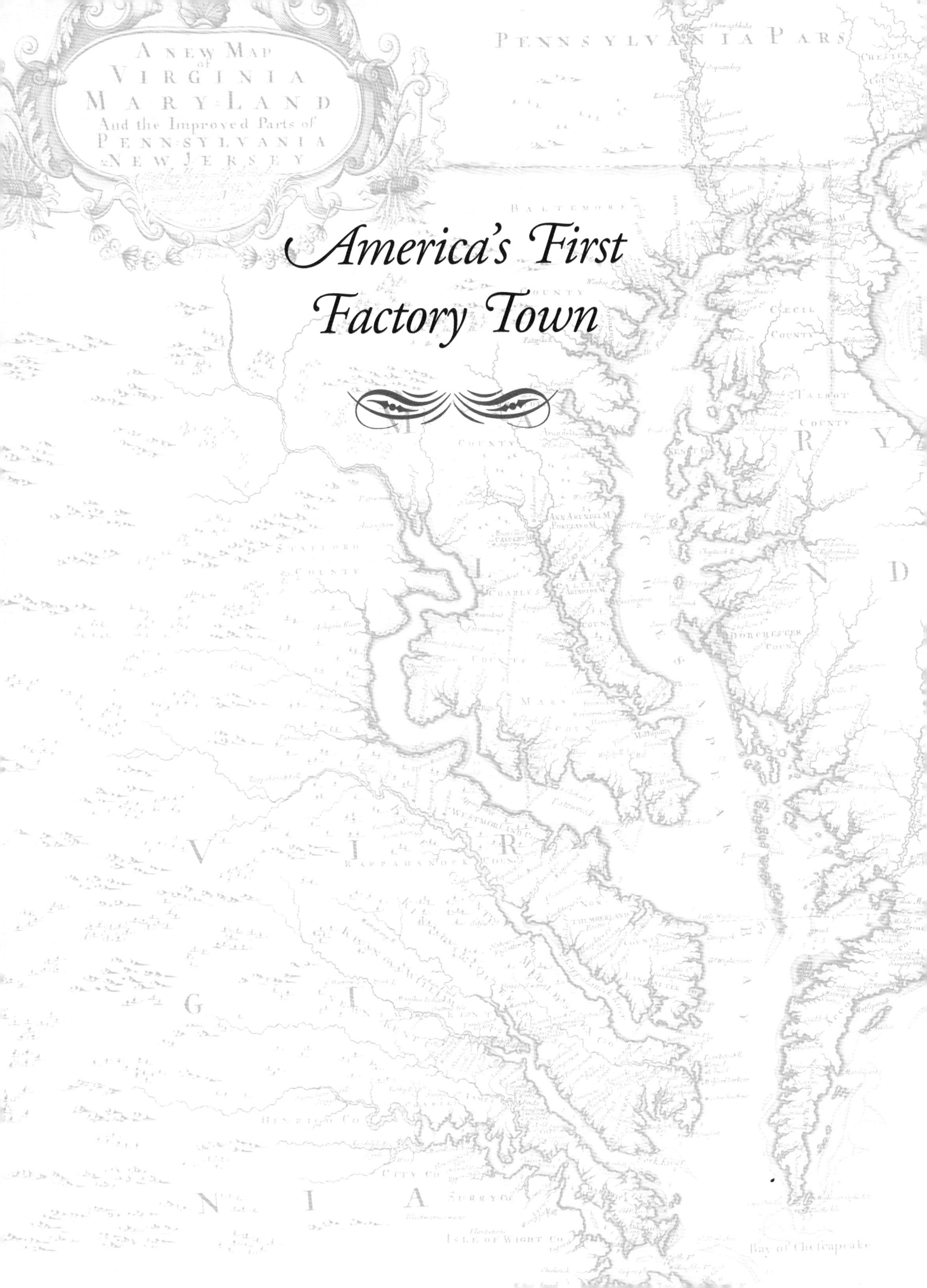

Agriculture

Industry

Allegories of Agriculture and Industry, sculpted in 1868 by Elias Robert,
stand high on the facade of the Gare d'Austerlitz in Paris.

Photograph by the author

Agriculture, Industry, and Architecture

OVER THE LAST EIGHT YEARS it has been my privilege to join the faculty of an architecture design studio in Paris, France. Each summer, my colleagues and I work with a small group of American students, and our wide-ranging explorations take us beyond the familiar places and promenades of the great city. One unsung building I enjoy revealing to them is the vast Gare d'Austerlitz, a railroad terminal completed in 1869. This magnificent industrial structure was one of the largest iron and glass railroad sheds at the time of its construction, as it is still. Along its flank, a boldly carved entrance pavilion fronts the quais on the river Seine. It is a grand gateway to the city. High above, on each side of the pavilion's limestone facade, two allegorical sculptures gaze outward: *Agriculture* and *Industry*. *Agriculture* stands before a wooden plow and grips a sickle in her right hand; her left cradles a sheaf of wheat. *Industry* leans against a steam locomotive, her stiffened right arm sustaining her weight as her hand rests on the engine's boiler barrel, a sledgehammer at her feet. Her left hand steadies an honorific antique vase at her hip. Scores of hastening passengers—and a few attentive architecture students—pass beneath these stolid, lofty figures every day.

Agriculture and *Industry* built a new world in the nineteenth century. They have underpinned all rapidly modernizing nation-states, and the potent symbolism that appealed to the builders of a nineteenth-century Parisian railway station is equally pertinent to our side of the Atlantic. In the half-century after the ironworkers and masons tightened the last bolts and struck the final mortar joints at the Gare d'Austerlitz, the United States matured into a world

power, a new nation raised on the foundations of *Agriculture* and *Industry*.

In America the broad brush of industry swept from New England across the upper Midwest, barely grazing the agrarian Old South and the new ground of the Great Plains. So our own geographic history depicts *Agriculture* and *Industry* as complementary but distinct regional entities, the sibling allegories set at opposite corners of an imposing stone facade. *Agriculture* feeds the population that *Industry* employs. *Agriculture* supplied the essential commodity for the *Industry* that brought New England's factories and factory towns to national dominance: cotton.

Yet the view of *Agriculture* and *Industry* as correlative but distinct agents of American modernization does not present a complete picture. In the lands surrounding the Chesapeake, agriculture and industry proved far more closely interwoven than in New England, and the character of that web of relationships marked the industrializing landscape of the colonies, and then of the new nation, in distinctive ways. Early in the history of America's industrial development, a full generation before the textile industry gave its more extensive imprint to Narragansett and Massachusetts Bays, factories and factory villages reshaped the Chesapeake. Those factories were large-scale flour mills.

Flour milling for the international market sparked a region-wide dynamic for substantial and rapid urbanization, the likes of which the Chesapeake had never before experienced. For more than a century, colonial authorities had attempted to impose an urban framework on the region's widely dispersed settlements, an effort that was almost universally unsuccessful. Even the first purely industrial process to take root—iron manufacturing—failed to yield the hoped-for impetus for urbanization. Chesapeake iron conformed to an agricultural model, while wheat garnered sheaves of mill villages and towns, and, in the case of Baltimore, whole cities.

It seems counterintuitive, but the assertion that the American factory system developed from wheat rather than iron even finds an unintentional reflection in the hands of our Parisian allegories, with the tasseled wheat stalk *Agriculture* cherishes and the iron boilerplate at *Industry's* touch. These attributes are reversed in our story—one paradox of the many that make historical inquiry such a challenging and fascinating project. In early America, the processes and forms industrialization took had a wider scope than first meets the eye.

The classic narrative of the American Industrial Revolution begins in late-eighteenth century Rhode Island. British immigrant—and industrial spy—Samuel Slater used his specialized knowledge of British textile equipment and systems to assemble the precision machinery for the earliest successful cotton thread mill in America. The cascading waters of Rhode Island's Blackstone River turned the wheels and gearing of his mill at Pawtucket for the first time in 1793, and the remarkable survival of this small, wood-frame factory building has only enhanced its position as progenitor of an entire industry, and of the industrial transformation of America. From Slater's diminutive factory, the chronology advances to the innovative organization of Francis Cabott Lowell's Waltham, Massachusetts, cotton-fabric factory of 1813, then attains early fulfillment in the immense success of the textile mills in the Boston Associates' planned industrial city of Lowell, begun nearby in 1822.

Pawtucket, Waltham, and Lowell; they are the triumvirate of early American industrial architecture, and their importance is indisputable. The textile technology imported from Britain in the period of the early Republic unleashed upon the American landscape a teeming progeny across New England and the upper mid-Atlantic. Within three generations the giant factories of the textile juggernaut gathered up some poor Southern relations and culminated in the smoky cities of heavy industry and the immense corporations embodying and embodied in Pittsburgh, Pullman, and Detroit: steel, railroads, and automobiles.

But New England textiles did not progress into the expansive reality of industrial North America unaccompanied; the story reaches more deeply and broadly into the American colonial experience. America's industrial origins and the origins of America's industrial architecture do not reside complacently in Slater's building and in the textile factory precedents of the British midlands. Our industrial genesis begins earlier, and farther south.

We find it in colonial and early republican Maryland, on the banks of the Patapsco, the great river descending to Baltimore harbor and the Chesapeake Bay. The "great falls of Patapsco" drove textile mill wheels before Waltham and Lowell, and at a scale larger than Slater ever imagined. Even so, that achievement occurs not at the beginning but at the end of our story. The arc of the Patapsco's industrial history reaches back to the large-scale enterprise for merchant flour milling the Quaker Ellicott brothers established in 1771, and lengthening still, makes landfall among the antecedent grist mills, ironworks, and tobacco plantations of the colonial landscape.

Here is the Chesapeake paradox: the Industrial Revolution emerged in a manner that was not at all revolutionary. Iron-making accommodated itself completely to the dispersed, non-urban, agricultural landscape that tobacco cultivation had fostered. Wholesale flour production and its commercial connections brought, instead, a new urban mentality and expression to the region: a spectacular architectural, economic, and cultural transformation.

The trajectory of the Chesapeake's transformation leads to five young men. In effect, these Quaker brothers, natives of Bucks County, Pennsylvania, were brilliant and prescient systems engineers. Joseph, the eldest, and Andrew; Nathaniel, Thomas and John . . . the Ellicott brothers set their sights on the falls of Maryland's Patapsco River in the spring of 1771. Their incisive and far-reaching achievement is the heart of this book.

No part of that achievement would have been possible without the topographic conditions particular to Chesapeake Maryland. But the falls that produced the driving force of that industrial and urban revolution could as readily turn against the human hands they aided. The tragic losses that a devastating flood carved onto the heart of the Ellicott brothers' industrial town nearly a century after its founding is a sobering coda to this new and significant story. And that history cannot be neglected for long.

A NEW MAP
of
VIRGINIA
MARY-LAND
And the Improved Parts of
PENNSYLVANIA
& NEW JERSEY

PART I

Tobacco and Iron

Nicotiana major latifolia. C. B. Pin. 169. — J. 117.
Ant. Tabacco. — Gall. Nicotiane ou Tabac.
Tobacco Plant. New York Public Library.

John Senex, *A new map of Virginia, Maryland and the improved parts of Pennsylvania & New Jersey,* 1719. Boston Public Library.

CHAPTER ONE

Topography makes everything happen

Most picturesque and attractive of all these waters are the estuaries called the East and Middle Branches of the Patapsco. The first of these reaches from the harbor of Baltimore to Chesapeake Bay, a distance of twelve miles; its greatest breadth being at the mouth, between North Point and the Bodkin, a distance of nearly five miles. After leaving the Lazaretto, just outside of the harbor, it is a lovely sheet of water, having undulating banks of various-colored clays rising on both shores somewhat abruptly, sometimes to a height of twenty feet above the water-level, with the tides of the Chesapeake rolling through every part of it in dark-green waves.[1]

DOES GEOGRAPHY MAKE HISTORY? Undeniably, its role is critical. Thomas Scharf acknowledged as much by devoting the opening pages of his monumental history of Baltimore City and county to a detailed discussion of topography. Published in 1881, Scharf's tome runs to a daunting 947 pages, yet at rare moments his sometimes oppressive thoroughness rises to the level of poetry—here, for example, in his description of the tidewater Patapsco, the roads beyond Baltimore harbor.

The Patapsco River opens to the expanse of the Chesapeake near the far northwestern shore of the bay. Like all the other great western shore rivers, the Patapsco reaches northwest, through the tidewater and the piedmont to the front-range hills of the Appalachians. From the northerly Susquehanna to the southerly James, rivers course through the land like so many parallel ribbons and find near symmetrical reflection in the smaller streams of the eastern shore. Together they form the myriad inlets and coves well known to sailors of the dark green waves.

The bay's intricate coastline greatly influenced the nature of colonial settlement and development. Myriad inlets and rivers enabled widespread and ready access to rich agricultural lands not only by shallow-draft sloops and flats, but also by the tall ships of the Atlantic sea lanes. Vessels could moor at innumerable wharves and landings and take on hogsheads of tobacco direct from planters. Profitable trading existed without the need for centralized urban markets, and ambitious, individualistic tobacco planters felt little impetus to create the town-based social, religious, and economic organization common to New England. Despite official efforts to create a system of towns, topography and tobacco kept the Chesapeake population dispersed.[2]

Sailing inland from its wave-ridden expanse at the bay, one finds the wide Patapsco diverging into three branches. The easternmost—also called the "Northwest Branch" since it turns west from an opening on the northern side of the river—terminates in the basin of Baltimore harbor. Around this "inner harbor" the city of Baltimore began to develop in 1730, initially bounded to the north and east by a small tributary called Jones' Falls. So long as the tobacco regime held sway, Baltimore Town remained small and underdeveloped.

The Middle Branch, leading west to Gwynn's Falls, departs from the Patapsco below the peninsula that shapes the southern bounds of Baltimore harbor. It, too, opens from the northern side of the

Tides: Benjamin Henry Latrobe, *First View of the Coast of Virginia, Hazy Morning, 1796.* Maryland Historical Society.

river and tends toward the northwest. On its shores in 1731 the Baltimore Ironworks took form, an early example of Maryland's first industry.

Past the Middle Branch, the Patapsco proper curves briefly southwest, then west, then regains its northwesterly course shortly before the fall line, the terminus of river transport. Here colonists cleared a beach on the southern bank of the river and called it Elk Ridge Landing, after the high ground looming to the west.

Through these high western hills the Patapsco flows to the tidewater. Again under Scharf's pen, its descent from the Appalachians takes on a poetic character:

> Most of [the Patapsco's] tributaries belong to Carroll County, and the principal ones rise in Parr's Ridge, at a distance of twenty-five to thirty miles northwest of Baltimore City. These streams have frequent bends, and plunge rapidly over beds of broken rocks in ravines between the high, abrupt hills. After reaching the border of the Second District, the [North] Branch becomes a wide, rapid creek of clear water, running through a more open country, with beds of limestone near on the one hand, and with the dark, forbidding hills of the Soldiers' Delight region on the other. After reaching the vicinity of Marriottsville, it unites, forms a fork with the West Branch, and then with redoubled energy rolls through a wide channel between the high domes of dark-gray rock until it reaches its extreme expanse among the bo[u]lders at Ellicotts' City. At this point it plunges over a great dam (no longer a natural one), and furnishes power for several of the largest flour-mills and cotton-factories in the country. From thence, after being somewhat contracted by the rocky barriers which arrest its expanse near Ilchester, and passing through the deep trough to Orange Grove Mills, it opens out into a beautiful, wide, deep valley until the wide gap is reached at the Relay House. From that point it flows steadily, and more narrowly, on through an alluvial plain until it is lost in the broad estuary at tide-water.[3]

These becalmed waters wash the shoreline at Elk Ridge Landing. Upstream, the tumbling north and west branches of the Patapsco enter a region where the dramatic change in elevation gives the rapids a drop of 193 feet over approximately ten miles.[4] The power of falling waters like these ruled American industry through more than its first century of development. Expressed in terms of cumulated annual horsepower, steam engines surpassed waterfalls only in the 1870s, the decade before Scharf wrote, and within a generation electricity would rise to displace steam.[5] It was water, then, that drove the industrial history of the Patapsco Valley, and that water possessed a dual nature: falls and tides. These two states conditioned a pair of cultures, one driven by mechanical motion from the force of cascades and the other fostered by ready shipping on placid channels.

At first industry occupied a place and scale well within the long-established realm of Tidewater tobacco culture. Later, like the new nation just then forming, it grew into something very different, with a pronounced urban form. Tobacco culture had proved resolutely rural, and when iron first came to harness the region's falls, it too failed to bring the cities that colonial authorities had tried for decades to create. The colonial iron industry remained as distant from urban sources and influences as had tobacco.

Agriculture, though, was not yet done with *Industry*. The region-wide shift from tobacco to wheat brought about more far-reaching changes and provided the basis for the culturally transforming union of industry and urbanism. Wheat gave America its first industrial towns. The falls and tides of Maryland's eloquent Patapsco recount this critical but neglected aspect of the nation's industrial origins, and that story is not simply local in nature and significance. It begins with tobacco and iron.

Falls: Benjamin Henry Latrobe, *Sketch of Washington's Island, James River, Virginia, 1796.*
Maryland Historical Society.

Topography makes everything happen 7

All aspects of the Chesapeake tobacco economy are depicted here in "A Tobacco Plantation": enslaved Africans at work assembling, packing, and rolling hogsheads; a wealthy planter seated at a table, pipe in hand, with a Chinese export porcelain punch bowl beside him; a merchant standing with quill pen at the ready, his ledger open on the table; tobacco fields overlooked by a Virginia house beyond; and, in the distance, a forest of ships' masts rising out of the bay.

From F. W. Fairholt, *Tobacco, Its History and Associations* (London, n.d.). George Arents Collection, New York Public Library.

A TOBACCO PLANTATION

Printed for & Sold by BOWLES and CARVER, Nº 69 in Sᵗ Pauls Church Yard. LONDON.

CHAPTER TWO

Tobacco planting
defeats town planning

BY THE TIME THE Lords Baltimore formally established the proprietorship of Maryland on their New World lands in 1634, staple-crop agriculture dominated the landscape. The near-catastrophic seasoning that ravaged the first European settlers in the Chesapeake also darkened glittering colonial dreams of acquiring eastern spices, native gold, and exotic agricultural produce. Faced with an increasingly sober analysis of regional prospects after Jamestown's visionary founding in 1607, King James himself revoked the Virginia Company's charter in 1624 and ordered lands that were to have been held by the company and tenanted to be released to the public. Similarly, inducements of property for immigrants to Maryland undermined the medieval notions of land tenure maintained by the Lords Baltimore. Their "quasi-feudal society" fell of necessity to colonial survival.[1] Tobacco supplanted them all.

The promise of fee-simple land ownership in both colonies enhanced immigration and dispersal as settlers acquired lands on or near the Chesapeake's abundant waterways. English merchant houses commissioned sailing ships at London or Bristol or Liverpool to collect Chesapeake tobacco prepared for sale. Planters consigned their harvests — dried, stemmed, and pressed into hogsheads — to these

A Map of Virginia and Maryland, made by John Speed in 1676, gives a schematic representation of the plantations seated all along the Chesapeake's waterways and optimistically locates a number of towns that failed to develop, including the original site of Baltimore Town.

Norman B. Leventhal Map Center Collection, Boston Public Library.

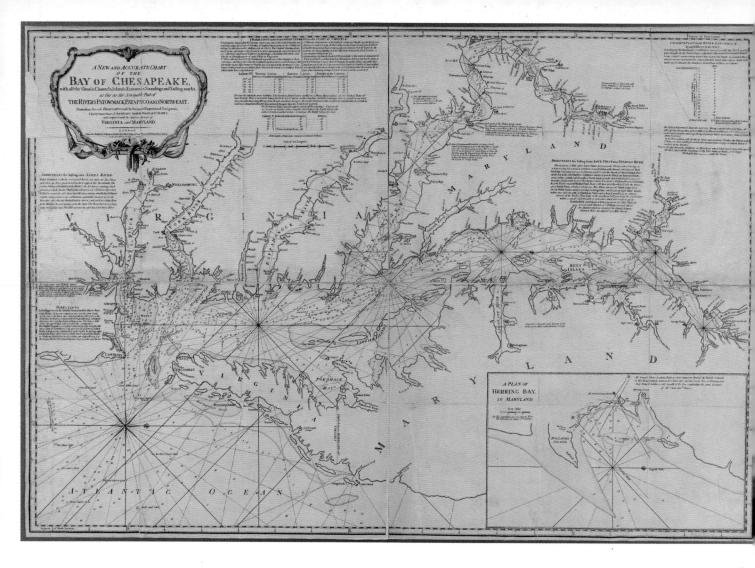

A new and accurate chart of the Bay of Chesapeake: with all the shoals, channels, islands, entrances, soundings and sailing marks as far as the navigable part of the rivers Patowmack, Patapsco and northeast (1776).

Lionel Pincus and Princess Firyal Map Division, New York Public Library.

merchants or their agents, often ship captains, who glided up the rivers and inlets to the wharves and landings serving one or more plantations. Subsequent to transport and sale in England, the merchant house allotted a credit to the planter's account, less freight charges and commission, against which the planter could draw for goods to be delivered the next season. This consignment system suppressed the growth of a local merchant class, and, where such individuals can be identified, colonial records indicate that seventeenth-century stores carried no permanent inventory of merchandise. Shipments from England extended only so far as the sales of tobacco hogsheads would allow. Neither economics nor agriculture gave an incentive to concentrate the colonial Chesapeake population in towns.[2] At the end of the seventeenth century, the market for tobacco stagnated. Oversupply, international trading battles, and outright war disrupted exchange, but naval confrontations between England and France in those years yielded an indirect but critical result. French interception of English merchant ships introduced continental authorities to the profits Chesapeake tobacco could bring. After 1713, the French tobacco trading monopoly opened to Chesapeake produce, and through the 1770s planting experienced a renewed vigor in the colonies as prices followed a long-term upward trend.[3]

Marketing evolved in the eighteenth century, as well. With the 1707 British Act of Union, Scottish merchants gained the right to participate in colonial trade. But rather than join the established system of their English brethren, Scots merchants organized a parallel market based in a network of strategically sited local stores with resident managers. These Glasgow merchants, backed by French buyers who paid a set price, took colonial tobacco not on consignment but as an outright purchase. Planters who heretofore had to bear the whole risk of freight, loss, and uncertain future pricing, now enjoyed immediate and steady credit. Unlike their seventeenth-century counterparts, Scottish-owned stores retained goods all year, as sales of merchandise accounted for a substantial component of Scots merchants' in-

come. Moreover, the Virginia Tobacco Inspection Act of 1730 and the similar Maryland act of 1747 instituted a state-controlled mechanism to regulate the quality of tobacco sold. These measures gave legal as opposed to customary standing to a specific number of collection warehouses per county, sited near wharves or landings. At these points of consolidation, state inspectors rejected inferior leaf and guaranteed higher prices by grading tobacco approved for sale. They issued tobacco notes or scrip as legal tender, and this negotiable paper permitted planters of any size to make purchases valued at less than a whole hogshead from any merchant or store. Currency freed them from total dependence on a single shipper, merchant house, or large planter.[4]

Despite these centralized collection warehouses and the growing "store system" of trading, the architectural environment remained, like the population, diffuse. The very few "clustered settlements" that developed in the region filled limited economic functions, and most lacked the varied craft, religious, and political activities common to urban life.[5] This is not to say that colonial authorities failed to try. Maryland instituted a series of new town proclamations and acts beginning in 1668, subsequently rewritten, enlarged, and reorganized for the next forty years. Each successive act reworked the previous town list, retaining or expunging some old names and adding new ones. These earnest attempts to establish an urban framework for colonial life by limiting shipping to authorized ports were roundly ignored at every stage in the debate. Lacking sufficient economic reasons to centralize shipping, colonial Chesapeake citizens made no effort to do so.[6]

The majority of commissioners appointed to design the wished-for towns employed a standard grid plan. In only a few cases did surveyors apply more sophisticated baroque elements, such as axial avenues terminating in public buildings, squares, or monuments, as typified in the colonial capitals of Annapolis and Williamsburg. Of all the towns authorized, a relative few actually came to be organized on the ground, and of those fewer still matured beyond a simple grid of mostly empty one-acre grassy lots.[7] Colonial building in this overwhelmingly rural society was largely limited to the plantation structures tobacco culture required.

The buildings developed organically, one might say, out of the peculiar geographic and economic environment of the colonial Chesapeake. The greatest number were "earthfast" structures—posts set in the ground—with relatively light frames that reflected the abundant timber and limited labor and capital of the colonial environment. Chesapeake builders dug holes for posts, mortised uprights to ground-laid sills, or affixed sills to wooden blocks set into the ground. Of these structural variations the common feature was an impermanent foundation, or none at all. Most floors consequently were earthen. Where builders did employ sills, plank floors were possible. Lateral stability for walls and roof framing depended not on complex diagonal braces integrated with the frame, but instead on a tightly nailed sheathing of riven clapboards. Lapped to shed water, these clapboards served as both shingle and siding. Chimneys, for the most part, were even more perishable than earthfast posts. Laborers built them up of wood daubed with clay. These methods saved builders the time and expense of preparing stone or brick foundations, and significantly reduced the number of labor-intensive carpentry joints traditionally required to secure a structural

Brigs ride at anchor in the placid summer waters of the Chesapeake Bay in this sketch made by Archibald Robinson entitled, *View of the Head of Chesapeake Bay, shewing Turky Point, Elk River, Sassafras River, Spesuti Island. 22nd August 1777.* Spencer Collection, New York Public Library.

Spencer Hall Shipyard, Gray's Inn Creek, Kent County, Maryland, ca. 1760, depicts a mid-eighteenth-century Chesapeake river landing with limited development. Maryland Historical Society.

Patent Certificate for Talbott's Vineyard, 1689. Maryland State Archives.

frame.[8] Thus was born the "Virginia House," and with judicious repairs this economical structure could last more than half a century.[9] The more resources a planter might devote to tobacco production instead of building, the greater his profits.

Edward Talbott, of Anne Arundel County, was one of those planters. Among the first to settle the Patapsco Valley, Talbott obtained a warrant in December 1688 for a survey of a tract "Lying in ye woods on A Ridge Called Elk Ridge . . . by ye main branch of Patapsco River."[10] The clerks at the proprietary land office dutifully recorded the certificate for 2,900 acres in 1689, and may have smiled at the felicitous name the applicant had chosen: "Talbott's Vineyard." Genesis relates of the great deluge: when the refugees on the Ark stepped down to dry land and began to repopulate the Earth, "Noah, a man of the soil, was the first to plant a vineyard."[11] As with Father Noah, reclaiming high ground from the flood, so with Edward Talbott and his plantation clearings in the dense woods of Elk Ridge.

Talbott's new ground took shape in two lots, a home plantation of some seventy acres, and an outlying quarter of twenty. For thirty years Talbott lived in a Virginia house with two principal rooms, a common type called a hall-chamber dwelling. He raised a family and hung his tobacco to dry in several large earthfast barns. Talbott's son John shared one of the dwelling's two low, garret bedrooms with his siblings, and wandered the forests and fields above the Patapsco as a boy. He obtained title to the plantation in 1726, and six years later applied for a renewed patent.

Toward summer's end, 1732, some forty-five years after the elder Talbott had begun to fell that ridgetop woodland, Deputy County Surveyor Henry Ridgley described the Vineyard's plantation buildings and organization in remarkable detail. Ridgley explored both parts of the plantation, marking the metes and bounds of John Talbott's patent and describing the improvements already in existence. On the larger parcel of "a boute 60 or 70 acres" of cultivated land, he found an "Endeferent Old Worm fence in Corne feilds and paster ground." Adjacent "a paild garden 80 foot Squar [and] a Small paild yard," stood "One Old Dwelling house With posts in the ground & almost rotten 2 Roomes plank floors above and below 30 foot Long 18 foot Wide." His inventory continued: "one other Old Dwelling house for a Kitchin 25 foot Long 16 foot Wide Very Much Out of Repair and Decay,"

with the typical earthen floor, since Ridgley did not specify "plank." An "Old Milk house" and an "Old hen house" stood nearby, then followed "4 Old 50 foot Tobacco houses 22 foot Wide Very Much Decay'd and Some of them Blown aside"—large but lightly framed gable-roofed structures fallen into disuse and, dare we say it, gone with the wind.[12]

While the construction date of Talbott's plantation buildings cannot be known with absolute certainty, a reasonable supposition places them shortly after he acquired the property in 1688, right at the beginning of the tobacco depression. His near forty-four-year-old structures showed their age. These observations conform in every respect to the economic realities of Chesapeake tobacco culture: investment in hogsheads not houses. By 1732, though, a shadow of change was crossing the land, and Ridgley observed this, too, at son John Talbott's cornfield and pasture land. Of all of the buildings he described, in fact, the only one Ridgley did not disparage as being "old" or "rotten" was a "Corne house 30 foot Long 12 foot Wide."[13] Like Ridgley, we, too, can see this conspicuous juxtaposition of deteriorated, late seventeenth-century tobacco buildings with a new, well-maintained corn house—and the word "corn" here doubtless used in the British manner for cereal harvests in general, not simply Indian maize. The future, critically, no longer belonged exclusively to tobacco but now also to grain. Over the course of a generation, the grain trade would lead a dramatic economic and architectural transformation of Maryland.

Talbott's plantation was situated on high ground above the falls of the Patapsco, in Anne Arundel County, and like others put into cultivation at this time had to make use of "rolling roads" descending to the river channel below the ridge. Talbott and his distant neighbors would have pressed their tobacco into hogsheads and rolled them down to the river for shipment.[14] An exact founding date for the Elk Ridge Landing is not known, but the settlement and cultivation of terrain rising to the west presupposes access to river transport back at the fall line. The landing consequently must have been in use in the last quarter of the seventeenth century; in any case, by 1746 it was called "old."[15]

Our county surveyor Henry Ridgley visited the landing in March 1729, three-and-a-half years before he measured out John Talbott's patent, and there he inventoried "one 40 foot Tobacco house" in a small glade in nearly six hundred acres of unclaimed for-

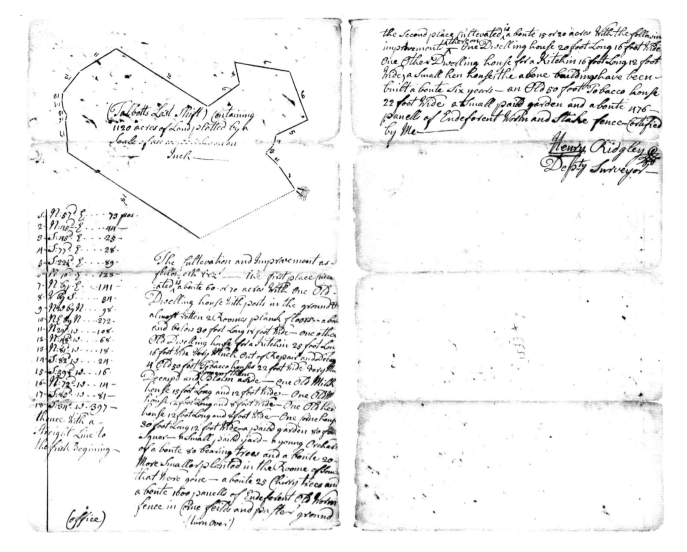

Deputy County Surveyor Henry Ridgley's notes describing Edward Talbott's deteriorated earthfast buildings and son John Talbott's new corn house in 1732.

Maryland State Archives.

est land. "I take the building to be a boute half Worn," Ridgley observed, implying a construction date of around 1710, if Talbott's deteriorated forty-year-old structures are a reasonable guide.[16] All five of Talbott's tobacco houses had a footprint of fifty-by-twenty-two feet, slightly larger than the landing warehouse, which probably conformed to the more common forty-by-twenty-foot dimensions found in medium-sized tobacco houses elsewhere in the Chesapeake.[17] Whether this tobacco house served as storage pending shipment for a single planter or several is unknown. No other buildings stood at the landing.

Ridgley surveyed the Elk Ridge Landing tract in 1729 for a patent called "Hanover," to be granted to Dr. Charles Carroll of Annapolis (d. 1755). After a long delay the land office assigned the patent to Carroll in 1737.[18] Perhaps their unusual tarrying resulted from uncertainty relative to the formation of a town at the site, which the colonial assembly had chartered in response to a petition of backcountry residents in 1733. Janssen Town was to contain "Forty equal Lots" on thirty acres "as lies most con-

venient to the Water . . . at and about the Landing, called, The Elk Ridge Landing."[19] By "October next," the assembly ordered, the purchase agreement with Carroll should be confirmed. But the deadline passed without action, and petitions to revive the town act failed in 1738, 1749, and 1762–63, despite the establishment and staffing of a public tobacco inspection house at the landing in 1748.[20]

In addition to the usual regional difficulties of town-founding, another factor peculiar to the Elk Ridge Landing site must also have come into play. Dr. Carroll had joined with his cousins and other prominent men to found the Baltimore Ironworks in 1731.[21] His Hanover patent contained beds of iron ore, and Carroll certainly resisted expropriation, an action that would have denied him control of natural resources in the form of ore, and of the site's development potential as the fall-line terminus of river transport for tobacco shipment.[22] Over the years of his ownership, Carroll sold or leased several lots, carefully retaining mineral rights to these parcels, and when he finally divested himself of the entire Hanover tract—if not the iron ore underground—he also retained the capacity to profit from the site's other major topographic reality. Carroll reserved to himself and his estate in perpetuity the five-acre lot containing the river landing.[23]

It was in fact around "Carroll's Reserve" that the town of Elk Ridge Landing finally did take shape, thirty-one years after the original legislation.[24] In 1764, Charles Hammond Jr., then owner of the Hanover tract, established the town privately and on his own terms by offering ninety-nine-year leases to lots, rather than the outright fee-simple ownership the public town act had contemplated and its multiple petitioners had desired. In this manner, Hammond, like Carroll, retained ultimate control of his property, and the rates and income from his leases, while shifting the risk of development to his lessees. Hammond commissioned draughtsman Richard Shipley to draw the town plan, which encompassed Carroll's five-acre waterfront commercial reserve and the informal lanes serving it, regularizing them into a rectangular grid in which lots were arranged according to the "golden section," an architectural ratio most simply rendered as five to eight. Shipley's conceptual organization of five-by-eight one-acre-square lots did in fact vary on the ground, where Shipley lengthened and narrowed several adjacent lots to give a greater density at the commercial center, but the overall configuration of lots yielded a regular grid of blocks ordered by three streets parallel to the river and two perpendicular.[25]

The Patapsco determined the northeast boundary of the town, with Carroll's reserve occupying roughly the center of this side. Hill Street marked the opposite side of town, the southwest boundary; between it and the river lay a street with two names: Falls Street, to the north, an old road leading to the lowermost ford on Patapsco Falls, and Fish Street, to the south. Between Falls-Fish Street and the river lay the optimistically named Market Street, interrupted by Carroll's reserve. These parallel streets ran with the long side of the rectangle. The two streets perpendicular to the Patapsco delimited each end of Carroll's reserve, while the lot boundaries alone described the northwest and southeast sides of town. The street on the lower, or southeast, end of Carroll's reserve extended by the public tobacco inspection houses at Market Street and the intersection of Falls-Fish Street. It was here that Shipley modified his standard square lot to maximize street frontage for a larger number of leaseholders, producing the typical long, narrow lots of a main-street commercial district at the town's principal intersection, the cross street linking the river landing to the old falls road. In fact, Shipley's plan interpolated the river itself into a major town avenue, an attribute underscored by its parallel reflection in the three major streets: Market, Falls-Fish, and Hill.

All this, however, was for naught. Shipley's grid, inflected by a little baroque idealism in its proportions, never fully developed, nor did the planned commercial district, and the speculator who had leased the best lots both at the center and on the periphery saw his envisioned real-estate empire collapse in 1787 and 1788.[26] A wharf, warehouse, and store constructed next to Carroll's reserve also entered default in 1788.[27] In the few heady early years, Carroll's heirs constructed a hundred-foot wharf on the reserve before 1770, and in that year a lessee built a forty-by-twenty-six-foot frame warehouse; these still stood in 1798, though by then the wharf was "very old and out of Repair."[28] But for these riverside improvements and a small, unoccupied one-story log dwelling, the rest of Carroll's reserve remained undeveloped at the end of the eighteenth century, and the village a quiet backwater on a silting channel.[29]

The regular grid plan of Elk Ridge Landing Town and the plan's unsuccessful realization were typical offspring of Tidewater tobacco culture. Only in exceptional circumstances did the imposition of a system of towns on the tobacco landscape lead to fully successful urban development.[30] Although Hammond's and Carroll's cupidity may have inhibited sufficient external investment to fill out Shipley's planned streets and lots, the longstanding history of tobacco shipments from the landing demonstrates that Shipley's carefully ordered architectural and commercial environment was unnecessary to the tobacco economy, even as that culture expanded into the piedmont, nor did it seem to be a prerequisite for the lately developing iron industry.[31]

The first steps toward industrializing iron production in the colonial Chesapeake were taken within the confines delimited by tobacco planting. In the middle of the eighteenth century, the tobacco and iron country of Elk Ridge and the lower Patapsco falls took on more than a peripheral role in this aspect of colonial Maryland's industrial development, but it did so without an underpinning of urbanization.

CHAPTER THREE

Iron City? . . . not yet

CEASELESSLY TURNING below the Patapsco falls, eddies in the river current had been eroding the mine banks at Elk Ridge for longer than any European could remember. Dr. Charles Carroll, the shrewd Annapolis surgeon, tobacco planter, and businessman scouted these likely concentrations of ore in the region's riverbanks as he prepared to invest in the Baltimore Ironworks. Perhaps he even walked the metes and bounds of his Hanover patent with county surveyor Henry Ridgely in 1729, studying the Patapsco's shorelines and confluent stream beds. But whether or not he actually ventured so far from his refined Annapolis rooms, what is certain is that very soon afterward, the Baltimore Company's crews of indentured servants and enslaved African miners began to dig the riverbanks for ore.

Dr. Carroll's Baltimore Ironworks, in operation by 1731, prolonged a wave of substantial investment in sustained, large-scale iron production that had begun in the 1710s. That decade ushered in not only a reinvigorated Chesapeake tobacco market, but also the Tuball, or Germanna, Ironworks in Virginia and the Principio Ironworks in Maryland, soon followed by many others, including Dr. Carroll's, and, at mid-century, four installations on the Patapsco.[1]

The earliest successful iron smelting in British America began in the seventeenth century at a number of small-scale bloomery forges scattered across the countryside near sources of iron ore and wood. These forges enabled blacksmiths to refine a "bloom" or ball of iron on a hearth not much larger than the fireplace of an ordinary kitchen or dwelling.[2] In fact, the formal establishment of the

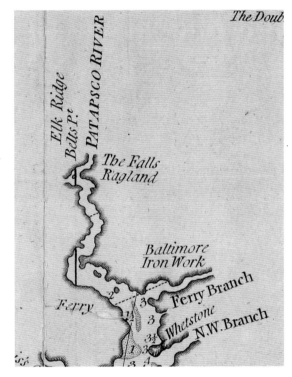

Detail from *A new and accurate chart of the Bay of Chesapeake,* showing the location of the Baltimore Ironworks.

Principio Company, which pooled the resources of a number of British investors, was contingent upon a successful trial of bloomery iron, subsequently approved in England. Bloomery methods, though, were insufficient for large-scale production, so the Principio investors employed the blast furnace process in their permanent facilities on the western shore at the head of the bay, as did Virginia's Governor Spotswood at Germanna, and Dr. Carroll at the Baltimore Company.

The blast technique comprised two stages of production: the smelting of iron ore into raw blocks of iron, or "pigs," at a furnace, and the successive reheating and hammering of pigs into a more stable

and pure form called "bar iron" at a forge. During the conversion of pig to bar, a block of pig iron might lose a third or more of its weight. Bar iron itself might be hammered to varying degrees of purity, and a bar in a lesser state of refinement was called an "ancony." Iron could enter the market in any of these three preliminary states—pig, ancony, or bar—whereupon castings might be made from melted pigs, for instance, or rods slit from bars and wrought into nails. Falling water pumped the bellows that raised a furnace temperature to "blast," and as well drove the massive, refining hammer of a forge. Blast furnaces and forges consequently required a greater initial investment in physical plant than did the bloomery method, which transformed ore to bars in a single step, but the blast-furnace/ refinery-forge process rendered much larger quantities of superior quality iron.[3]

Iron production thus required a highly specialized building. The intense heat of smelting and forging dictated the use of masonry, for example, and the chemical process yielding iron from ore required a uniform furnace configuration. So long as the technology remained the same—and it did over the eighteenth and early-nineteenth centuries—a standardized architectural concept prevailed. Just as certain English stone types best served to line the bosh, or crucible, of a furnace, so too did imported expertise guide colonial build-

ers in the specifics of constructing furnaces and forges. A class of transient European ironmasters disseminated the principles to colonial investors.[4] And yet the industrial processes of iron production did blend seamlessly into Chesapeake tobacco culture. The long-standing trading relationships that had arisen over time to handle the transport and sale of tobacco readily adapted to another staple. Iron easily fit the pattern of seasonal shipments supported by credit, well-established contacts with British merchant houses, and a shared language and legal system. Like the largest and wealthiest tobacco planters, who continued to use the consignment system throughout the eighteenth century to the Revolution, Chesapeake ironworks undertook large-scale production for the British market, and consigned iron to many of the same houses that managed planters' accounts.

The nature of iron production itself, in addition, paralleled tobacco culture. Smelting and forging required not simply the specialized skill of an iron master, but also a quantity of unskilled and trainable labor together with a specific combination of geographic attributes, similar to that of a tobacco plantation. Of course, falling water, ore, and wood had to be found in relatively close proximity to wherever iron would be made, but in the Chesapeake, the organization of labor on isolated, often large plantations and the employment of in-

Detail of a casting arch with a portal to the bosh.

Historic American Engineering Record, Library of Congress.

dentured servants, convicts, and, above all, enslaved Africans had come to be critical for tobacco culture. Furthermore, once specialist iron masters set the requisite structures into place, the same labor and expense-saving practices already well established for tobacco culture prevailed in Chesapeake ironworks. Colonial builders raised dams of wood, earth, and gravel—instead of stone—and employed the common repertory of wooden structures to shelter not only men, animals, and materials, but also the machinery and workspaces unique to ironworks. The mentality of a *tobacco* plantation readily translated to that of an *iron* plantation. Industrial iron followed an agricultural model.[5]

As with tobacco, transatlantic economic interests decisively shaped Chesapeake ironmaking. Simmering conflict between Britain and Sweden—one of the Crown's major iron suppliers—culminated in 1717 with a complete retaliatory trade embargo.[6] British attention quickly turned from Scandinavia to new iron sources across the Atlantic. It can be no coincidence that in 1718 the trial run of iron bars produced in Maryland for the Principio investors reached England, evidently the first such shipment of bar iron from the American colonies to Britain. Nor can it be coincidental that in 1719 the colonial assembly of Maryland passed "An Act for the Encouragement of an Iron Manufacture, within this Province."[7]

The Maryland Iron Act permitted prospective builders of ironworks to receive a writ of condemnation for one hundred acres of land to be held in fee—that is, in absolute ownership, with right of inheritance—after the payment of damages to the original owner. The colonial bill became law a month after King George I rescinded the two-year-old Swedish embargo, but the die was already cast. Within a decade after the newly organized Principio Company exported its first shipment of pig iron to London—probably in 1724—three more Maryland ironworks were planned or under construction. By 1767 at least twenty-three of the Maryland Iron Act's *ad quod damnum* writs had been issued, and,

A nineteenth-century engraving of a casting house interior, with the portal visible at the base of a blast furnace, pig iron casting underway. *Scribner's Monthly*, 1875.

as the Revolution began, some thirty-six ironworks had been put into operation.[8]

Crown policy also induced competition on the Patapsco. The British Iron Act of 1750 removed duties on all American pig iron exports to Britain, and also lifted duties on bar iron off-loaded at London quays. At the same time the act expressly prohibited new colonial facilities from finishing iron by slitting, rolling, or plating, or by conversion into steel for small, fine tools. In response, local investors on the Patapsco established the Elk Ridge Company to produce duty-free pig iron in 1756. When a royal decree in 1757 abolished all duties on American bar iron, regardless of port of entry, two Patapsco Valley forges began to hammer out duty-free iron bars in the early 1760s.[9] And about 1770, a fourth enterprise on the Patapsco entered the iron business, this time

to mold cast-iron wares from melted pigs, a method of finishing not specifically prohibited by the British Iron Act. Although the enumeration of iron in 1764, which required importation to be handled by British merchants, may have offended colonial pride, for Chesapeake producers it actually did no more than ratify the established trading regime. As tobacco long had been, Chesapeake iron was transshipped through British merchant houses.[10]

All told, from 1731 to 1775 combined iron exports from Maryland and Virginia varied in general between two and three thousand tons of pig iron annually, many times more than any other North American region.[11] Nevertheless, just as tobacco culture had provided no incentive for urban development, so iron production, too, induced no urban manifestations. The four mid-eighteenth-century ironworks that tobacco men established on the Patapsco did not vary from the tidewater standard, as their stories show.

The success of British-owned Principio, and more important still, that of Dr. Carroll's locally owned Baltimore Ironworks, inspired other ambitious Maryland men to enter the race to industrialize. Among this class of citizens, whose wealth, like that of the Baltimore Company investors, derived from tobacco planting, mercantile activities, real-estate speculation, and, now, the potential returns from iron production, was Caleb Dorsey (1710–1772).

Dorsey's father, Caleb Sr. (1685–1742), maintained a home plantation called "Hockley-in-the-Hole," which skirted the waters of the Severn River above Annapolis. From this seat at the historic center of colonial power, Caleb Sr.'s prospect also took in new western lands, and in 1722 he speculated on 200 acres across the heights of Elk Ridge.[12] "Dorsey's Chance" was the father's aptly named patent, but it was the son who drew out profits from ventures in the piedmont. In 1742 and 1743, Caleb Jr. patented his holdings on the Patapsco, amounting to some 2,000 acres in his own name and 2,500 acres with his brother Edward, most of these lands given the brothers "for love and affection" by Caleb Sr.[13]

The largest of the Dorseys' various tracts adjoined "Talbotts Vineyard," John Talbott's plantation, extending southeast from the Vineyard along Elk Ridge and the Patapsco falls. This 1,766-acre parcel, resurveyed as "Moore's Morning Choice Enlarged," encompassed "Dorsey's Chance" and an adjacent seventeenth-century tract originally patented as "Moore's Morning Choice."[14] Inside the southeastern limits of Dorsey's enlarged patent a sizable stream traversed the ridge and descended toward the Patapsco. Rockburn Branch met the river outside of Dorsey's tract, where it flowed through a one-hundred-acre patent called "Hockley." On a hill above, before the branch crossed into Hockley, Dorsey built the very fine two-story brick residence called Rockburn facing the ridgetop fields to the south. Rockburn's southern façade still boasts the masterful brickwork patterning Dorsey's masons employed, an extravagant and instructive display of social capital and economic prowess compared, for example, to John Talbott's older and much more typical wooden, earthfast dwelling that was slowly settling into genteel deterioration on the plantation next door. Just below Rockburn house, on land de-

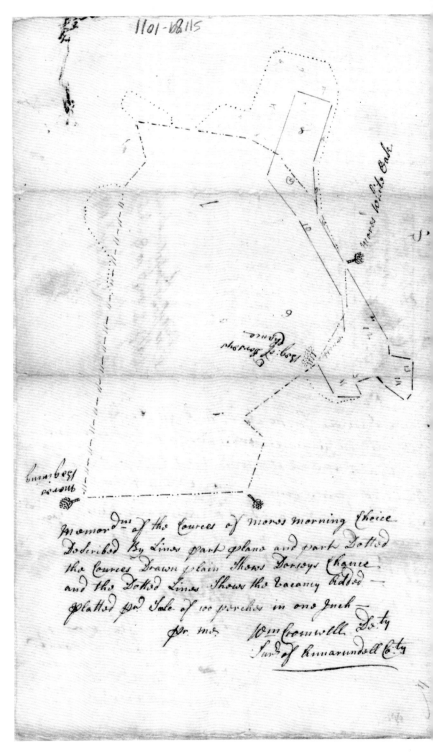

scending to the north by the edge of the branch, Dorsey chose the site for an iron furnace.[15]

In accordance with the provisions of the Maryland Iron Act, the justices of the Chancery Court issued a condemnation writ for one hundred acres on July 29, 1755. Their judgment gave Dorsey's project legal imprimatur, and insured that the site could not be taken from him by a competitor.[16] Writ in hand, Dorsey and his brother Edward mortgaged

Plat showing Dorsey's Chance and the patent boundaries for Moore's Morning Choice, where Caleb Dorsey built his dwelling, Rockburn, and the Elk Ridge Company Furnace.

Maryland State Archives.

most of their Patapsco lands at summer's end, and the following spring formalized a partnership with Alexander Lawson. The Elk Ridge Company came into being on April 5, 1756, each of the three partners holding an equal share.[17]

Lawson, an ironmaster with long regional experience, had been employed at the Baltimore Company Ironworks from 1736 to 1748 at least, and had formed a partnership that organized the Nottingham Ironworks on the bay northeast of Baltimore Town, probably before 1746.[18] Now in another partnership uniting tobacco money with production expertise, Lawson and the Dorseys impounded the "fine constant stream" of Rockburn Branch and built the Elk Ridge Company furnace below the pond, sending the tail race to the Patapsco just upstream of Hockley, near the lowermost ford through the falls before the deep and brackish tidewater. After company laborers erected the substantial stone "furnace, bridge casting and wheel house, with a bridgeway," they built ancillary structures in wood and planted an orchard. They cut a road and cleared the river landing, then began to unearth the site's "very fine iron ore."[19]

The presence of mine banks along Rockburn Branch recalls the ore deposits washed by the Patapsco along Dr. Carroll's Hanover patent, just downstream. There, miners excavated pits into the gray-brown river banks and loaded the "red and yellow petrified iron" ore into sloops that sailed down the Patapsco as far as the Middle Branch, then ascended to the Baltimore Company's furnace on Gwynn's Falls.[20] The Elk Ridge Company's laborers, instead, extracted ore directly from the furnace property, though they did eventually ship ore downriver as well. Some years after completing the Rockburn Branch site, the Elk Ridge Company built a second furnace much closer to the bay, on a stream joining the tidewater Patapsco, and called that installation the Curtis Creek Works.[21]

Dr. Carroll's accounts for his own ironworks describe facilities that give us a good idea of the Elk Ridge Company's architecture. Specifying "a furnace 24 by 26 feet," our precise Annapolis physician ordered "a house, warehouse, stable, kitchen, [and] coal house" as well. Carroll engaged masons to lay the courses of the furnace under the supervision of an expert founder, and charged a carpenter "to build a coal house, a bridge and bridge house, a casting house, a wheel and wheel house, the 'moving gear'

of the bellows, and a dwelling for the founder."[22] Each of these architectural elements fit together to make an industrial system.

The capacious base of the iron furnace held a container, or "bosh," about eight feet in diameter. Above, the stack narrowed and rose to near thirty feet.[23] "Myne burner[s]" and "breakers and cleaners"—so these laborers were called at the Baltimore Company—prepared the iron ore, and "carters" delivered it to "fillers," who charged the furnace from the top with measured proportions of ore, charcoal, and an oyster-shell or limestone "flux" that bonded with impurities in the ore once the charcoal was ignited.[24] Often the fillers worked from a bridge or bridge house that for ease of access ran at a level span from a bank or slope above the furnace to the top of the stack. Such a span, essentially, was a covered bridge wide enough to accommodate the carts and floor space necessary to sort and hold materials in readiness for filling. Siting a furnace in a swale or valley enabled this highly functional configuration, availed by Dorsey at Rockburn branch.

In the wheel house, waterpower drove the mechanical bellows that sustained a sufficiently hot fire in the furnace for the chemical reaction of smelting to occur. Red-orange molten iron collected in the bottom of the bosh, to be periodically drawn off by the "founders" and run into casts shaped in sand in the casting house. These were arranged like piglets nursing at a mother sow, hence the colorful name. Slag boiled to the top of the of the searing pool in the bosh and could likewise be drawn off from a higher opening and discarded, or drained from the bottom after the full quantity of iron had been channeled into the sand molds. Once ignited, a furnace might require a week or more of burning to achieve sufficient blast temperature, and once reached, a blast could be sustained constantly for six to eight months. The founders would cast pigs twice a day.[25]

A northern visitor to the Principio Company in 1749 marveled at the "30 piggs now cast [that] ly hot in the sand," he recounted in vivid language, ". . . & the fire goes not out after it is once blown up untill the Season of ye year comes about. The furnace I suppose is 20 foot high or more," he estimated,

> & is fed with oar [ore] & coal &c at the Top as if it were the Top of a Chimney all put in there. These they bring in Horse Carts the

oar the Coal & oyster Shels & there Stayd two men Day & night. The top of ye furnace is about breast high from the floor where they Stand to Tend it & ye flame Jets out continually[,] extinguishe[d only] by the oar, Coal & Shels as they feed it. Each Couple Tend 24 hours in which time they Run or Cast twice.[26]

The immediacy of Joshua Hempstead's diary entry gives some color to the arduous labor which, at the Elk Ridge Company furnace, yielded about five hundred tons of pig iron per year.[27]

Dorsey's Elk Ridge production meshed neatly with his long-established method of tobacco merchandizing: "I have Sent you 6 hhds [hogsheads of tobacco] on my own Account Marked thus C/D," Dorsey wrote to a British merchant in 1754, the year before embarking on the ironworks project,

> & 14 hhds In Partnership With Edward Dorsey . . . As you Will find by the Ships Manifest. . . . Desire you Would Sell My tobacco the first Good Opportunity, & If find able Incoragement Will Do all In My Power to Promote your Consignments.[28]

Dorsey operated at a level of trading sufficient to handle local sales of imported merchandise beyond his own needs—the British merchant's own "consignments." Indeed two years later, by February 1, 1757, London merchant John Buchanan would address "Caleb & Edward Dorsey & Alexander Lawson, Merchants, Annapolis" to inform them that goods ordered the previous November would be shipped on "the Betsy, Capt. White" in March. "Your assistance to give my Ships a quick dispatch will oblige [me]," Buchanan concluded.[29]

When Captain White and a colleague, Captain Johnson, sailed from Patapsco docks for Britain the following September, their brigs contained sixty tons of Elk Ridge iron in addition to the partners' hogsheads of tobacco.[30] Dorsey's account book reference for those September voyages establishes 1757 as the earliest securely dated production year for the Elk Ridge Company.[31] Captains White and Johnson again embarked for London laden with Elk Ridge iron and tobacco in August and September of 1758 and September of 1759. Another conveyance weighed anchor for London in September 1761. The "season of ye year" for the Elk Ridge furnace, to use

Joshua Hempstead's poetic language for the duration of a blast, must have run from mid-winter to near summer's end.[32]

As on a tobacco plantation, Dorsey hired a white overseer to supervise laborers at the Elk Ridge Company's furnaces. Christopher Gardner received £24 in 1767 "for two year's Oversight at [the Curtis Creek] works."[33] William Williams held the same responsibilities at Elk Ridge furnace from 1759 to 1768; George Teall succeeded him in 1770. Williams took on at least one apprentice, and though Dorsey also paid wage and day laborers, he made use of convict and white-servant labor from the earliest years of the company's existence.[34] An English convict seized the moment and escaped in 1756, probably while the furnace was still under construction, though certainly the labor of mining, woodcutting, and charcoal burning must have been well underway for the 1757 production season.[35]

By far the largest cohort of furnace laborers were enslaved Africans, who occupied both skilled and unskilled positions. Assessors for Dorsey's estate in 1772 enumerated "24 Negroes at the [Elk Ridge] Furnace" that year, and Dorsey's own accounts frequently record payments to slaves for overwork and their subsequent purchases. Tasks involved the whole range of labor undertaken at a furnace: £7.12.0 to "Thomas Dorsey's Joe . . . for cutting seventy-six cords" of wood, and £4.12.9 to "Boy Jack . . . for making castings . . . beyond his regular work assignments."[36] There is virtually no information in the scholarly literature concerning the housing provided for these various iron plantation workers;

September 30, 1756.

RAN away laſt Night, from the *Elk-Ridge* Iron-Works, a Convict Servant Man, named *Richard Snailum*, born in *Lancaſhire* in *England*, a Man of a whitiſh Complexion, about 5 Feet 9 Inches high, and pretty well made for his Height: He had on and carried with him, an old Beaver Hat, a dark cut Wig, a large Linen Handkerchief ſtrip'd with red, a grey Coat with a Cape and white Metal Buttons, a Pair of old Leather Breeches, a Pair of Hempen-Roll Trowſers, Country-made Shoes, two Oſnabrigs Shirts almoſt new, and one Dowlaſs Shirt. He is a cowardly and deceitful Fellow; and is ſuppoſed to be gone towards the Head of *Gunpowder* River, having formerly attempted to eſcape that Way.

Whoever apprehends and conveys the ſaid Servant to the ſaid Works; ſhall receive Three Pounds Reward, and reaſonable Charges.

CALEB DORSEY.

Caleb Dorsey advertised for help finding a runaway indentured servant, escaped from the Elk Ridge Ironworks in the *Maryland Gazette,* October 7, 1756.

Maryland State Archives.

nevertheless, one may safely assume that the hierarchy of status imposed by white authority on tobacco plantations also had its parallel on iron plantations, as did the patterns of personal competition within enslaved communities recently observed in anthropological studies of agricultural plantation labor.[37]

Competition for the Elk Ridge Company, itself, arrived in 1760–1761, shortly after the repeal of British import tariffs on colonial bar iron. "Charles Carroll Esqr & Company," the next generation of Baltimore Company owners, moved to expand operations to the Patapsco. The metes and bounds for the hundred-acre parcel condemned for them under the Maryland Ironworks Act marked a tract including part of the Hockley patent and the neighboring low ground that ran north and east to the river, adjacent to Dorsey's furnace land.[38] Although the forge they planned to build would have complemented the Elk Ridge Company's production, it seems more likely that their application for a writ of *ad quod damnum* was a preemptive measure, designed to secure for themselves this valuable tract so close to the Elk Ridge furnace. Carroll and Company let out the condemned land, and only after the death of the lessee three years later does it appear that the forge construction was genuinely begun.[39] The single-story stone structure "now building at the Head of Patapsco River" in November 1763 was the heart of a complex called the Hockley works, employing as many as thirty-nine slaves in and about the forge in 1783. No whites resided on the property, much like the outlying quarter of a tobacco plantation.[40]

Dorsey himself entered the forge competition rather late, and evidently by chance. Directly across the Patapsco from Hockley, and extending upstream along the north bank of the river opposite Dorsey's own condemned land, local ironmaster Edward Norwood received an *ad quod damnum* writ for another hundred-acre forge tract, to be named Avalon later in the nineteenth century. Like Charles Carroll, Esq., Norwood must also have condemned the land in 1760, but by August 1761 he had entered into discussions with Dorsey for the Baltimore County parcel. "Since I saw you I have Considered the Trouble I am in with [my] Distressed Children," Norwood reflected,

> if it will Suit you to come down to my house
> to morrow morning I will Lett you se[e] a
> List of what things I have got for the forge

which you may have if you please with the Land & building place as I am Shore that I Cant Run the Resque of a partnership in so Great an Affair without pigg Iron to Carry it on[. Y]ou have now an Opportunity of Serveing your Self if you think proper[,] if not I have an Officer [offer] for the land.[41]

Dorsey did attend Norwood the next day at his dwelling, and there the troubled would-be forgeman issued a bond to ensure that title to the condemned land would eventually convey properly.

Dorsey immediately set to building, or took up the project Norwood had commenced. Laborers set a log formwork across the Patapsco, and filled it with earth and gravel, a typical method of dam construction again reflecting the regional realities of abundant timber and limited labor and capital: a wooden dam was serviceable while a furnace or forge had to be constructed of stone. The funneled waters ultimately put into motion the shafts and gearing inside a substantial one-story stone forge building, its dimensions perhaps as large as seventy by forty-five feet, with an adjacent stone coal house sixty by thirty feet.[42] The great forge hammers began to pound Elk Ridge Company pig iron into bars the following spring. Local merchant Jonathan Pinkney confirms the event for us in his April–May 1762 store accounts, setting down the following transaction: "Bought of Caleb Dorsey 1 Ton 36 Bar Iron at £32 pr Ton £36.16.00."[43]

By the early 1770s, masons had built the last of the four major colonial-era ironworks to operate in the Patapsco valley. Dorsey's second son Samuel leased the east corner lot of Elk Ridge Landing Town in 1769: lot five contained 1.5 acres between Market Street and the Patapsco.[44] Here, almost certainly with Dorsey's assistance, Samuel built and operated an "air furnace," in which pigs were melted to make cast-iron objects. Along with the forge, this was another operation complementary to the manufacture of pig iron. Samuel's was a "reverberatory furnace," as a Swedish visitor to the site termed it, a furnace in which the charcoal fire did not mix with the iron but reflected intense heat upon it. Such a furnace would have been staffed by potters, or cast-iron pot and utensil makers.[45]

The details of such an air furnace in operation at Germanna, Virginia, are offered us by the garrulous and good-humored Virginian, William Byrd,

whose extraordinary and wide-ranging diaries make for fascinating reading:

> Col. Spotswood . . . received us with open arms, and carried us directly to his air furnace, which is a very ingenious and profitable contrivance. The use of it is to melt his sow iron, in order to cast it into sundry utensils, such as backs for chimneys, andirons, fenders, plates for hearths, pots, mortars, rollers for gardeners, skillets, boxes for cart wheels; and many other things, which, one with another, can be afforded at twenty shillings a ton, and delivered at people's own homes. And, being cast from the sow iron, are much better than those which come from England, which are cast immediately from the ore for the most part. Mr. Flowry is the artist that

directed the building of this ingenious structure, which is contrived after this manner. There is an opening about a foot square for the fresh air to pass through from without. This leads up to an iron grate that holds about half a bushel of sea coal, and is about six feet higher than the opening. When the fire is kindled, it rarefies the air in such a manner as to make a very strong draught from without. About two feet above the grate is a hole that leads to a kind of oven, [on] the floor of which is laid shelving towards the mouth. In the middle of this oven, on one side, is another hole that leads into the funnel of a chimney, about forty feet high. The smoke mounts up this way, drawing the flame after it with so much force, that in

An iron forge by an English river, similar to those Caleb Dorsey and Charles Carroll built beside the Patapsco.

Paul Mellon Collection, Yale Center for British Art.

less than an hour it melts the sows of iron that are thrust towards the upper end of the oven. As the metal melts it runs towards the mouth into a hollow place, out of which the potter lades it in iron ladles, in order to pour it into the several molds just by. The mouth of the oven is stopped close with a movable stone shutter, which he removes so soon as he perceives, through the peep holes, that the iron is melted. The inside of the oven is lined with soft bricks, made of Sturbridge or Windsor clay, because no other will endure the intense heat of the fire. And over the floor of the oven they strew sand. . . . The potter is also obliged to plaster over his ladles with the same sand moistened, to save them from melting. . . . The Chimneys and other outside work of this building are of free stone.

Byrd concluded this meticulous and highly precise discussion with characteristic wry humor, no doubt sharing a dram of his "respects" with Spotswood's men:

> The potter was so complaisant as to show me the whole process, for which I paid him and the other workmen my respects in the most agreeable way. There was a great deal of ingenuity in the framing of the molds, wherein they cast the several utensils, but without breaking them to pieces, I found there was no being let into that secret.[46]

A fully functional air furnace thus operated without a water-driven bellows, since the tall chimney was sufficient to maintain the requisite draft. Samuel Dorsey's "Elk Ridge Air Furnace," sited at the edge of the Patapsco, consequently had no need for waterpower, and was not accompanied by a dam and millrace. Instead, proximity to the water gave ready access to shipping, as Byrd had observed at Spotswood's Massaponax operations: "Just by the air furnace stands a very substantial wharf, close to which any vessel may ride in safety."[47]

Although production records do not survive for Samuel Dorsey's air furnace, correspondence with the Maryland Council of Safety during the Revolution sheds light on castings that must have supplemented the more mundane fabrication of frying pans and fire backs. Dorsey "cast a few small guns,"

as early as December 1776, and wrote to the council that he "should be glad you would apoint sum person to prove them this next weak that in case they should not answer we mite make another mixture of mettle."[48] In June the council inquired after "the Cannon and Swivels you agreed . . . to make."[49] By that time Dorsey had cast twenty-eight cannon of forty promised and an unspecified number of movable guns mounted on platforms; some of these were ready to be proved that month.[50] Samuel's untimely death in debt and intestate on September 11, 1777 led ultimately to the sale of the Elk Ridge Landing air furnace after 1780. In 1789, a surveyor called the ruins, which stood beside the former colonial road running through the landing from Annapolis to Philadelphia, an "old furnace," and by 1798 federal assessors found nothing of value to record on the lot.[51]

The iron plantations that smelted pigs or forged bars along the Patapsco and the other waterways of the Chesapeake mirrored in critical aspects the fundamental economic operations and organization of tobacco culture. Largely supported by capital derived from tobacco planting, Maryland's colonial ironworks shared tobacco's dispersed placement of facilities, organization of labor, and sales overseas through British merchant houses. Even the specialized masonry architecture of furnaces and forges all fit readily within the existing economic and cultural framework. If much cast ironware sold locally, none of this industrial production required an urban environment more sophisticated than the river landings and wharves that had been in use for a good century. Most important of all, and notwithstanding the underground economies within enslaved communities, the crippling attributes of slave labor and plantation ownership stifled the natural momentum toward urbanization that occurs with more open, wage-based, industrial operations. The colonial Chesapeake iron industry led to no more extensive villages and towns than had the tobacco economy.

Maryland iron retained its agricultural origins and dimensions throughout the colonial period. Though iron-making was in fact the earliest industrial process to exist in the Chesapeake, a more obvious agricultural component of the colonial economy proved more important to the development of American industrial towns and factories. That element was wheat.

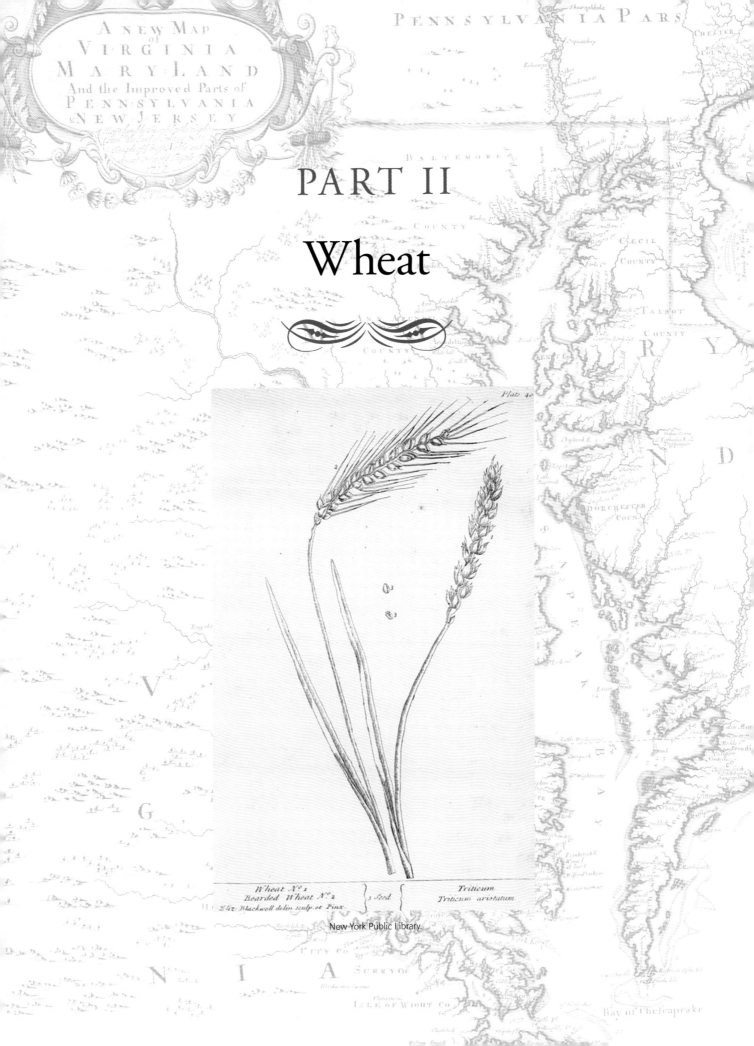

PART II

Wheat

Plate 40

Wheat Nº 1
Bearded Wheat Nº 2 | 3 Seed | Triticum
Eliz. Blackwell delin sculp. et Pinx. | | Triticum aristatum

COUNTRY CHURCH-YARD. 151

Oft did the harvest to their sickle yield,
Their furrow oft the stubborn glebe has broke:
How jocund did they drive their team afield!
How bow'd the woods beneath their sturdy stroke!

Let not Ambition mock their useful toil,
Their homely joys, and destiny obscure;
Nor grandeur hear with a disdainful smile,
The short and simple annals of the poor.

The boast of heraldry, the pomp of power,
And all that beauty, all that wealth e'er gave,
Await alike th' inevitable hour.
The paths of glory lead but to the grave.

Nor you, ye proud, impute to these the fault,
If Memory o'er their tomb no trophies raise,
Where thro' the long-drawn aisle and fretted vault,
The pealing anthem swells the note of praise.

Can

Wheat at the harvest.

Yale Center for British Art.

CHAPTER FOUR

New Polestar — New Direction

A S EARLY AS THE mid-seventeenth century, the second- and third-generation political leaders of the colonial Chesapeake began to imagine a mature society on the Atlantic main. For these planter merchants, bound by commerce and culture to Europe's great cities, that meant an urban form. The Burgesses of Virginia drafted "An Act for Building a Towne" in 1662, followed by more legislation from 1680, and Maryland's assemblymen initiated their own series of new-town proclamations and acts beginning in 1668.[1] Nearly exclusive reliance on tobacco put the whole region at risk, they reasoned, and the campaign to encourage town development walked hand-in-hand with the parallel goal of a diversified agricultural economy. In 1662, Maryland attempted direct promotion of "English Grayne" harvests by elevating "wheat, barley, peas, and rye" to "legal tender," like tobacco, but the new additions to monetary exchange had little effect.[2] With no mills to grind grain, tobacco planters did not diversify. Lacking grain for mills to process, investors did not build.[3]

Solving the conundrum involved an even more pronounced intervention. Colonial authorities enabled prospective mill builders to obtain privately held land along likely waterfalls by applying for a writ of condemnation, as the Maryland Ironworks Act was to authorize a half-century later. Virginia passed a mill act in 1667 and Maryland followed suit in 1669. The Maryland act permitted condemnation of ten-acre tracts — later enlarged to twenty — and established below-market levels of compensation to owners. In exchange, owners retained title to the land and issued instead long-term leaseholds for the condemned mill seats — eighty years, in Maryland.[4]

Since builders now needed less capital to bring a mill project to fruition, more mills might be built.

Like the long-standing struggle to impose an urban framework on a culture with little use for one, the Maryland Mill Act met with little success initially. Over its first fifty years, to 1719, the act provided legal grounds for only fourteen *ad quod damnum* writs. Yet this paltry total nearly doubled in the next decade, and multiplied eleven times over the subsequent thirty-five years, to 1766, the date of the act's repeal.[5] What happened?

Certainly the tobacco depression at the turn of the seventeenth to the eighteenth centuries changed the attitudes of some colonial citizens, among them John Talbott, who took to farming grain over planting tobacco in the 1720s. But other critical factors converged at this moment as well. The first was population. Pennsylvania's founding in 1681 and its rapid settlement by groups of English, Welsh, and German Quakers brought to the fore a large class of hardworking, ambitious farmers and merchants who gave the mid-Atlantic a prosperous colony with a diversified agricultural economy. Then came movement. Settlement of the Shenandoah Valley after 1730 extended the reach of the Pennsylvania Quaker grain-producing culture.[6] At the same time, trade increased. Expansion of Caribbean colonies increased the demand for grain, and also drew out indirect outcomes. New England merchants, who had already developed close economic relationships with the sugar islands, turned to mid-Atlantic farmers for harvests of wheat for local families and of corn for the enslaved Africans of the Caribbean, the ill-found refiners of tropical sugar.[7]

European developments also contributed to

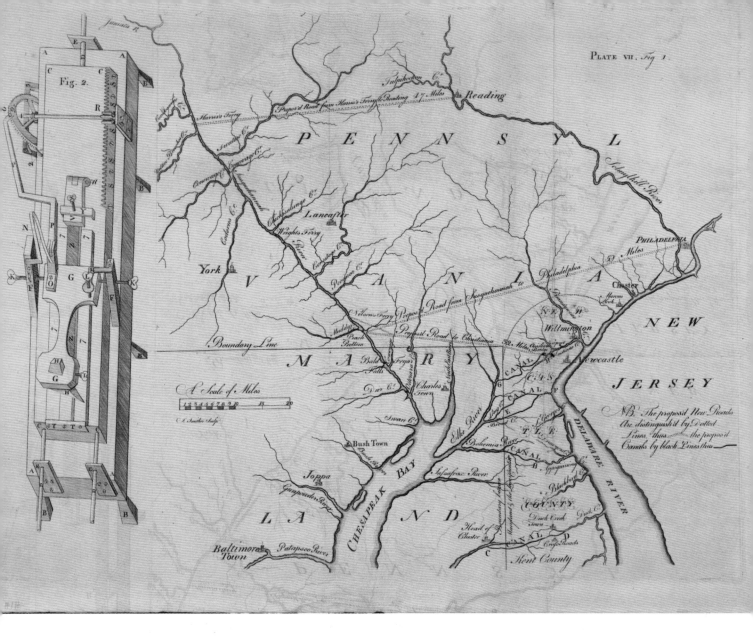

PLATE VII. *Fig. 1*

Baltimore Town is shown on the Patapsco in 1771, the year Ellicotts' Mills was founded. The configuration of the map is significant. Here Baltimore Town is cut off from tidewater tobacco lands to the south and is instead incorporated with mid-Atlantic wheat territory to the north.

New York Public Library.

change. Europe's population was growing at a time of failing wheat harvests in the Mediterranean region and elsewhere. The suffocating effects of wars and political strife on the cultivation of foodstuffs also increased European demand for grain dramatically over the eighteenth century.[8] By 1730, the largest market for Pennsylvania wheat was very likely centered in southern Europe, and during the two subsequent decades, Philadelphia doubled "the tonnage of ships trading [wheat] with Spain, Portugal, and Madeira . . . then doubled [them] again by the time of the American Revolution."[9]

Philadelphia's waterfront warehouses drew harvests not only from southeastern Pennsylvania and Delaware, but also from a steadily increasing ring that encompassed the eastern shore of Maryland and Virginia, as well as the northern and western portions of Maryland's western shore.[10] Baltimore

Town began to take on its own share of this grain trade in the decade of the 1750s and grew enormously as a consequence, because the grain economy did not simply require direct connections to British merchant houses but a far more complex network of financial and production relationships, among them: farmers, millers, distillers, bakers, shippers, "wholesalers, retailers, . . . bankers and insurers."[11] Each of these individuals had a hand in the process as the raw kernel came to be transformed into ever more saleable products.

Where a tobacco planter controlled all of the stages of production and typically traded directly with London, Bristol, or Liverpool merchants—or with a larger planter who did so—wheat farmers did not, because the market did not consist entirely of raw grain, and those grain and flour shipments did not go in greatest measure to Britain through the established trading houses, as tobacco did, but more significantly to southern Europe and the Caribbean.[12] Moreover the capital requirements of large-scale flour production for the international market and the greater uniformity of flour grades that market demanded could not be met by every person who swung a scythe through the golden stalks, nor by every local gristmiller. The consolidation of the various procedures as well as the division of labor present in large mills easily achieved heretofore unknown economies of scale. Thereafter, the specialized activities various independent handlers undertook to store, sell, transport, insure, and secure profits opened new business opportunities at every step. Most importantly, colonial ownership of this network of related production and shipping enterprises combined to keep income and profits local. In this way the tremendous forces that gathered to shove gearing and millstones into motion also propelled a dramatic, region-wide change in the long-standing architectural framework that tobacco planting had locked into place.

By 1762, the urbanizing potential of this agricultural and economic transformation was so palpable, that the increasingly dismayed citizens of Elk Ridge addressed a fourth and final petition for a new town to the colonial assembly, again unsuccessfully. "There is now a considerable Trade carried on [at the landing] and from its advantageous Situation would become a great market for Grain if Merchants could have ground on any Tolerable Terms for building Warehouses and other Conveniences for carrying on Trade there."[13] A regional displacement was underway, and the Elk Ridge petitioners saw it. The economic polestar of northern and piedmont Maryland shone no longer in the lower tidewater. It had traversed the bay to a mid-Atlantic center.

The "shift from tobacco to grain production redefined the regional identity of the upper Chesapeake," historian Charles G. Steffen observes.

One by one, the ties that fastened Baltimore County to the Greater Tidewater stretched and then snapped as northern Maryland was

Deputy County Surveyor Henry Ridgely mentions Charles Pierpoint's millrace on the Patapsco, March 1729, very likely the valley's first.
Maryland State Archives.

James Hood's Mill. From Catherine Van Courtlandt Mathews, *Andrew Ellicott: His Life and Letters* (New York: The Grafton Press, 1908).

pulled into the economic orbit of the Middle Atlantic region. Urbanization brought this underlying transformation into full view, because the backcountry wheat trade generated an unprecedented demand for mills, roads, bridges, ferries, and — above all — towns.[14]

If Elk Ridge Landing Town never became a second Baltimore, still the Patapsco Valley took the vanguard of this regional transformation. We are already acquainted with a very early emblem of it in the deceptively simple image of John Talbott's well-maintained corn house amid the wind-blown decay of his father's tobacco barns. Young John, a second-generation Patapsco landowner, fell squarely into the new regional type.[15]

Talbott's plantation on Elk Ridge extended northward to a bluff that fell to the river. Just upstream, the Patapsco cut a narrow S-curve through the steep hills, and on the inside edge of the upper bend, Charles Pierpoint, a Quaker miller and planter, built a grist mill. Pierpoint's narrow, fifteen-acre patent extended for almost three-quarters of a mile west along the river and the slope below Talbott's

bluff. Our county surveyor, Henry Ridgley, blazed the lines of the well-named patent, "A Stony Hillside," in March 1729, three years before he climbed to the ridgetop to retrace father Edward Talbotts' "Vineyard" for son John. At the far eastern end of "A Stony Hillside," where Pierpoint could take advantage of the angled turn of the river to dig the shortest possible millrace, Ridgley marked a pair of "White Oakes Standing Near a greate Stone in the Edge of the falls and Between the Said falls and a Race Dugg by the Said Pierpoint for to build a Water Mill thereon."[16]

Pierpoint had settled on Elk Ridge about 1714, on a 26.5-acre parcel next to the Talbotts' large plantation, and, like John Talbott's father Edward, Pierpoint had built Virginia houses. These, too, a successor deputy county surveyor carefully inventoried much later. After nearly thirty years had passed, William Cromwell found them all to be "very old and Indifferent." Although no description of the mill exists, Pierpoint's dwellings possessed features that suggest he had access to a mason, who probably laid up a secure lower story or foundation for the grist mill — which was right at the river's edge—and then replaced the perishable wooden chimneys of the ridgetop farm houses with brick at the same time, about 1730.[17]

When appraisers returned in 1749 to inventory the deceased Pierpoint's estate, their tally specified sixteen slaves and 2,600 pounds of tobacco in storage, 600 pounds of trash tobacco, and "9 rooms of Tobacco not Strip[p]ed." The mill, evidently, contained a "Parcell of Coopers Tools and 1 Old Hammer," and a grindstone.[18] Clearly, account credits from grist-mill operations alone were not sufficient to support Pierpoint's family and hands at this stage, though his financial resources had been adequate to the task of undertaking the enterprise without need of a condemnation writ for the mill seat.[19]

In 1766, some thirty-five years after Pierpoint's laborers dug that first colonial millrace beside the Patapsco, a second and larger-scale grist mill got underway in the valley on a condemned parcel about seven miles above Pierpoint's mill. James Hood also owned the tract surrounding the mill seat and briefly ground grists here before his death in 1769; he appears neither to have employed slave labor nor cultivated tobacco. The appraisers for Hood's estate listed a grindstone and "10 barrels of indian corn."[20] In addition to cooper's and joiner's tools, they found an iron for marking barrels and the tools and equipment for a functioning blacksmith's shop. The marking iron suggests a volume of activity that necessitated a delay between the delivery of corn or wheat and the return of meal or flour, a means to keep order among multiple accounts, or perhaps to indicate a "Hood brand." Nearby stood a fulling mill, for treating and dyeing woolen cloth.[21]

Here we can see a craft-centered settlement, if only a very few buildings, that catered to neighborhood trade beside a bridge crossing the Patapsco, mentioned in a later deed of sale. Hood died intestate, and it appears from the public records that the mill did not continue to operate while his estate was being settled. When after five years his heirs conveyed the "Mill[,] Dam and Bridge," the deed carefully specified the "Water Works, Millering Utensils and Implements thereto belonging or in any ways at any time had used or occupied [in or] about the said Mills," a jumble of language intending to encompass both the structures and the movable fittings, which during the interim of disuse may, in fact, have moved.[22]

lis, *for ready Cash only,*

A LARGE and valuable Assortment of well chosen BOOKS.
(t.f.)   WILLIAM AIKMAN.

THIS is to give Notice; that the Fulling Mill on the main Falls of *Patapsco,* near *Benjamin Hood's* Mill, formerly belonging to *Edward How,* now belongs to *Thomas Williams;* which Mill is new built, and in good Order For Fulling   All those that will favour me with their Business that Way, may depend on having it drest in the best Manner, from the coarsest to the finest that can be made, and have it dyed the best of Colours, as they may think proper to direct, on reasonable Terms   by
(w3)   FRANCIS BLACKBURN.

This notice concerning the fulling mill near James Hood's Mill, part of the craft-centered settlement on the Patapsco that Hood established, appeared in the *Maryland Gazette,* August 7, 1772. Maryland State Archives.

P. S. It having been reported at the last Sale, that this Land bore a Quitrent of 10 *per Cent.* we think it necessary to inform the Publick, that it pays no more than 4¾, which a Sight of the Patent now in our Possession will sufficiently shew.

TO BE SOLD,

A TRACT of Land, containing about 500 Acres, situate in *Baltimore* County, near to *Hood's* Mill, on *Patapsco* Falls, and within One Mile of said Mill, and within Four Miles of Two other Merchant Mills, that always give *Baltimore-Town* Price for Wheat, and within Ten Miles of said Town. The Soil is good for Grain or Grass, and has an extensive Range. For Particulars enquire of *Edward Cook,* at Mr. *William Otty's,* adjoining to said Land.

May 4, 1772.

RAN away from the Ship *Molly, William Maynard* Commander, then lying at *Benedict,* Two indented Servant Men: the one named ROBERT

Evidence of the new way. Farmland "good for Grain" is offered for sale near Hood's mill and "Two other Merchant Mills" in 1772. It likewise appeared in the *Maryland Gazette,* August 7, 1772. Maryland State Archives.

With these two small-scale grist mills and the scattering of corn houses and granaries that must have been spreading westward across the ridgetop farms, the well-established social and trading structures that had merged the Patapsco Falls with the tidewater began to change. Charles Pierpoint and John Talbott, the Elk Ridge petitioners and James Hood, each resolved to move in the new direction, but they took only small steps. Not two years after James Hood left his mill for the last time, and while Charles Pierpoint's son Joseph still ran his father's gristmill and contemplated a final threshold crossing himself, four Quaker brothers from Pennsylvania bought a mill seat on the Patapsco between Hood's and Pierpoint's, and gave the new way an even more brilliant gleam.[23]

Jones' Falls as seen in the early nineteenth century.
New York Public Library.

CHAPTER FIVE

The First Assay:
Joseph Ellicott, William Moore, and Baltimore Town remade

WHILE MARYLAND land-office clerks were transcribing the deeds and patents James Hood had assembled for his Patapsco mill tract, a Baltimore County registrar recorded an even more significant name in a heavy, leather-bound volume. Paging through "Deed Book L" to a clean sheet, the copyist began to write the text of an indenture, dated March 7, 1763. Joseph Ellicott, the eldest of five Quaker brothers from Bucks County, Pennsylvania, was a party to this and two other deeds copied into the book that month, the first appearances of his name in the land records of colonial Maryland.[1]

These deeds concerned a mill seat on Jones' Falls, the stream that had originally formed the eastern boundary of Baltimore Town but now coursed through a ravine that divided the eastern quarter of the town's land area from its western three-quarters. Ellicott joined a group of investors who were undertaking the transformation of a small gristmill into a major flour-milling installation. In this ostensibly prosaic act of reconstruction lay the heart of a social, economic, and architectural revolution.

Industry had come quietly to the colonial Chesapeake, its roar and clangor lost in the easy integration of iron with the routines and structures of tobacco culture. Wheat, instead, rang a clear peal across the Chesapeake landscape, and brought about the transformations of place and mentality that produced the first American industrial towns. The relatively straightforward production and merchandizing practices of colonial tobacco and

iron—plantations, enslaved labor, and direct sale to British merchant houses—concentrated profits and investment in the hands of a small class of local plantation owners and foreign merchants. Those conditions did not apply to the cereals trade, which required far more extensive overland networks of growers, processors, handlers, and shippers—the locally based, independent-but-coordinated farmers, millers, craftspeople, and merchants whom we have begun to meet as they established themselves in the Patapsco Valley. Each of these persons could profit individually and invest locally, to differing degrees, certainly, but the scale of their combined investment provided a tremendous impetus for development at major ports and in the villages centered on the mills.

The architectural framework of this cultural and economic change proved dramatically different from what had existed before, and is critical to understanding the course of American industrialization since. That importance is not simply the influence of the form of the merchant flour mill on the architecture of the factory building, but even more significantly, the conception of factory building and factory village as a unified industrial system. The Ellicott brothers saw it. They came of age in this resounding mid-century moment, and they applied their youthful energy and intellect to a realization of its potential. Joseph, the first-born, made the first assay on Jones' Falls at Baltimore Town.

Development of the Jones' Falls site had started on a very small scale a half-century before Joseph

Edward Fell. Colonel Edward Fell initiated the redevelopment of the Hanson's Mill site on Jones' Falls in 1758. He soon sold to Delaware miller William Moore, in 1762. Moore enlisted Joseph Ellicott and other investors to complete the facility known as Moore's Merchant Mills.
Maryland Historical Society.

Ellicott's arrival. Charles Carroll, Esq.—whose son Charles Carroll of Annapolis was to invest in the Baltimore Company Ironworks with his cousin Dr. Charles Carroll—sold the mill seat to "Jonathan Hanson, Millwright" for £15 in 1711.[2] Hanson probably erected a small-scale grist mill on the falls, intended to serve the lightly peopled territory back of the Patapsco's Northwest Branch before Baltimore Town ever existed—not unlike Pierpoint's mill on the main branch of the Patapsco, which drew custom from the diversifying farms of Elk Ridge. No

description of Hanson's mill survives, but the relatively low property values reported in subsequent real-estate deeds suggest that the facilities were small and local in character. Conveyances occurred for £40 in 1741 and £50 in 1758, when merchant and land developer Edward Fell took title.[3] Fell subsequently obtained a new *ad quod damnum* writ in 1760 and made substantial capital improvements to the Hanson mill tract, selling his lease two years later, in 1762, for £1020, a twenty-fold increase over the purchase price of the site.[4]

The facilities Fell constructed probably included a dam, mill pond, and race descending from the northern extremity of the parcel, while the man to whom Fell sold the lease appears to have undertaken construction of a mill at the southern end.[5] William Moore, the mill builder, was an Irish millwright recently arrived from the Brandywine, an important tributary of the Delaware River at Wilmington, a region also undergoing flour-mill development. Nine months after he bought the leasehold from Fell, Moore engaged partners in his mill-building project by subdividing the leased tract to permit construction of a second mill, to be driven by the waterfall from the existing dam, shared with his own mill. The Irishman realized £400 by conveying a one-half share in the dam—with its attendant waterpower and maintenance obligations—as well as a 9.5-acre lot above his own mill, to John and Hugh Burgess and their ambitious thirty-year-old colleague, Joseph Ellicott.[6]

In 1828 this old mill, similar to those built by William Moore and Joseph Ellicott, still stood beside Jones' Falls.
John Rubens Smith Collection, Library of Congress.

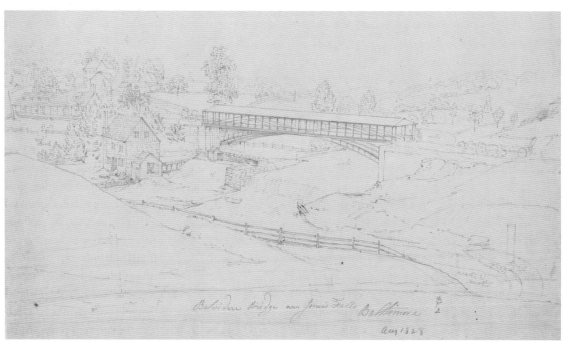

Ellicott and the Burgesses promptly set about construction of the second mill, but also simultaneously engaged in two complex property transactions to distribute unequal shares in the project among William Moore, themselves, and yet two more investors. Ellicott ultimately obtained a one-ninth share in the project, with a value of £500 out of a £4,500 total. If Moore's sister mill was worth the same amount, the sum for the whole enterprise would have yielded at least £9,000.[7]

Whatever the actual value, what we can say is that William Moore's own portion of the project not only included the value of the mill house itself and the other half of the dam with the remaining 10.5 acres of the twenty-acre tract, but also, very likely, a dwelling house, a cooper shop, a "beakhouse"—rather a "bakehouse" or bakery—stables, and other outbuildings, which were enumerated in a 1773 lease.[8] Moore introduced the term "merchant mill" to describe this facility in the lease, and his language served to distinguish the large-scale, wholesale operations conducted there from the small volume of grinding ordinarily handled by a grist or "country" mill.[9] Thus in three years—from Fell's 1760 condemnation proceedings to Ellicott's 1763 share transactions—a consortium of eight investors had enabled construction of what must have been for the time and place a coordinated enterprise of unprecedented commercial size. The Moore's Mills complex included a large dam and two capacious merchant flour mills, with facilities for barrel-making, bread-baking, and horse-drawn transport, located just outside the city limits of Baltimore Town.

The trajectory of the Hanson's/Moore's Mill site neatly mirrors that of adjacent Baltimore Town. Following its 1729 founding, Baltimore languished for nearly twenty years. Only twenty-one of its sixty lots had been sold by 1736, and in accordance with the provisions of the town act, in that year title in the remainder was to have reverted to the original landholder. This was Charles Carroll of Annapolis, who had owned the tract with his brother Daniel, by then deceased. Carroll evidently made an agreement with the town commissioners to take only two-thirds of the unsold balance, or twenty-six lots, while the commissioners retained the rights to thirteen. Carroll shrewdly sold none of his lots until 1745, while the commissioners gradually reduced their number; by 1752 both had nearly exhausted their stock. In that year, a young man named John Moale—who became a prominent Baltimore citizen and one of the town commissioners—climbed the rise later called "Federal Hill" and made a sketch of the town from the south, looking across the basin. The drawing illustrates some forty-five structures scattered over what were then 145 lots; "no more than a few hundred" residents populated the town.[10]

Yet it is at precisely this mid-century moment that Baltimore's fortunes began to turn. In 1745, the colonial assembly authorized annexation of Jonestown, an adjacent community of twenty lots laid out in 1732 along the east bank of Jones' Falls. Located across the ravine from the original area of Baltimore Town, the village lay just below Hanson's

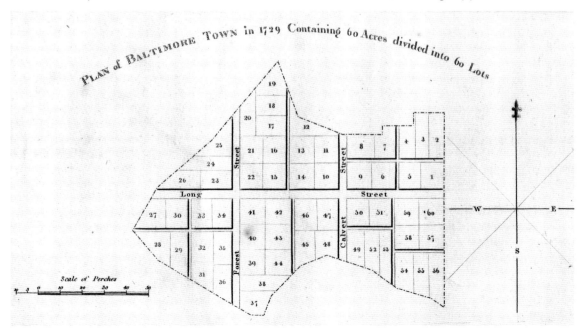

The Baltimore Town plan in 1729.

Maryland Historical Society.

John Moale's sketch of Baltimore Town in 1752, when it was populated by "no more than a few hundred" residents.
Maryland Historical Society.

Mill. The same legislation also created an incentive for improvements to the Baltimore waterfront by granting title to new land made by extending fill into the basin. Developers constructed parallel wharves alternating with alleys of water called docks. Two years later, the town commissioners added eighty-four lots to the north and east of the original Baltimore boundary, to order development in the area between Baltimore and Jonestown, and in 1750 they more than tripled the number of Jonestown lots. Baltimore enlarged its boundaries again in the opposite direction in 1753, around the basin to the west and south. Further expansion here pushed the limits in 1765, and by that year shipwrights were assembling and repairing vessels at Fell's Point, a bustling community that framed the basin's eastern side. The seat of the county court transferred to this burgeoning commercial center in 1768, and in 1773 Baltimore annexed the developed zone that extended all the way east to Fell's Point.

Unlike Richard Shipley's plan for Elk Ridge Landing Town, which confined the lots to a rectangle proportioned to the golden section, the boundaries of Baltimore kept to the contours of the terrain. Within that irregular margin, however, a strictly utilitarian organization of streets and lots prevailed—multiple grids without baroque embellishment.[11] Assessors inventoried 564 houses aligning the grids of the older town limits in 1775, sheltering a population of some 5,900 citizens, plus 800 more individuals at Fell's Point.[12] Baltimore Town

had sustained a remarkable increase over the quarter century from 1750.

Only a few years before the 1775 urban enumeration, a Philadelphian named Joseph Alibone traveled south to Baltimore before making his way to Quaker meetings in Annapolis and Frederick. "[A]fter tarrying a little" at the inn where he was lodged, Alibone set out on foot to explore:

> . . . we walk'd to see the Town, which contains near twice the number of Houses as Wilmington [Delaware], it stands at [the] head of a large Bason (coming from Patapsco River) in which we saw several large Vessels at Anchor which come here [frequently] Some for Tobacco, but cheifly for Wheat & Flour of which great quantities are brought to this Place from a fine Country that lies back of it; the town was formerly rather unhealthy arising from a large body of Marsh ground adjoining it which of late is surprizingly improved, being bank'd out & nearly filled up with Gravel which adds much to the healt[h] & beauty of the place, there is a brisk trade carried on here in most branches, being serv'd by a variety of Artificers from different parts, so that altho the Town has been but of trifling signification till about 15 Years since, yet at present they are well supply'd with matters in general either for use or elegance. Yet it is generally rema[r]k'd

that the manners of the People are abundantly vitiated; The Houses are [in] general neat & good being mostly built of Brick Some of which are very spacious & rent higher than in Philada, & were the Streets kept in better order it might justly be said to be a very pretty Place.[13]

Fifteen years before Alibone wrote, while Baltimore was still "of trifling signification," wharf hands loaded the first casks of flour on a schooner bound for the Caribbean. In 1768, just over a decade after that first shipment, exports of bread and flour from Maryland reached nearly 2,000 tons. Supplementing this figure with the export totals of raw wheat and corn shipped that year gives a sum for all forms of grain totaling nearly 13,000 tons, a volume that just exceeded the colony's tobacco exports. That year, tobacco reported an export value of almost £15 sterling per ton, compared to £3.85 for cereals, but the differential soon changed considerably.

Maryland's entire export volume of bread and flour reached nearly 3,700 tons in 1772, the year Alibone walked the rutted streets of Baltimore Town, while the export value of tobacco that year fell to £13.66 per ton and cereals rose to £11.75. The reversal was underway. By the turn of the century, annual shipments of bread and flour from Baltimore alone—that is, just from the city, not the whole state—ranged between 11,500 and 24,600 tons, roughly a quarter of the whole nation's total.[14] In the last decade of the century, the eighteen merchant mills operating within a four-mile radius of the city fostered an aggrandizement of the populace from 13,500 in 1790 to 31,500 at century's end.[15] This corona of merchant mills would permit Baltimore's quarter-share of the national flour-and-bread-export total to hold at least into the second decade of the nineteenth century, as the city's population swelled to some 63,000 people, and its tobacco exports fell to about two-fifths the volume of flour alone.[16] The growing-pains of manners and maintenance that Alibone observed in the midst of this headlong village-to-city trajectory seem entirely merited.

There is no question that the regional shift from tobacco to grain drove the exceptional intensity of Baltimore Town's urban surge, but the sources of that transformation had global reach. In Europe, the convergence of rising populations with increasing food shortages exploded demand, while, on the western side of the Atlantic, rapid colonial expansion into ever greater tracts of arable land proliferated supply. These bonded at an urban nexus.

Historian Joyce Appleby, among the most prominent scholars to have studied the era's fundamental economic and social changes, offers a trenchant analysis:

> After a century of stagnation, population began to grow again in Europe—in fact, worldwide. England, which had been a major exporter of grains, had barely enough food to feed its growing population. Other European countries, especially Spain and Portugal, that had not adopted harvest-enhancing improvements, felt the pinch even more keenly. The demand for food expressed itself most obviously in higher grain prices. After 1757 the terms of trade changed decisively in favor of grain. . . . The rise in grain prices translated itself in America into a sustained incentive to produce for this European market. . . .
>
> Unlike Europe with its underemployed poor, the colonies exhibited the remarkable phenomenon of a society experiencing rapid population growth without a decline in the standard of living. Instead of pressing upon the means of subsistence, Americans pressed upon fertile land. This was particularly the case after 1750 when European immigrants and internal migrants began moving through Western Pennsylvania, Virginia, and Maryland into the back country.[17]

This eighteenth-century warehouse on the Delaware waterfront in Philadelphia was similar to those lining Water Street in Baltimore.

Marian S. Carson Collection, Library of Congress.

was but the most conspicuous example of a city built on grain.[20]

Although Pennsylvania dominated colonial grain exports during the third quarter of the eighteenth century, the geographic circumstances of the small village port on the broad Patapsco enabled Baltimore Town to capitalize on the increasing grain cultivation of the Maryland piedmont and backcountry, and, as well, to siphon off a significant portion of Pennsylvania produce.

Baltimore's central position in a protected harbor on the western shore of the Chesapeake made it more accessible to those lands then entering cultivation than were the tidewater ports farther south. Moreover, as grain cultivation spread west in Pennsylvania, the overland route to Philadelphia became more arduous, and the Susquehanna—whose shoals made it unsuitable for large vessels—provided a serviceable riverine avenue for smaller craft laden with wheat and flour, southward bound to the bay and Baltimore's mills and warehouses. The expanse of the Chesapeake here rarely froze, presenting another advantage over the icy winter shoreline of the Delaware at Philadelphia. And since the sugar islands of the Caribbean absorbed at least half and often the greater share of Baltimore's annual exports, the Maryland port's position on protected water farther south than Philadelphia and New York and somewhat closer to the West Indies gave Baltimore traders a natural advantage.[21]

Marketing, itself, underwent a significant mutation. Cereals trading proceeded at variance with the traditional "consignment" system that bound most Chesapeake tobacco and iron producers directly to British merchant houses. The new method of merchandising—called the "cargo" system by historian Charles Steffen—embraced independent colonial citizens who developed their own networks of trading, managed between mid-Atlantic flour and grain producers, Caribbean sugar refiners, and suppliers

Baltimore's population grew from a few hundred residents in 1750 to almost 20,000 by the mid-1790s, when George Beck painted this view of the city. Maryland Historical Society.

From beginnings on the mid-Atlantic coast, where close-knit communities of Quaker immigrants had early recognized the superiority of the soil for surplus grain production and had elevated the modest profits and community stability to be garnered therefrom to the level of a religious calling, farmer-settlers brought wheat cultivation first to the territories of western Maryland and Pennsylvania, then extended to the great valley of Virginia and the Ohio River.[18] An expanding network of roads followed them. Merchant millers and tradesmen organized large-scale operations along piedmont waterfalls to process harvests and transport commodities, and coastal brokers built urban warehouses and wharves to manage interchange with diverse local and international ports.[19]

The preparation of harvests for international export required urban attributes. Appleby elaborates:

> Marketing food crops in America, even during the colonial period, had created a host of ancillary trades. Millers, teamsters, ship and wagon builders, bakers, coopers, and grain merchants sprang up to process, transport, and sell American grains. Where tobacco planters converted to wheat in the upper South urban networks appeared. Baltimore

of European consumer goods. Their numbers increased three-fold in Baltimore County from 1750 to 1775, and their activities demonstrate a maturing of the colonial economic system in which native rather than British-based merchants coordinated imports and exports of varied products from dispersed sources and destinations.

One may readily perceive the developing interrelationships among these merchants, millers, and farmers within the evolving international order. Since the sugar islands and southern Europe needed foodstuffs more than tobacco, Chesapeake tobacco planters had no incentive to adapt to this more complex method of trading, while native grain merchants had to do so in order to stay in business. The many such merchants resident in Baltimore Town invested heavily in urban development—not only in merchant mill villages like William Moore's, but also in counting rooms, warehouses, and port facilities on the basin; in shipbuilding and mercantile connections with other American ports; and in well-finished dwellings in town.

Moore himself built a warehouse near the basin on Gay Street, the main road descending to the port from the Jones' Falls mills. He held another lot in town and owned the Exchange Coffee House on Bank and Market Streets in Fell's Point. Certainly

Moore termed himself "merchant" long before the appellation appeared in a 1785 deed.[22] As Joseph Alibone noted, the wheat-producing farmers who settled the "fine country that lies back" of Baltimore had ultimately cultivated great urban change as well.

Although it would be a mistake to assert, as some local histories have done, that Joseph Ellicott and his brothers single-handedly cleared the Patapsco watershed of tobacco planting, it is no exaggeration to state that the Ellicotts were critical members of the regional vanguard. Their correct assessment of larger regional and international trends, and of the particular opportunities that Baltimore Town's rapid increase afforded, led them to throw the weight of their investment not on a partial share of an expensive mill village near town, but over a much larger area of a minimally developed waterfall ten miles distant.

Joseph Ellicott had learned well from his years at Moore's Mills: the conceptual leap from the small gristmills of Hanson and Pierpoint did not terminate at the larger, integrated facilities of Hood and Moore. That regeneration could go further still. In 1771, Joseph and his brothers did take a risk with their own merchant mill and village on "the great falls of Patapsco," but with the clear-eyed understanding that chance favored their convictions.

Baltimore in 1828, no longer a town but "a city built on grain." Until the decade before the artist John Rubens Smith made this drawing, one-quarter of the nation's annual flour and bread exports were shipped from Baltimore's wharves.

John Rubens Smith Collection, Library of Congress.

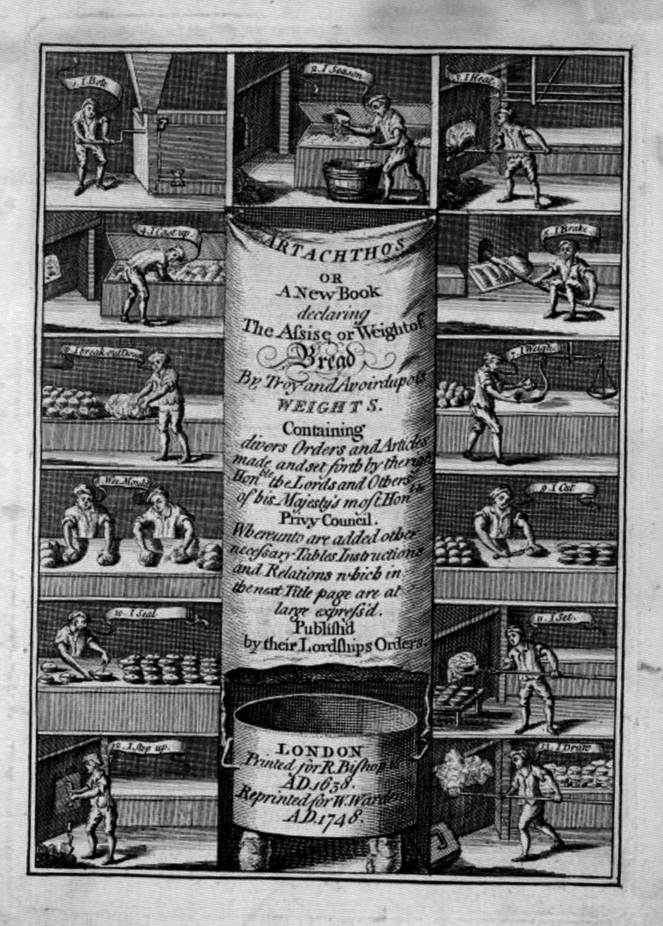

CHAPTER SIX

Ellicotts' Mills—An American first

In April 1771, Joseph and his brothers Andrew, Nathaniel, Thomas, and John ranged in age between thirty-eight and thirty, each one well settled in his respective vocation. Joseph and the youngest, John, called themselves millers, while Andrew and Thomas practiced the wheelwright's craft, and middle son Nathaniel worked iron as a blacksmith. All had grown to maturity near Solebury, Bucks County, Pennsylvania, in the gently rolling hills some two days' journey north of Philadelphia, where a wide bend in the Delaware River embraced an Arcadia of neatly kept farms. Each brother had married upon reaching majority, and, according to Thomas, all had come of age in various aspects of the milling business, which they must have entered as teenaged apprentices.

Andrew, senior — the immigrant—died in 1741 when his boys were still children. Though Ann Ellicott, the young widow of this English Quaker, soon remarried outside of the meeting, the brothers were not deprived of the community bonds Quakerism enforced. Their activities dovetail well with the larger Quaker story in the mid-Atlantic, and that story is critical to understanding how they came to design America's first factory town.[1]

Just as the sweeping arc of the Appalachians envelops the rich and extensive wheat country of southeastern Pennsylvania, so did the Quaker sense of community bind together the "sprawling townships . . . of contiguous farmsteads" that brought the Pennsylvania colony's greening meadows and woodlands into cultivation.[2] Quakers made these dispersed farms an unlikely but solid foundation for unifying institutions. Although they set themselves apart from the broader culture, and to some extent

were excluded from colony-wide positions of political and religious authority, they effectively nurtured a binding sense of community among themselves and excelled in commerce, a field open to them without restriction. Through devotion, piety, and attention to the accumulation of "decent wealth," they sought to rear children and keep them in the faith—a potent form of domesticity that had far-reaching social and economic ramifications.[3]

Quakers lived *in* the world, not apart from it, and the diligent cultivation of agricultural surpluses tallied with sagacious mercantile investments. Distinguished Quaker historian Frederick Tolles put it best: "Instead of rejecting the gross world of human appetites and passions, [Quakers] insisted that it was the material out of which the Kingdom of God was to be fashioned."[4] Quakerism acknowledged the sinfulness and depravity of fallen humanity but embraced the Puritan notion of God's calling to a

profession of both work and faith, the immediate and the ultimate, earthly profit exalted and tempered. By 1769, Quakers were about a seventh of Philadelphia's population, yet numbered "more than half of those who paid taxes in excess of one hundred pounds," an exemplary statistic, as is this: twelve of the city's seventeen wealthiest citizens were Quakers.[5]

The Ellicott brothers' Quaker roots instilled in them a pronounced awareness of their place in the world as productive individuals and an appreciation for extended commercial and religious relationships. Those relationships defined and integrated personal and group identity. Doubtless the Ellicott boys were apprenticed to Quaker millers, learned trading from Quaker merchants, and entered upon their professions not only with secure contacts to Quakers already well positioned, but also, and more importantly, with an innate understanding of what the idea of "community" could actually achieve. The worldview the Ellicott brothers learned as young men gave them a conception of community, both earthly and spiritual, that predisposed them to imagine and implement what came to be the central organizing concept of their industrial village: the animation and coordination of a network of complementary, mutually supporting activities. Joseph's experiences at Moore's Mills not only offered him specific operational and managerial lessons in a large-scale facility, his experiences also positioned him to apply the special concept of Quaker community to the terrain of Chesapeake Maryland. That terrain was human and economic as well as topographic. Joseph and his brothers succeeded brilliantly.

Thomas Ellicott was the only one of the five to write, even briefly, of their experiences. "It is now upwards of 38 years since I first began millwrighting," he stated in 1795, when he was fifty-seven:

> I followed it very constant for about ten years, making it my particular study. Several of my brothers being also mill-wrights, we kept in company; and were often called to different parts of this, and the adjacent states, to build mills of the first rates, in their day. Some of them entered into the manufacturing line, but I continued at mill-wrighting, and other business connected therewith; such as rolling screens, and fans, and making them go by water, in merchant and grist mills; also farmers fans, for cleaning grain, being the first, I believe, that made these things in America: but for several years past, have done but little else, than build mills, or draught to build by.[6]

So Thomas took to his career at age nineteen, and in 1763, when he was twenty-five, joined his brother Joseph on the initial family foray into Maryland, where he witnessed one of the deeds for the extensive Moore's Merchant Mill project on Jones' Falls.[7] By the end of that decade, Thomas was applying his joining skills not only to wagon making but also mill-machinery fabrication, and in the winter of 1773–1774, back in Pennsylvania, he built three water-powered rolling screens and fans, including wire sieves, for his brothers' merchant mill.[8] Notwithstanding his earlier presence in Baltimore, Thomas opted not to join his brothers in their partnership on the Patapsco, which began to take shape in 1771. Certainly, though, his hand at drafting mill designs "to build by" must have proved useful to his brothers as they engineered their own exceptional mill and the machinery and motive systems necessary to power the enterprise.

When Joseph, Andrew, Nathaniel, and John, "all brothers in company," proceeded "into the manufacturing line," they raised funds for the Patapsco venture by standing security for one of four total shares of company stock, valued at £500 per share, coincidentally the amount of Joseph's investment in Moore's Merchant Mills. These instruments did ultimately report dividends as with modern corporate stock, but for the individual who did not initially make available to the company the full cash value of his share, interest accrued to the company's account on the outstanding balance "short of stock."[9] This method of organization gave the company itself an identity beyond that of its individual owners and perhaps lessened the operational complexities of divided proprietorship. At Moore's Mills, for example, or Caleb Dorsey's Elk Ridge Company, these ownership relations appear to have been ordered through real-estate indentures alone.

Scholars of American corporate-industrial history have tended to seat the origins of the nation's corporate capitalism with the immensely successful New England textile companies of the early nineteenth century, yet the Ellicotts' organization shows that a kind of corporate model held some currency for private business investors a generation earlier.[10] The Ellicotts' prescience and sophistication here in terms of company design mirrored that applied to the architecture of their industrial community. Nonetheless, the brothers never expanded this nascent joint-stock system to additional investors, either among the public or to other family members. Sons inherited portions of their father's allotment, and successor company operations evidently proceeded as partnerships, alone, without further stock issues. When the initial company required capital supplements, the four brothers raised funds through loans.

The first of these, in 1775, took a traditional form: "Richard Gibbs, gentleman," a successful Bucks County farmer with an eye for business opportunities, supplied £1,200 cash secured by a mortgage of all company holdings. Almost certainly Gibbs was one of those well-positioned members of the Society of Friends whose connections proved so formative for the Ellicott brothers. The second loan not only demonstrated the brothers' persuasive abilities, but also, notably, their astuteness in obtaining investment from influential persons outside the Quaker community. In 1777, Charles Carroll of Annapolis agreed to deliver his harvests of wheat over one season at a set price. The quantity totaled 2,665 bushels, worth almost £1,000, which the Ellicotts repaid over time with interest, as they did the mortgage to Gibbs. The confidence of a leading Maryland family—arguably the most influential of all Maryland families—doubtless persuaded others to bring business to the fledgling enterprise, a fact as significant as Carroll's in-kind loan itself.[11]

With the initial capital raised and the methods for future investment understood, the brothers took the leap. On April 24, 1771, the four young men signed several Baltimore and Anne Arundel County deeds. The two adjacent tracts they purchased extended west across Patapsco falls from Baltimore County to Anne Arundel, about five miles downstream from Hood's mill and two miles upstream from Pierpoint's.[12] Just there, the Patapsco opened into a wide curve, the narrows upstream and down relented, and the valley broadened. The inner curve of the falls faced Baltimore County, and a length of level ground beyond the low bank on this side rose just above the shoals, while the strength of the current cut deeply into the shore opposite, making for a more pronounced drop to the water on the Anne Arundel side. On this western slope, a "small Draft"

A page from Thomas Ellicott's essay in Oliver Evans, *The Young Millwright and Miller's Companion.*

and its several tributaries cut a defile that ascended as high as the ridge top.[13] This, too, opened the valley at the curve of the falls, and yielded a passable grade for a road west. Toward the east, in the direction of Baltimore Town, the best road trace ran south along the level by the river, then climbed by turns to the broad plateau above.

The Patapsco bisected the greater part of these eighty-four acres. The lower of the two tracts comprised fifty acres, laid out as a rectangle perpendicular to the river, through which the Baltimore road would begin its ascent to the plateau, while the contiguous upper tract ran lengthwise upstream and encompassed most of the inner curve of the falls. Adjacent to its upper end, the brothers discovered an odd configuration of unclaimed land, a "vacancy" not included in earlier surveys, that extended fully around the curve of the falls and also included more of the defile and a part of its northern slope. In 1773 the colonial land office issued a warrant for resurvey of this upper tract, to be patented "Mount Unity," ultimately securing 19.5 additional acres to the Ellicotts; the next year they purchased from a local planter some thirty acres that filled the spaces between the arms of the former vacant land.[14] The

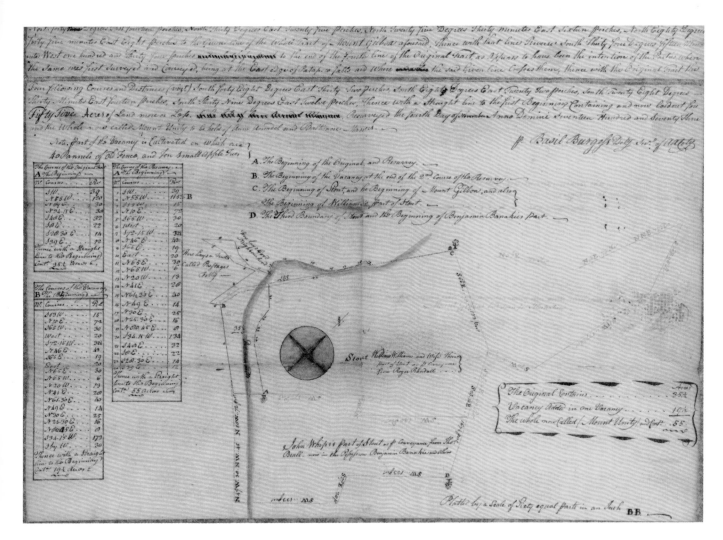

The plat of the original Ellicott patent, describing the family's first tract, purchased from William Williams in 1771.

Maryland State Archives.

resulting 135.5-acre tract ran the length of the valley bottom for more than a mile, ascended the pass to the west at the upper end, and climbed to the east at the lower, assuring the Ellicotts control not only of the mill seat itself but also of the areas on both sides of the river best suited for access to it. The ordered siting of multiple components of the enterprise lay fully in their hands.

Even in the configuration of their original tract, the intentions of the Ellicott brothers were evident. No merchant mill could function without ready access to expansive farm lands and nearby urban market halls, and few transactions could occur in a cash-poor economy without inventories of goods for trade and the presence of services, likewise dependent on complementary development and reliable contacts. A road was crucial. No inconvenient lane would suffice either, this road, but a public highway grafted to the existing network, however inchoate, which by virtue of an easy river crossing would generate traffic that would be the lifeblood of the mills.

The rockbound, densely wooded ribbon of the valley must have opened to wide clearings on the high

grounds in 1771, the year of the Ellicotts' purchase, but all these lands, high and low, had been patented by then, and some low grounds fenced and cultivated.[15] Although they may not have had to cut a swath into the "dark 'mill hollow' . . . through regions where the sound of the axe had never before been heard," as John Ellicott Tyson's picturesque 1847 history of Ellicotts' Mills claims, the brothers early occupied themselves with building a road and bridge.[16]

Before springtime came to the valley again, the Anne Arundel County Court allocated funds to John Ellicott & Company "for maintenance of Ellicotts Bridge over the great falls of the Patapsco River," the earliest surviving record of any work done on the site.[17] Instead of simply holding a likely piece of real estate against ill-defined prospective improvements, as had happened with Carroll's Reserve at Elk Ridge Landing, the Ellicotts engaged in an active and carefully planned project founded on connection between the populating lands to the west and the Atlantic world. Before the mill, before the workshops, before the store and warehouse, the brothers built a road and a good river crossing.

If the four Ellicott men assembled on the brisk unpaved streets of Baltimore Town in the early spring of 1771 to sign the deeds or to ride out to examine their property, they did not all remain. In May, Andrew sent word to Quaker merchants in Philadelphia: "Friends, Holinsworth & Rudolph Please to forward that pork Samuel Har[?]de put in your Care for Andrew Ellicott and John Ellicott as Soon as Possible to Baltim[ore] Town thy frd Andrew Ellicott May ye 17th 1771."[18]

As early as a month after the April deed signing, partners Joseph and Nathaniel were perhaps no longer in Baltimore. In any case, by 1773, only John and a colleague named Samuel Godfrey were present on site, along with Andrew's eldest son Jonathan, who turned seventeen that year, and a man named Michael Monks. These were among the first employees of "John Ellicott & Company." From the beginning, the formal distinction between all levels of employees within the company was clear: everyone earned wages. Godfrey assumed a variety of mercantile responsibilities at £30 per year, while Monks worked for John Ellicott & Company only periodically, and at a rate of pay equivalent to Jonathan's as a miller and family member, £36 annually. John Ellicott drew £90, an amount that clearly enforced his status as owner relative to the others.[19] Their numbers on site increased a year later, in 1774, as John's household of taxables expanded from four to seven unnamed individuals. That year, work on the merchant mill commenced.[20]

Like his brother John, Joseph Ellicott also drew a £90 annual salary from the company, but he missed the 1773 enumeration of taxables that Constable Abraham Walker took in Patapsco Upper Hundred, as well as the 1774 census of heads of households for Saint Paul's parish, likely because he made several trips to Philadelphia and Baltimore on company business during those early years. Joseph earned a credit on his company account for cash spent "going down wt. our wives" in mid-summer 1773—to accompany them on the move from Pennsylvania to Maryland—and early the next year he purchased and probably transported Thomas Ellicott's mill machinery from Pennsylvania. Joseph also acquired books for the company in Philadelphia; although unspecified, it is possible these were blank ledger volumes bound by a city bookseller.[21]

As important as the Ellicotts' real estate transactions are to understanding the premises of company operations, even more telling are the multifarious financial accounts maintained in the library of company ledgers. These books reveal critical components of the financial, occupational, and architectural organization of Ellicotts' Mills. Just as the boundaries of the original tract display the Ellicott brothers' conceptions that a merchant-mill community have a basis in ready access to traffic and extensive, even exclusive, company control of the landscape, so too do the ledgers disclose something of the mentality that underlay the brothers' earliest activities. Indeed the quintessential organizing principle of the enterprise—its expansive framework of flour processing, support services, and trading—finds an apposite symmetry in the three initial company ledgers, each one evidently devoted to an individual component

of the enterprise: milling, smithing, and mercantile activities. Together, these operations attracted and retained a loyal and extensive community-wide following for the entire company.[22] Significantly, no account lists a payment to an architect or a professional designer, yet the Ellicotts built a complex array of structures and organized them in a sophisticated, effective, and consciously hierarchical town plan. Nor does any entry concern a reservoir of enslaved labor, yet a diverse and hierarchical range of wage and salaried employees stride across the ledger pages as they must have trod the floorboards of the mills and shops and dwellings. The laconic Ellicotts left few letters, but their real-estate indentures and company accounts make their industrial village live again. These commonplace records give Ellicotts'

Mills dimension and extent, chronology and routine, voice and mentality, purpose and connection. The brothers' designs are unmistakable.

Having cleared a road into the valley and spanned the Patapsco with a bridge, John Ellicott and his young crew turned first to putting ancillary services into operation and to constructing a permanent dwelling for the household. Thus the drays and wagons that began to cross Ellicotts' bridge in 1772 and the clipped or plodding treads resounding with them represented movement turned into commerce. And commerce consisted of more than grain harvests carried to a mill; the Ellicotts viewed that fundamental exchange as part of the constellation of transactions given shelter and stimulus in a mill town, not simply by a mill. On June 1, 1772, Samuel Godfrey began to draw a salary as the storekeeper, and, on a date now unknown but probably the same year, also became the first account holder recorded on page one of the Smith's book.[23] In spring 1773, a local small planter and builder named Bartholomew Balderson began to cut lumber in the Ellicotts' water-powered sawmill, and for just over a month during the succeeding winter rented the sawmill for his own use. Balderson supplied "timber for [the] Coopers Shop" and within five days of that May 1773 delivery had built it. His handiwork appeared the same month in repairs made to a dam and race and to a set of bolting gears, the machinery of a flour mill.[24] When company accounts transferred to a different ledger on September 8, 1774, a schoolmaster, a tailor, a baker, and a number of teamsters had balances carried forward to the new book, indicating still more village activities pre-dating construction of the Ellicotts' merchant mill, detailed in account entries dated after September 1774.[25]

These later account entries show that Balderson's "mending" of the millrace and gears the previous year must have occurred elsewhere than at the Ellicotts' merchant mill, which had not yet been constructed. Upstream stood the likely site: James Hood's mill. This enterprise had been dormant since Hood's death in 1769, and a lease from Hood's heirs could have provided the Ellicott brothers with a readily operational facility for grinding the flour that Ellicott & Company accounts show they sold before completion of their own mill. Lease or no, James Hood's son Benjamin opened the very first company account of all, recorded on page one of the earliest ledger, and at the end of 1774 sold the

Details from George Ellicott's drawing of Ellicotts' Lower Mills. FROM LEFT TO RIGHT: the saw mill, the merchant mill, and the storehouse.

Ellicotts his father's mill.[26] Thenceforward, Hood's came to be known as "Ellicotts' Upper Mill," and it operated as a subsidiary enterprise of John Ellicott & Company until Joseph bought it outright when the original partnership formally dissolved in 1778.[27]

Certainly, company laborers proceeded to raise a dam and excavate a millrace-canal on the Ellicotts' original tract some years before the Hood's mill purchase and before the Ellicotts' merchant mill went into service because the operational sawmill Bartholomew Balderson used in 1773 presupposes a functional power supply. In addition to sizing lumber for the company, Balderson made "4 pair [of]

The original Ellicotts' Mills storehouse was configured very much like the lefthand wing of this warehouse in Fredericksburg, Virginia, with a flight of steps climbing to a center door on the upper story.
Library of Congress.

An eighteenth-century warehouse on Philadelphia's Delaware waterfront, with two hoods for hoists at each side of the façade. This double building was a larger and more elaborate version of the type the Ellicott brothers built on the Patapsco, which had a single hood at the peak of the gable.
Library of Congress.

bedsteads," credited on August 17, 1773, coincident with the mid-summer arrival of John's and Joseph's wives on the site, doubtless to occupy John Ellicott's dwelling, newly completed.[28] This story-and-a-half stone house stood back from the river, at the foot of the slope that together with the curve of the falls bounded the level ground on the Baltimore County side of the Patapsco. John had a front porch built for his dwelling, and if Leah and Judith Ellicott paused there at the railing to look up the valley, across the level ground bestirring with activity, they would have seen the millrace descending toward them alongside the new road to a location a bit short of their vantage point. There the race angled beneath the road's surface into an underground trunk line to reach the wheel of the sawmill before splashing back into the falls.[29] The road continued parallel to the Patapsco, past the steps the women climbed to the porch, before ascending eastward toward Baltimore Town.

The greatest extent of the low ground along the inner curve of the falls lay between river and

road, while John Ellicott's house and yard pressed against the eastern hill and held the southern end of the developed area. At the northern end, where Ellicotts' bridge spanned the falls, the road inclined on a ramped embankment contained within stone retaining walls, so that the grade of the crossing could gain the elevation of the higher western bank opposite. This ramped eastern embankment may also have doubled as an abutment for the Ellicotts' wooden dam, spanning the Patapsco at an angle to drive the current into the millrace, which kept to the eastern side of the road for nearly three hundred yards before turning west to the mills, above John Ellicott's dwelling.[30] Here, between the dwelling and the turn in the millrace, the builders erected the stone storehouse, also a story-and-a-half structure, raised above the flood-plain on a full-height cellar, with paired flanking steps rising on the gable-end facade to the center door. The gable roof projected in a hood over the centered garret opening above. This large structure, thirty-three feet on its gable end, and deep fifty-three feet on its flanks, was a variation of an urban warehouse form, examples of which lined the Delaware waterfront in Philadelphia, certainly a type and location familiar to the Ellicotts.[31]

Across the road, where the covered trunk line of the race emptied back into the river, the builders raised the frame sawmill parallel to the Patapsco and cleared the site for the merchant mill, which was to stand perpendicular to it. Above these, at the river's edge, the builders aligned a wooden coal house and the single-story stone blacksmith's shop. These two structures closed the river-side of an expanse of space open to the Baltimore road, delimited on one end by the mills and on the other by the teamsters' stable. The flank of this massive stone stable fronted the road, and a longitudinal center aisle opened to the exterior on each gable end through a tall segmental archway. The stable walls attained sufficient height to accommodate not only these two arched gable-end openings, but also a mezzanine over the stalls, with a lighted garret above all, probably containing a threshing floor and storage rooms. The generous size of this building must have enabled the teamsters to roll tall-sided wagons loaded with barrels and casks down the central aisle unimpeded. These containers the coopers assembled in their log or frame shop, probably located along the Baltimore road on the far side of the mill seat, by a small stream later called "Coopers' Branch."[32]

No record survives of the temporary structure or structures John Ellicott and his crew and laborers erected to shelter themselves, their draft animals, and equipment during the initial staging of the project. Earthfast methods cannot be discounted, though log construction is equally probable, since the Ellicotts did not come to the piedmont from the dominion of tidewater tobacco. Furthermore, scholars have generally agreed that the practicality and

cost savings of log building quickly took it beyond specific immigrant traditions.[33] In fact, three log dwellings already stood on valley lands in 1761 and 1762, adjacent to what became the Ellicotts' tract, and in 1798 several single-room log dwellings and a log stable were numbered among the company-owned rental housing grouped on both sides of the Patapsco.[34]

Since the long-term success of the Ellicotts' enterprise depended on a substantial investment in infrastructure and a commitment to multiple community-based enterprises—in contrast to the largely insular local economies centered on Chesapeake tobacco plantations and ironworks—one may consequently presume that the brothers built more permanently, if not always at the greatest possible level of security and stability, which would have been stone. Certainly all of the most important early buildings were stone, and the appeal of such structures on a flood-plain was obvious. The presence of good building stone on the valley slopes may have been one of the factors that influenced the Ellicotts' choice of site, yet those same slopes held abundant timber. The fact that the Ellicotts chose the more difficult process of quarrying and working stone into blocks signals intention, and reveals their confidence in the greater solidity and long-term economy of masonry. While one may read into their choice for stone an affinity for the valley's earlier stone forges, more certain is the link to stonemasonry in merchant-mill buildings themselves. Given the anticipated scale, expense, and duration of their operations, the brothers doubtless chose to allocate their resources as efficiently as possible.

Precise construction dates for the full range of these first village buildings, temporary or permanent, are not known, neither then are their number and function, since only three or four of them remain standing.[35] Yet the Ellicotts' organizing plans are clear, and clearly illustrated. A priceless drawing

Details from George Ellicott's drawing of Ellicotts' Lower Mills. FROM LEFT TO RIGHT: the stable with Jonathan Ellicott's house behind, the smith's shop, and the coal house.

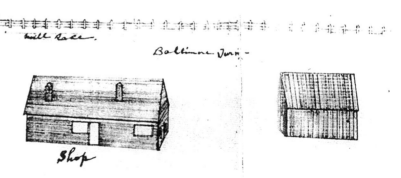

Jonathan Ellicotts house 1782

Shop

Baltimore Jun

mill race.

from the hand of a son of Andrew Ellicott depicts many of Ellicotts' Mills' earliest permanent structures. Once operations got underway, Andrew apprenticed several of his eldest son Jonathan's younger brothers at the Patapsco mills, among them George, four years Jonathan's junior. Like Jonathan, George was to make his career at Ellicotts' Mills, and while a still a teenaged apprentice in millwrighting, he also became an accomplished surveyor.[36] In the 1780s, George applied his drafting skills to create a highly accurate perspective of the mill complex as seen from the heights on the Anne Arundel side of the Patapsco. This panorama displays the range of buildings from John Ellicott's dwelling on the south to the teamsters' stable on the north. It is through George's hand that the configuration of the buildings already discussed is manifest.[37]

A decade or so later, in 1798, the Federal Direct Tax assessor for Baltimore County inventoried all the structures George had drawn plus several others built later. Fortuitously, the surveyor produced a sequential list, identifying the dwellings and outbuildings that appeared at his right hand as he walked up the Baltimore road from John Ellicott's toward the Patapsco bridge. Then, after an about face, he registered the buildings of the industrial zone on the west side of the Baltimore road, again at his right hand as he walked south. The store, which was on the east, he included with the grouping of industrial structures, but it, too, fell with them in proper sequence. The federal assessor for the Anne Arundel district may have registered his entries in sequence, too, proceeding from the bridge westward, up the ascending road, though the lateral disposition of the buildings is not fully known. The early village, now almost entirely vanished, appears in these sources.

A close reading of documents and images in light of the company labor records contained in the ledgers allows us also to repopulate these village places.[38] Three distinct zones emerge, ordered by status, function, and architectural form. To the east of the Baltimore road lay the upper-level residential quarter, along with the company store, its inventory and storekeeper under the Ellicotts' watchful eyes. At the end of the eighteenth century, a row of six multiple-story dwellings faced the road and river here. In addition to their dimensions, elevations, and materials, the plans of these dwellings expressed and enforced the social status of their occupants. The northern four dwellings presented two-story facades

of stone, symmetrical compositions of imposing scale, though without high-style classical detail. The smallest stood directly opposite the Patapsco bridge, and was probably a two-room structure without a central passage, that is, with a winder stair in the larger of the two main-floor rooms.[39] This dwelling was under ground-rent to a man named Samuel Smith, who operated a tannery. Doubtless Smith steeped his tannins out of bark shorn from timber at the sawmill, and produced leather not only for shoemaking, horse tack, and harnesses, but also for belt drives in the flour mill.[40]

First employee Samuel Godfrey occupied a larger, three-bay dwelling next to the south, and its more generous size reflected his higher status within the company. In addition to his early responsibilities as storekeeper, Godfrey built a malt-house and distilled whiskey, an enterprise, like that of the tanner, complementary to the principal activities of the company. Later he managed the company's warehouse operations on Baltimore basin.[41] This dwelling, too, lacked a central passage on the principal floor, where a paired hall and chamber plan followed the classic, eighteenth-century usage.[42]

Godfrey's dwelling, also under ground-rent from the company, angled slightly toward those of his employers, Jonathan and George Ellicott, paired farther down the Baltimore road.[43] Jonathan occupied a still larger three-bay dwelling, and its increased dimensions suggest the space for social sorting accommodated in a central passage. An inference of formal room, passage, and principal chamber plan is not unreasonable, given the known configuration of George's dwelling, next door. Here, Jonathan's younger brother inhabited a five-bay house, the most substantial domestic building in the village. George's house still stands, and its plan does reveal a more socially sophisticated eighteenth-century interior, comprising parlor, central passage, and principal bed chamber on the first floor, with a dining room, added later, behind.[44]

Beyond a large garden to the south stood the fifth two-story dwelling, an amalgam of frame on stone about the same size as the tanner's dwelling, its configuration probably representing an enlargement of an original one-story stone structure with a frame second.[45] This house the storekeeper leased. Next stood the storehouse, then John Ellicott's story-and-a-half dwelling. Though the plan of this house is not known, its footprint was slightly larger

than that of Jonathan's house, and its front porch, unique among village dwellings in the eighteenth century, must have been intended from the beginning to serve as a semi-public gathering place for the interaction between community and company, a critical aspect of the entire enterprise.[46]

West of the Baltimore road lay the industrial zone, headed on the north by a two-story frame dwelling, probably a boarding house for the millers and apprentices, perhaps in care of a senior miller. Then came the substantial stone stable for the teamsters; the stone smith's shop with its wooden coal house; the frame sawmill and the stone merchant mill; two more stables, of frame construction; two more stone shops, and an unspecified stone house. Beyond these, where the Baltimore road began its ascent, stood the single-story stone dwelling of the principal cooper, along with a stone coopers' shop and two single-story log dwellings for his men.[47]

The workforce living and working in these structures comprised several groups. Tradesmen, such as the coopers, smiths, and wheelwrights, generally maintained a permanent presence in the community and mobilized their own assistants, still on the company payroll. Transient workers, who might stay for a period (or periods) of months or years, principally included the millers and teamsters but also such specialized individual laborers as the tailor, baker, teacher, and the women who took in charge washing, mending, and cooking, and in some cases baking and spinning. Day laborers were migrants and neighborhood residents who worked only occasionally for the company on short- or long-term tasks.

Over the first winter of merchant mill operations, 1774–1775, some eighteen individuals outside of the family circle found employment in the village, their rates of pay indicating a well-established social hierarchy. Senior millers Samuel Cooper, Hezekiah Dean, and Moses Pitcock earned fifty shillings a month, equivalent to Samuel Godfrey's £30 annual wage. Journeyman millers Joseph Cornelious and Matthew Boys earned forty-five and forty shillings, an older apprentice, Patrick Nowland, thirty, and a boy, Carlisle Porter, twelve. Teamsters Robert Stewart and Thomas Griffin earned fifty shillings. Washerwoman and cook Ruth Young began for a few months at fifteen shillings and after a month's break returned at twenty-five; could she have struck the company for a higher wage? William Dillworth and his team of coopers earned eighteen to twenty-two pence by the piece, and some seven or eight laborers, among them "molattoe" Henry Howard, also worked by the task or by occasional days, generally earning from fifteen pence to two shillings per occasion. This work included reaping, raking, and binding wheat and oats on the ridgetop fields, threshing the harvest, cutting cords of firewood, burning charcoal, butchering animals, roadwork, and other projects unspecified. George Matthews took a commission on casks of Ellicott flour sold in Baltimore.[48]

Doubtless the transient members of this workforce lodged wherever space was available, perhaps in a proper boarding house but also scattered among other dwellings in the village, including, for "sundry hands" at the end of the century, in care of Jonathan Ellicott.[49] The day laborers must

This mid-nineteenth century engraving depicts part of the upper level residential quarter at Ellicotts' Mills. Almost out of view on the left is the head miller's dwelling in the industrial zone. Across the millrace, on the left is the house of Samuel Godfrey, then Jonathan Ellicott (ca. 1780), and George Ellicott (ca. 1792). The porches are nineteenth-century additions.

From Allison Ellicott Mylander, *The Ellicotts: Striving for a Holy Community* (Ellicott City, Md.: Historic Ellicott City, 1991).

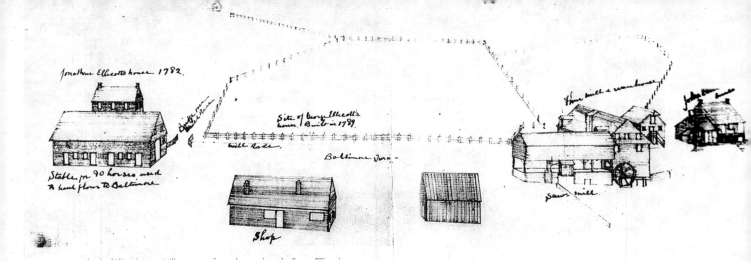

Various handwritten labels on the drawing: "Jonathan Ellicotts house 1782.", "Stable for 90 horses used to hand flour to Baltimore", "Site of George Ellicott's house Built in 1789", "Mill Race", "Baltimore June –", "Shop", "flour mill & ware house", "Saw mill"

George Ellicott's drawing of Ellicotts' Lower Mills.

Maryland Historical Society.

have walked to the village from the neighborhood. Contracted tradesmen rented shop space from the company, and while some of these individuals took company dwellings as well, others boarded. In rare cases, transient workmen "found themselves" housing, food, and washing in the neighborhood, and certainly by the end of the century also made use of four small, single-story log dwellings on Bartholomew Balderson's property by the Ellicotts' tract across the river.[50]

There, on the Anne Arundel side of the Patapsco, the village's third zone lay, comprising ancillary activities and humbler housing. Closest to the Patapsco stood the one-story frame dwelling of the principal blacksmith and a one-story stone dwelling occupied by a man who later contracted to build and run a linseed oil mill on the site. Like the tannery and distillery, the oil mill was yet another enterprise complementary to company operations.[51] Then stood a two-story frame tavern with a two-story stone kitchen and a log stable. Farther up the road, two frame shops, wheelwright's and blacksmith's, were accompanied by the one-story log dwelling for the blacksmith. Bartholomew Balderson, himself a joiner, probably ran the wheelwright's shop, in which case his log dwellings may have housed his own crew, like the cooper's across the river. A stone schoolhouse topped a low rise north of the road, and across to the south, on a yet higher hill silhouetted in the west, in alignment with the road's approach from the Patapsco bridge, was "a House of Worship and Discipline [also built of stone]; and a Burying Ground for the Society of people Called Quakers."[52] Quiet above all.

The hilltop remove of the meeting house and school house distanced their contemplative pursuits from the raucous distractions of the village below. But the greater and lesser hilltop sites also put on explicit display the Quaker affiliations of the company, expressed in terms of faith and the communion of saints on the one hand and of useful knowledge on the other. The meeting house, the burial ground, and the school house, literally ascendant over the village, served also as figurative guides, their relative elevations reminders of the ever-present unity of the spiritual and earthly communities and of the hierarchy of persons and values composing both. The importance of that theological foundation for the community, expressed in architecture, was intentionally juxtaposed with the dominant position, size, and finish of the Ellicotts' dwellings opposite, at a level with the village on the other side of the river, where management and ownership authority lay.

These relational motifs play out in other architectural variations as well, and may be plotted in terms of square-footage of dwelling space. It is critical for our understanding of the Ellicotts' accomplishment to recognize that these distinctions in size were not haphazard productions of chance but functions of an intentional and globalizing design crafted by the Ellicotts as they brought the idea for a mill village into reality. Virtually every facet of the enterprise was reflected in architecture.

The range of spaces begins, of course, with little or none—the condition of the boarders and day laborers—and doubtless proceeded from the sharing and position of now unknown rooms. For us the spatial distinctions emerge, imperfectly, with the calculation of 168 square feet, contained within the smallest of Bartholomew Balderson's four log dwellings, twelve by fourteen feet. The more important frame and stone dwellings by the river in the Anne-Arundel zone attained 540 square feet, while the tavern-keeper kept the largest building in the neighborhood, just above 1,000 square feet on two floors, with a supplement of 900 in his substantial kitchen.

In the industrial zone by the mills, the cooper's

workmen occupied 256 square feet, equivalent to the largest of the log dwellings in Anne Arundel, and the cooper himself, 600, a bit more than his fellow tradesmen across the river, excepting the tavern keeper. The frame millers' house contained 640 square feet on two floors, a little more still, but only half that of the store-keeper's stone and frame dwelling sited across the Baltimore road. The six dwellings here, exclusive of garrets, cellars, and kitchens proceeded from 1,200 to 1,300 square feet for the three rented houses, and from 1,600 to 2,100 square feet for the three Ellicotts. From shared room to log house to capacious stone residence, each person occupied a home equivalent to his or her position in the clockwork universe of Americas first industrial town.

No part of Ellicotts' Mills ever conformed to the exactions of a grid, but the village took shape according to a fundamental organizing principal in every respect as deliberate and hierarchical as an overlay of avenues, alleys, and lots ordered by the right angle. Yes, the plan was opportunistic, as the Baltimore road followed the easiest grade the terrain dictated, but the community's organization and development were never haphazard, undirected, or unplanned. The Ellicotts jealously guarded their investment through the extensive acquisition of land and the regulation and ordering of improvements, yet they also exercised a pronounced and even sophisticated understanding without the direct involvement of an architect wielding compass and rule over a set of comprehensive specifications. In this respect, the Ellicotts' exceptional project was of a piece with its place and period, and as will be evident in the form of the mill, belonged to a vernacular tradition of building without involvement of formal architects. This tradition was shaped as much by opportunity and experience as by social and economic ambition.

Ellicotts' Mills was a tangible expression of an idea of Quaker community, one that readily encompassed the farming and mercantile interests that were the principal components of the wheat and flour trade in the eighteenth-century mid-Atlantic.[53] The concept of Quaker community also prepared American ground for that element of the nineteenth-century architectural and industrial landscape called the factory town.

The lesson of Ellicotts' Mills is this: do not mistake the lack of regularity and uniformity in the "vernacular order" of the early mill village for a lack of conscious, comprehensive design.[54] The Ellicott brothers' project aimed just as pointedly at social control and the generation of profit as did those nineteenth-century company town builders more commonly recognized as the originators of the type in America. A more subtle reading of the brothers' mill village reveals the Ellicott Company's attempt to organize and express the hierarchical components of a new kind of industrial community just then developing, freed from the hermetic mentality of a plantation—tobacco or iron. As much as company ownership of land and the means of production resembled the hierarchical universe of the plantation, this new, more dynamic system, founded on wage labor, contracted services, multiplied sources of capital investment, and broad-based local and international economic connections, shed the stifling character of the plantation, and by its nature opened itself to urbanizing transformations. The plantation, in contrast, merely *resembled* a village. In the same way, the numerous seventeenth- and eighteenth-century tidewater towns that possessed the formal attributes of urban design without any real economic outlining remained only dim, uncolored likenesses of urbanism.

"The plantation, in contrast, merely *resembled* a village." Detail from Francis Guy, *Slave Quarters with Field Hands at Work,* c. 1805.
Maryland Historical Society.

The clockwork gearing of a flour mill.
Library of Congress.

The Ellicotts' Mill—architecture, ambition, and inspiration

THE ELLICOTTS' VILLAGE beside the Patapsco took shape from wood and stone—and a new mentality. In quite an inspired way, the brothers translated the intricate, clockwork gearing of a flour mill into a still larger and more complex system. The mechanism became an instructive metaphor: the cooperative and extensive connections among Quaker farmers and merchants that shaped the Ellicott brothers as they entered life in southeastern Pennsylvania enabled them to visualize how well the coordinated movement of mechanical components could inform a broader organization of cooperative human systems.

In this way, the "Parcell of Coopers Tools and 1 Old Hammer" that Charles Pierpoint wielded as he bound staves into flour barrels a half-century before the Ellicotts came to the Patapsco Valley—these tools may be seen as an element of the system of flour production that could be separated from the work of the miller himself.[1] As merchant milling—we might say "the flour industry"—began to distinguish itself from grist milling, other distinct yet still integral components of the larger process came to have separate practitioners. William Moore's "beakhouse" for his bakers, and the coopers' shop, stables, and other outbuildings at his Jones' Falls site gave a new architectural dimension to this division of labor.[2] Even James Hood's smaller-scale operation on the Patapsco likely combined some merchant with country work, and the ardent "marking iron" heated to brand his barrels may have helped order that diverse production. Hood also undertook coopering, joinery, wagon-making, and blacksmithing at

his mill, all beside a bridge over the Patapsco.[3] The Ellicott brothers gave each of these elements—nascent at Hood's and in more developed form at Moore's—greater elaboration and coordination. They gave them an industrial scale.

The American Industrial Revolution finds its origins not only in such indisputably "industrial" actions as iron smelting (a technical operation), or in large-scale structures that sheltered and drove mechanical yarn spinners (a technical building), but also in the venture of merchant flour milling—a technique of coordinated actions that together comprised a centralized system, a system that not only engendered great urban convergence, as at Baltimore Town, but also the kindred network of urbanizing communities, the villages centered on the mills that made the whole process possible.

At Ellicotts' Mills, none of the ancillary facilities and activities—like the sawmill, woodworking and metalworking shops, the tannery, the linseed oil mill, the tavern, store, warehouse, and school—none of these could have sustained the company's wholesale milling operations uniquely, but instead—and perhaps more importantly—they offered an array of complementary services useful both to the company and to the larger community of farmers and planters, small-holders and large-holders, whatever the commodity produced. The convenience of the Patapsco bridge generated traffic flow, to this the shops and services near at hand supplemented their own production efficiencies and traffic-generating capacity, and all of these served as foundations for the Ellicotts' great merchant mill in a manner every bit

A French burrstone from the Carew Tidal Mill in Wales, UK.
Wikimedia Commons.

as real as the literal stones quarried at last from the valley slopes.[4]

From 1774 through the spring of 1775, a substantial amount of building took place in the village, centered largely on the great mill. John Ellicott opened pertinent accounts for lumber production, joinery, carpentry, and masonry work in the ledgers; these detail the production and assembly of building materials over many months—sizing of plank, boards, "scantling" (or studs), and "saw timber" (or beams) in the sawmill, riving shingles, and kilning bricks, as well as multiple periods of "maisoning," to lay up walls of stone, augmented where necessary with precision brickwork. The most significant of these account entries records the expense of £100, registered in January 1775, for "a pair of French Burr millstones 5 feet Diameter," purchased from merchant John Brown in Philadelphia, and the payment to joiner John Botts the same month for "laying 30 Square Floor, and making stairs & fraims on the Husk," that is, for flooring the mill, building its staircase, and assembling the complex framework that secured the run of millstones, gearing, and other equipment contained within it.[5]

Detail of George Ellicott's drawing showing the original 1774 merchant mill.

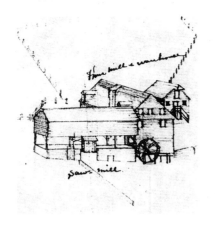

George Ellicott's perspective drawing depicts this substantial merchant mill perpendicular to the river, just below the bend in the millrace. The structure brought a footprint thirty-six feet by a hundred under roof.[6] Masons laid up its stone walls to the height of two stories above a low cellar; these the carpenters topped with a long gable roof terminated at each end by gabled dormers. At the center of the western pent, an oversize shed-roofed dormer framed a large opening which certainly contained a windlass for raising bags of wheat and other materials to the garret, illuminated further by gable-end windows. Three of these are visible on the south and must have corresponded to windows in the northern, or road-side gable. The horizontal line George drew at the base of the river gable, between these three garret windows and the two upper-story windows high in the southern wall, suggests that the stone walls of the mill rose to a uniform height and that the garret gables were frame. This lighted and accessible garret provided a full working floor for the mill, and almost certainly accommodated the extent of open space necessary to strew the quantities of damp, warm flour fresh from the millstones to dry out before bolting, the process of sifting and mixing to achieve a consistent grade of saleable produce. The frame gables permitted greater air circulation for this purpose.

Although the precise configuration of the mill's interior spaces is not known, a general idea may be inferred from the standard processes in operation. First, harvested wheat would be threshed—at another location—to separate most of the stalks or chaff from the kernels. The threshers may have worked in the garret of the Ellicotts' large stone stable nearby, as was the case in another stable the company built on Gwynn's falls in the 1790s.[7] Then, at the mill, Thomas Ellicott's three water-powered rolling screens and fans with wire sieves would have winnowed the wheat in the second stage of the cleaning process. Winnowing removed the remaining chaff from the wheat kernels, a service likely not offered at a smaller grist mill, or, perhaps, only available with a hand-turned wheat fan. Ideally, wheat would be weighed at this point since cleaned grain gave a more reliable measure, though often enough the millers' men filled the scales with wheat not yet fully cleaned and the clerks wrote out a deduction for the burden of the unusable chaff.[8]

Convenience probably dictated that the fans, scales, and some storage bins were located on the first floor of the building. Here also was the husk, the heavy frame containing the complex wooden gearing that transferred and reoriented the motion of the water wheel to the stones, fans, and bolters. The stones themselves, and the wooden hoppers that fed grain to them would have opened above onto the second floor, which also would have contained wooden bins, or garners, for the cleaned wheat awaiting grinding. The bolters could have operated

on this floor or the one below, or both, turned, like the fans, by a long shaft geared to the main drive train. The relative tightness of the weave of the bolting cloths used in this mechanism determined the grade of the flour produced: from superfine white flour to coarser mixtures called middlings, shorts, and tailings, which included progressively greater quantities of the bran and germ that caused these lesser grades of flour to go rancid more quickly. In the final production stage, the millers gathered up this graded flour from the bolting chests and sealed it into barrels for shipment.[9]

If the entire village of Ellicotts' Mills was the factory, then the merchant mill itself was a machine, regardless of the degree of automation present in its first incarnation. The millers' men and boys hauled baskets, sacks, and barrels; raked, swept, and shoveled flour; bore it on their backs or ran the hoist lines of the windlass, all between each stage in the

The ruined Adelphi Mill in Prince Georges County, Maryland, clearly shows the structure of the frame gable building form.
Library of Congress.

BELOW: The lower wing of this large, eighteenth-century flour mill on Delaware's Brandywine River was similar to the Ellicotts' original merchant mill. Note the frame gable and the widely spaced dormer windows. Here the left-hand dormer had a hoist, and was positioned above large openings in the lateral wall. The Ellicotts placed this element in the center of their exceptionally long mill's lateral wall, between the two dormer windows. The taller wing on this Brandywine mill almost certainly reflected Oliver Evans's mechanical innovations at the end of the eighteenth century. These automated milling processes, arranged over multiple stories, allowed millers to construct taller buildings on smaller footprints.
Courtesy Hagley Museum and Library.

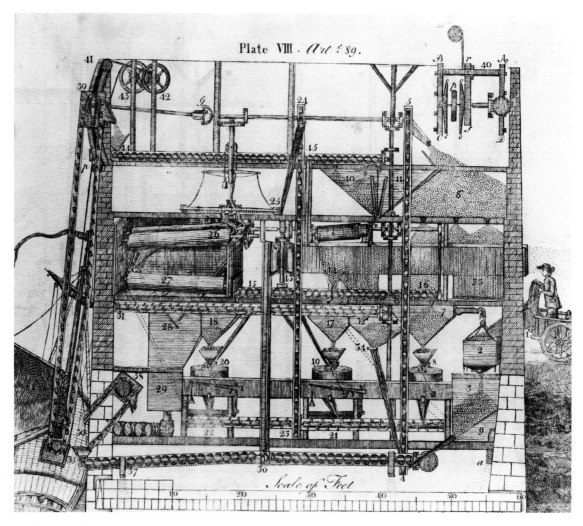

Plate VIII. *Art. 289.*

Scale of Feet

Schematic for a late eighteenth-century merchant mill, showing the automatic mechanisms patented by Oliver Evans. From Evans, *Young Millwright and Miller's Companion.*

process. Perhaps later Jonathan Ellicott installed garners in the garret, to permit gravity to fill the hoppers over the stones on the second floor; certainly in the 1780s he devised a mechanism to mix bolted flour automatically, but in any case the design and configuration of the mill reflected the high degree of manual labor required to produce the desired quantities of superfine flour.[10] It was above all the volume of production that the Ellicotts sought to increase in their enterprise, and this they accommodated in a building of exceptional horizontal extent, not unusual height. Certainly its gearing and shafts were of wood, like other fourth-quarter eighteenth-century mills, and reason dictates that the Ellicott brothers built at a scale that did not exceed the physical capacities of the materials available to them. The large, exterior waterwheel, low on the river-end of the building, did ultimately turn a greater number of millstones than the pair of five-foot French burrs paid for in January 1775: six pairs were in operation in the mid-1790s.[11] Clearly,

the Ellicotts built large enough to accommodate a substantial augmentation of grinding capacity, but the means of power generation and transfer rested securely on a well-established system.

A more dramatic innovation came to the industry in the 1790s, with Oliver Evans's integrated mechanisms—elevator, horizontal conveyor, and flour dryer (or "hopper boy, named after the young men who spread out freshly milled flour on the floor of the garret to dry). These mechanisms permitted almost complete automation of the entire process, obviating the need for human porters and the waste associated with them. Modern mills thus required fewer employees, and an even higher volume of production could take place in a taller, less extensive building than the Ellicott brothers had imagined in 1774, since the mechanisms could quickly raise large quantities of grain or flour through multiple stories in a manner that would not have been efficient by hand. In short, Evans's innovations proved quite influential for merchant milling, and when the Ellicotts replaced their original structure after a fire in 1809, the company erected a new building with five working floors on a much smaller footprint.[12]

Nevertheless, the Ellicotts' original conceptual innovation yielded a facility that was impressively modern in its own generation. With as much as 10,800 square feet of interior space distributed over three levels, the Ellicotts' mill was a grand building by any local measure, exceeding even the contemporary stone merchant mills gathered along Brandywine Creek, where William Moore had practiced the craft before organizing his Jones' Falls enterprise.[13] The Brandywine flowed through the wheat lands of southeastern Pennsylvania to the Christina River at Wilmington, where it joined the Delaware, a river drainage that had been under extensive flour mill development since mid-century. By 1772, eight flour mills turned stones in the Brandywine valley above Wilmington.[14] In the Patapsco watershed, of the twelve flour mills assessed in the Federal Direct Tax districts embracing the river's main branch—twenty-four years after workmen completed the Ellicotts' merchant mill—only two rivaled the square footage, and none the footprint area of this exceptional building.[15]

Almost certainly the two rival mills had been built with Evans's new mechanisms. In 1787, the new states of Maryland, Pennsylvania, and Delaware granted Oliver Evans patent rights, subsequently enlarged to federal patent protection in 1790.[16] Evans's equipment could be retrofitted into older mill buildings—as the Ellicotts did with their own merchant mill the year of the federal patent—but builders of new mills could exploit Evans's systems to change the building form.[17] Thus in the mid-1790s investors at the Hockley Forge property built a four-story brick merchant mill containing at least 10,500 square feet on a footprint of forty-four feet by sixty, and the third-generation Ellicott & Company built in the decade between 1795 and 1805 two four-story brick merchant mills on Gwynn's Falls, sheltering as much as 12,800 square feet on footprints of forty feet by eighty.[18] Recall that the Ellicotts' original merchant mill was two-and-a-half stories on a footprint of thirty-six by one hundred.

Of the twelve Patapsco mills assessed in 1798, before the full measure of Evans's architectural impact could be felt, the wide variation in building form is significant. Hood's mill, re-christened Ellicotts' Upper Mill, and two others—including a replacement for Charles Pierpoint's erected by Baltimore investor John Cornthwait—sheltered a little more than 2,500 square feet each. Two of these were two-story stone structures and one a three-story frame. The four largest mills of the twelve, all masonry of two, three, or four stories, ascended from 4,500 square feet to the Ellicotts' 10,800, and the five smallest of the twelve descended from 1,800 to 400 square feet. Like the mid-sized mills, their materials were wood and stone, but in two- and one-story forms.[19] The relative smallness of the eight lesser mills suggests that they were not constructed primarily as merchant facilities, and their considerable range of magnitude and materials confirms that among grist mills operating at the end of the eighteenth century a unique form was not necessary.

However, among the early class of merchant mills, a standard regional form did develop. This type began to appear in southeastern Pennsylvania about 1750, concurrent with the period of rapid population growth and expanded wheat cultivation.[20] These mills conformed to rectangular, multiple-story dimensions, with stone walls completed by a gable roof. The characteristic feature was an internal waterwheel driven by a millrace that penetrated the building across its short axis, most often through arched openings located at the back of the longer lateral walls. A hood projected over the garret opening of the gable-end facade, much like the warehouse type present on Philadelphia's Delaware waterfront and erected in the storehouse at Ellicotts' Mills.[21] More than fifty of the type survive today along the region's streams, including those flowing through the Ellicott brothers' home county of Bucks.[22]

The internal waterwheel framing of the LeVan Mill, Berks County, Pennsylvania, shown with the millrace entering through the arch below.

Library of Congress.

Griesemer Mill, Berks County, Pennsylvania. The standard southeastern Pennsylvania merchant mill type, developed from about 1750. Note the hood and hoist at the peak of a frame gable, and the arched opening for the millrace at the back of the lateral wall, for an internal waterwheel.
Library of Congress.

The nearly intact internal waterwheel gearing of the eighteenth-century Thomas Mill, Chester County, Pennsylvania.
Library of Congress.

This type of "old fashioned grist mill . . . that may do merchant-work in the small way," as Thomas Ellicott stated, later found its most recognized expression in Ellicott's idealized mill plans and elevations, published in 1795 with Oliver Evans's manifesto on flour-mill automation, *The Young Millwright and Miller's Guide*, one of America's longest lived mechanical pattern books, released in fifteen editions until 1860.[23] A similar stone mill form with an internal waterwheel also existed among the eighteenth-century merchant mills of Brandywine Creek—descending from southeastern Pennsylvania through Delaware—a plausible case of a type following the waterpower present in a regional river drainage. If, as Thomas Ellicott related of his own experience, millwrights "were often called to different parts of this, and the adjacent states, to build mills of the first rates, in their day," one may readily form an idea of how this early merchant mill form spread.[24] Transient experts, then, likely gave a common form to particular classes of mills sited across a larger region, rather than building every kind of mill in a more localized area. The rising importance of mid-Atlantic and Chesapeake merchant milling certainly must have generated such a cadre of experts, including among them Thomas Ellicott.

Significantly for our story, the threads that run through Bucks County and the Brandywine Valley also wound a new strand on Jones' Falls. Although William Moore left no description of his paired 1763 merchant mills and though the assessors' notations from 1798 have been lost, landscape painter Francis Guy very likely depicted the pair in the middle-

ground of a view of Jones' Falls he put to canvas in 1804. Guy juxtaposed two mills standing in the ravine at the water's edge with a much larger new merchant mill set higher up on the opposite slope, the composition a romantic expression of progress which Guy reprised in a second view that gave even greater emphasis to the bulk of the new mill.[25] In the painting of the Moore's complex the impounded waters of the falls splash down the rocky embankment of the head race canal leading to the upper of the two mills, a rectangular, two-story stone structure with frame gables, the ridge of its gable roof perpendicular to the falls. At the lower corner of the longer lateral wall, towards the falls, a low, squared bay opens to the interior wheel pit and allows water exiting the mill to stream back into the falls below. Another opening in the wall immediately above this tail race gives on to an elevated wooden flume exiting the upper mill in the direction of the lower one. The flume evidently channeled the current from a forebay that parted the waters on the head-race or upstream side of the upper mill's wheel pit, thereby conducting the flow either to one mill exclusively or to both. In the painting, water courses down the flume to the lower mill, where it drops onto an external wheel at the gable end of that building, otherwise configured as its twin—two-story stone, frame gables, ridgeline perpendicular to the falls. Thus did these two mid-century merchant mills share waterpower, the lower mill slightly less expensively constructed with an external wheel, and the upper a modification of the internal-wheel type

In 1804 English painter Francis Guy depicted William Moore's Merchant Mills, by then considered small and old-fashioned. The upper mill of the two is the Pennsylvania/ Brandywine internal waterwheel type, while the lower mill has a more economical external waterwheel. Both mills have frame gables, facing the river.

Maryland State Archives.

known from experience to Joseph and Thomas Ellicott, and to William Moore.[26]

If Joseph Ellicott and William Moore brought the Pennsylvania-Brandywine merchant-mill type to Baltimore in 1763, the Ellicott brothers chose not to adapt the internal-wheel to their first Patapsco mill.[27] This apparent contradiction finds a rational basis in the Ellicotts' ambition to erect a building that would double the size of the established type, which in Thomas Ellicott's idealized ground plan possessed dimensions of thirty-two by fifty-five feet.[28] Essentially, the program for a mill building of thirty-six by one hundred feet combined Moore's two mills into a single structure, a conceptual reconfiguration that concurrently maintained productive capacity and reduced construction costs, but did pose some architectural challenges.

Use of an external wheel spared John Ellicott & Company the considerable expense of additional wall length and roof area, and postponed greater maintenance costs to a potentially brighter financial future, when replacing a wheel would be less expensive than enlarging a small building too quickly grown to capacity. The gamble of visionary industrial scale carried more weight than did the prudence of Moore's smaller, more customary forms. Mary-

land's flour and bread exports doubled in less than a decade after 1763, when Joseph Ellicott joined the Moore's Mills project. That increase—and the expectations it fostered—must have proved a significant factor in the configuration and extent of the brothers' own mill.

Several other elements present in the Ellicotts' merchant mill give us an idea of the brothers' design process and sources. The frame gables Francis Guy depicted at Moore's Mills were also employed on the Ellicotts' merchant mill. Images of mills surviving into the photographic era show frame gables posed on the uniform-height masonry walls of numerous Virginia, Maryland, and Pennsylvania mills, suggesting a derivation that does not have antecedents unique to local conditions. If frame gables did permit greater air circulation in the garret and promoted faster drying of freshly milled flour laid out in this space, as already suggested, this architectural solution, while not universal, did have currency across the larger region.[29]

Two other elements the Ellicotts incorporated into their mill appear to have had more focused sources. The first of these is the shed-roofed dormer centered on the lateral elevation of a rectangular, gable-roofed structure. Here the large dormer frames an opening into the garret and surmounts a bay of similar large doorways aligned below for access to lower floors. This element appears to have been more common in the southeastern Pennsylvania mills than among those in Maryland and northern Virginia, and it is quite reasonable to suppose that the Ellicotts brought the idea for this attribute with them from Pennsylvania.[30] The lateral entry not only neatly joined the Ellicotts' two conceptual structures derived from the Moore's Mills project, but quite practically permitted efficient distribution of materials to any level from the midpoint of their exceptionally long building.

The second element is the gable-roofed garret lighted by a pair of dormer windows pushed toward opposite ends of the pent, present in only a few Baltimore and Brandywine mills.[31] For these it is productive to revisit young John Moale's 1752 sketch of Baltimore Town. In his drawing, Moale rendered the town's first tobacco inspection warehouse as a large, single-story rectangular structure under a gable roof, with a garret lighted at its extremes by dormer windows. The design handily prefigures the roofline of the Ellicotts' merchant mill, and offers a reminder that the substantial utilitarian buildings once standing beside now silted-up riverine landings or long replaced in nineteenth- and twentieth-century urban redevelopment campaigns were once abundant examples of extensive, unencumbered interiors—models, like merchant mills themselves, not sufficiently recognized in the history of industrial architecture. John Talbott's four earthfast versions were twenty-two by fifty feet, and the public inspection houses assumed still greater scale and

The oversized dormer above large openings on each floor is shown here in an early nineteenth-century Philadelphia warehouse (left). The configuration also appeared in earlier southeastern Pennsylvania flour mills (right), and the Ellicott brothers adapted it to their own mill.
Library of Congress.

more substantial form than those of the planters. How, then, to light this long merchant mill's somber garret? The Baltimore inspection could well have suggested a solution to the young men whose eyes were already focused on the port and the opportunities it made possible.

The dimensions and attributes of the Ellicotts' great merchant mill ably testify to its designers' capacity for critical analysis and ready adaptation. Their imagination produced the pivotal machine that made the much more extensive factory of the village hum. In 1783, a decade after the stream of commerce began to cross their Patapsco bridge and scarcely over a year after British General Cornwallis surrendered his sword to an army of ambitious

Detail of John Moale's sketch of Baltimore Town in 1752 showing the tobacco inspection/warehouse with two widely spaced dormer windows, perhaps a model for the roof configuration of the Ellicotts' mill. See also the photograph of the eighteenth-century Brandywine River flour mill on p. 57.
Maryland Historical Society.

former colonists, John and Andrew Ellicott commenced development of a waterfront district on the Baltimore basin. In the parallel rows of two- and three-story brick warehouses fronting Ellicotts' Dock, "plain finished for storage with compting room on lower floor," was also lodged the fulfillment of the Ellicotts' own expansive view of the industrial process.[32] Here:

> Muscovado sugars of different qualities, in hogsheads;
> West-India and New England rum; molasses
> RICE, by the Cask;
> Chocolate, by the Box;
> Cordial, by the Keg;
> and Pork, by the Barrel

returned for the flour that itself streamed out of their merchant mill like the Patapsco's waters over the wheel.[33]

The Ellicotts' mill building and the village of Ellicotts' Mills were, in fact, not separate entities, but new, integral architectural types that reflected and shaped the cultural transformation taking place in the eighteenth-century Chesapeake and

This interior view of a Fell's Point warehouse gives an indication of the largely unencumbered interiors of colonial Chesapeake tobacco warehouses and storehouses—like the Baltimore inspection house—which may have served as models for the Ellicott brothers as they designed their own merchant mill.
Library of Congress.

The Ellicotts' Mill—architecture, ambition, and inspiration ❧ 63

the larger Atlantic world. The Ellicotts expressed in architecture the various but unified systems and connections of these evolving economic and material conditions. As perceptive American builders had done for years, the Ellicott brothers combined regional and individual experience with the contingency of inspiration, and in so doing, they produced a prophetic version of an architectural form—the factory town—that would attain proportions even they did not foresee.

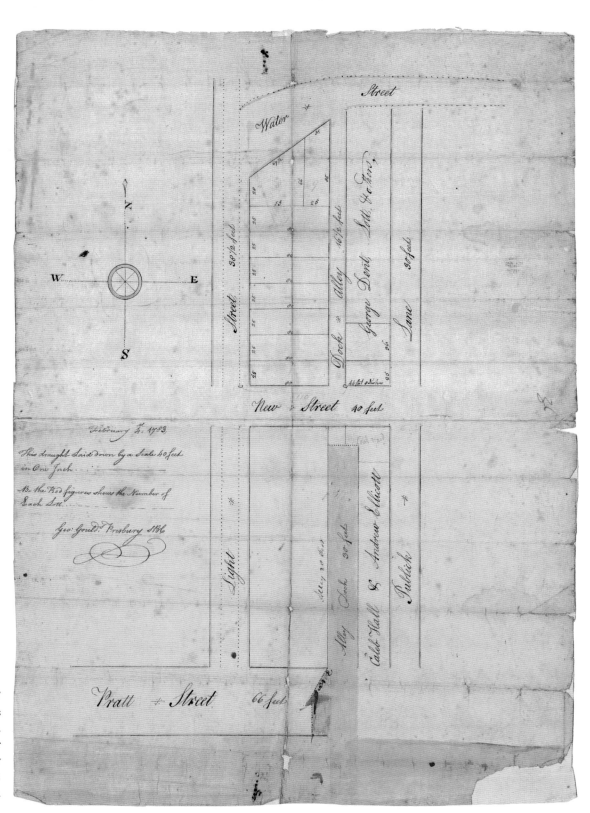

The plat for Ellicotts' dock and warehouses on the Baltimore basin, developed in 1783 after the Revolutionary War victory.
Maryland Historical Society.

PART III

Cotton

Cotton Plant. New York Public Library.

Cotton sailcloth was a critical commodity in the Atlantic world, and its production was a powerful incentive for American manufacturers.

New York Public Library.

CHAPTER EIGHT

The First Factory—
The Family Tree

*ELLICOTS-MILL is a small village whose principal establishment is a
large flour mill, belonging to Mr. ELLICOT, from whom it receives its
name. This mill has six pairs of stones, and is constructed as well as any
of those of the Brandywine, whose improvements it shares. The situation
of this place, serried among the mountains, is romantic. The water there
is clear, the rocks there high and majestic, the trees noble, and I would
have loved to enjoy one day longer that view, a little melancholy and well
enough suited to my disposition, if the heat which oppressed me had not
compelled me to gain more temperate regions.*[1]

FRANÇOIS ALEXANDRE FRÉDÉRIC, Duc
de la Rochefoucauld-Liancourt, undertook
extensive travels through the United States
in the middle years of the 1790s, and offered to
end-of-the-century French and English readers his
voluminous perceptions of American society and
culture. The new nation's attitudes and manners,
landscape and agriculture, commerce and industry ranged through his purview, and the perceptive
Frenchman's critical examination reveals the largely
agrarian republic embarking with energy and confidence—if not always success—on the path of industrialization:

> Several manufactures of sail cloth have been
> established in the United States with toler-
> able success, but have been carried to no
> great extent. Every year also some spinning
> establishments, and even cotton manufactu-
> ries, are attempted to be set on foot; but the
> following year they are sure to fall; for no
> other reason than the high price of labour,
> which is itself a consequence of the general
> system of taxation.[2]

Shortage of labor and lack of protective tariffs may
in fact have handicapped American industrial development, but in terms of the movement to large-

scale cotton textile manufacture, limited expertise
and imperfect technology also undermined the
profitability of these early operations.

The quality and functionality of mill machinery proved critical to the nascent American cotton
industry, and, perhaps without recognizing this
condition, the French visitor observed one newly
established cotton mill whose success derived from
the apt combination of direct experience and technical knowledge. On his way to Boston, la Rochefoucauld crossed the Blackstone River at Pawtucket,
Rhode Island, where a water mill owned by Quaker
merchants William Almy and Moses Brown had recently opened. "Here are established," he remarked,
"the cotton works which appear to succeed better
than any other manufacture established to the present time in America."[3] Englishman Samuel Slater
had fitted out this mill with precise and functional
machinery on the British model and began to produce yarn there equal to British quality in 1793, after several years of productive trials in a pre-existing
fulling mill.

Accurate replication of British carding and yarn-
spinning machinery threw open a door against
which would-be American textile manufacturers
had been pushing since before the Revolution, and
the effects of the technological training Slater pro-

Samuel Slater's spinning frame, the first commercially successful cotton textile machine in America. Smithsonian Institution.

Samuel Slater's original 1793 factory still stands at the core of this larger building on Rhode Island's Blackstone River. It was of wood frame construction, 26 by 40 feet, two stories with a garret. Library of Congress.

vided in Almy and Brown's water mill cannot be overestimated.[4] "Mechanic after mechanic who had learned or practiced in their plant left their employ and set up in business for himself," Caroline Ware states in her classic study of New England industry. Twenty-seven cotton textile mills spun yarn in "Rhode Island, southern Massachusetts, and eastern Connecticut in 1809," and Ware attributed the majority of them to the knowledge and experience disseminated from the Pawtucket mill.[5]

Yet Slater's extraordinary success with the processes and mechanics of cotton yarn spinning, and his consequent position as the progenitor of the New England textile industry, have led generations of scholars to conflate the immense importance of that industrial achievement with the presumed importance of his building as the architectural progenitor of the American System of factory production.[6] But the complex processes of American industrialization and urbanization did not center on a single industry or region. The Englishman's building, we can now see, was of less consequence than the machinery it contained.

Slater had joined the enterprise of Almy and Brown not long after he immigrated to America in 1789, having served a seven-year apprenticeship with

Jedediah Strutt at Belper, Derbyshire, in the rapidly industrializing English midlands. There he learned the intricacies of cotton textile production, both at the level of the machine and the factory.[7] Slater evaded British restrictions on the export of industri-

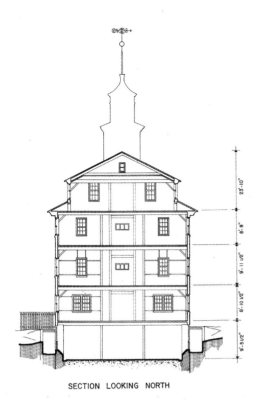

SECTION LOOKING NORTH

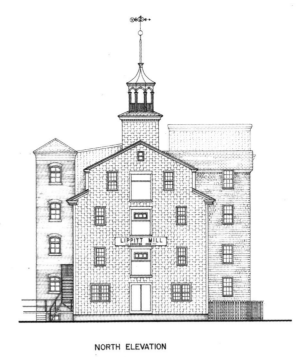

NORTH ELEVATION

The Lippitt Mill, organized in 1809 in West Warwick, Rhode Island, was wood frame construction, 30 by 104 feet, three stories with a clerestory monitor roof. Library of Congress.

al technology and remained with Almy and Brown to run the textile factory he built with them on the Blackstone at Pawtucket. It is this still-standing facility that many architectural historians consider the first true factory building in America.[8] Slater's two-story frame structure stood perpendicular to the river, twenty-six by forty feet long, sheltered by a simple gable roof.[9] The mill's significance to the American textile industry is indisputable, but the building itself was smaller than Hood's Mill on the Patapsco—in terms of total square footage—and constructed of the same materials. In 1793, Slater opened the doors to his new building, sheltering 2,080 square feet on two floors, compared to the 2,688 over three levels at Hood's, whose gambrel-roofed garret and frame principal story seated on a frame and stone lower floor had been washed by the Patapsco for twenty-seven years.[10] Slater's was hardly a revolutionary structure.

Indisputably, the wooden tradition was dominant in early American building at all levels, and timber would have presented significant practical advantages to Slater and other early factory builders: availability, economy, and easy workability, as well as a familiar assembly method suited to open interiors of increasing extent, and an ability to withstand vibration. Yet these convincing attributes had not dictated a form to ambitious merchant millers farther south.[11] Although it is possible that the scale and frame construction of the Slater mill bought greater

social acceptance for a controversial intrusion into a conservative, agrarian culture, significantly larger and more obtrusive structures had already accompanied a successful and dramatic challenge to the plantation system in the colonial Chesapeake.[12] It was not, in fact, a lack of native masonry models, building skill or a fear of being radical that dictated the exclusive use of lumber in the Pawtucket mill, but a rational desire for economy: the cotton textile enterprise in America had not yet rewarded its investors. Time and again, American yarn and fabric enterprises started up and failed with astonishing regularity and, it seems, increasing frequency up to the time Slater imported British technology.[13] It was thrift that drove Almy and Brown to fund that small wooden building.

Indeed seven years later, in 1800, Slater built for himself a second mill of identical materials and dimensions.[14] The subsequent year, Almy and Brown more than doubled the length of the original Slater mill with the first of several frame additions, extending its footprint by fifty feet to yield overall dimensions of twenty-six feet by ninety. In 1809, the investors who organized the Lippitt Mill in West Warwick, Rhode Island, pressed this larger frame model further to produce a three-story structure surmounted with a clerestory monitor roof—which added almost a full fourth story—within overall dimensions of thirty by 104 feet. Four years later, the 1813 brick mill of the Boston Manufacturing

The Waltham Mills, Waltham, Massachusetts, as painted by Elijah Smith. Francis Cabot Lowell's original 1813 mill (Waltham I) is the structure on the left built of brick, 40 by 90 feet, four stories with a two-story clerestory monitor roof. The later mill building to the right (Waltham II) is 40 by 150 feet.
Gore Place Museum House, Waltham, MA.

Company at Waltham, Massachusetts, did attain four full stories on a similar footprint of forty by ninety feet, this elevation surmounted by a two-story gambrel modified to contain a narrow horizontal monitor window at the intersection of the two roof planes. Soon the Boston Associates added a second four-story brick mill at Waltham, in 1816, expanding the form to 150 feet, to be driven by the same power source. The Associates subsequently undertook development of Lowell, Massachusetts, in 1821, where they greatly amplified the Waltham plan, providing factory sites for multiple interdependent textile companies along a waterway managed by the Lowell Lock and Canal Company. The organization of uniform four-to-six story brick mill buildings, forty by 150 feet long, housing all of the components of cotton textile production, from bale to bolt, proved to be immensely profitable. A generation after Slater's small yarn-spinning factory first put its machines into motion, the Lowell type set the standard for large-scale American corporate capitalism, an industrial design that soon dominated the world economy.[15]

Notwithstanding the apparent soundness of this genealogical succession—carrying frame construc-

tion from a scatter of small, New England grist mills to Slater's purpose-built textile factories, then gathering up the Slater form to be amplified in wood and further enlarged in masonry—this classic but narrowly focused developmental view disregards significant components of the American industrial story that do not correspond to the pattern. The first Waltham mill was constructed of brick in 1813, at forty by ninety feet, and it did presage the large, brick, nineteenth-century American textile factory type. Yet its footprint area did not exceed that of the Ellicott brothers' 1774 merchant mill: 3,600 square feet. Had its builders looked to the south, the renowned Massachusetts factory would have found a pair of close rivals in the two four-story brick merchant mills, forty by eighty feet, that the third-generation Ellicott Company had built on Gwynn's Falls beginning about 1794, and the smaller-scale four-story brick merchant mill of forty-four by sixty feet that the owners of the Hockley forge site on the Patapsco constructed the same year.[16]

Oliver Evans's automated, flow-technology mechanisms enabled the four-story form of these mills, and their scale testifies to the importance of the flour industry in late-eighteenth-century Baltimore.[17] Furthermore, the choice of brick over stone in these large mills indicates the ready availability of local building supplies and the recognition that brickmasonry offered certain construction economies in terms of greater regularity of coursing and easier modification, where stone required more laborious quarrying and dressing before it could even be laid up. Joseph Alibone had noted in 1772 that Baltimore's houses were "mostly built of Brick," and merchants had constructed brick warehouses on the waterfront at least by 1790. The city grew so extensively and rapidly over these years that Baltimore's building trades must have been highly developed by the last decade of the eighteenth century.[18] To state as a distinguished New England architectural historian does that the use of "brickwork [in 1813] . . . at Waltham represents the first major application of the material to industrial building, and thus establishes an early date for the type of masonry which was to become characteristic of the nineteenth-century factory" is simply incorrect.[19] The claim of northern supremacy in terms of materials, size, and chronology rests uneasily on sandy ground. In fact, before the turn of the eighteenth century—twenty years before the first Waltham factory began producing yarn and fabric—a number of capacious, masonry industrial buildings with water-powered equipment had already been constructed outside of New England, and not only for the merchant milling of flour.

The most extensively planned of these took form on the heights above the falls of the Passaic River in New Jersey, where the project directors commis-

sioned the new town of Paterson to be laid out. Organized in 1791 under the leadership of Alexander Hamilton, Secretary of the Treasury, "the Society for Establishing Useful Manufactures" purchased the riverfront acreage and undertook development of an extensive manufacturing complex, to be powered by water from a single, lengthy canal. The "New National Manufactory," in Hamilton's view, was to contain facilities for thirteen distinct branches of production, ranging from paper to sailcloth and sheetings, pottery, hats, shoes, and fine metalwork, capitalized by joint-stock subscriptions to one million dollars.[20] The facilities for cotton carding and yarn spinning, fabric weaving, and printing obtained authorization to be erected first—all multiple-story stone structures—along with fifty double houses for workmen, to be built "of stone or clay [i.e.: brick], and pointed . . ." the directors' resolution ran, "unless the expense of such material shall exceed by thirty per cent. the expense of a house of the same dimensions in wood."[21]

A financial panic in 1792, cost over-runs, and fraud on the part of some of the contracted managers led to crippling investment shortfalls in the Society, but the cotton mill did go into operation in 1794, winding yarn in a four-story stone mill building, forty by ninety feet long. The two authorized facilities ancillary to the cotton mill—"a printing

ABOVE: Middlesex Mill, Lowell, Massachusetts. Lowell is founded in 1821, and its brick factory buildings generally conformed to the large Waltham model: 40 by 150 feet long, four to six stories tall, with a clerestory monitor roof.
New York Public Library.

LEFT:
The independent Lowell Lock and Canal Company provided waterpower to the independently organized Lowell Mills, which together shared a product distribution network. This innovative and efficient corporate arrangement conserved capital and contributed significantly to the immense success of the Lowell factories.
New York Public Library.

Owings Upper Mill is perhaps the last surviving brick flour mill from the 1790s in Baltimore County, Maryland – it stands three stories tall, 60 feet long. The Ellicotts' contemporaneous brick flour mill on Gwynn's Falls was larger still – four stories, 40 by 80 feet, nearly as large as Waltham I. Their second Gwynn's Falls mill, completed by 1805, was identical to the first. Waltham I dates from 1813.
Library of Congress.

and cal[e]nder house" and "a carding and roping house"—were to have been large stone structures as well, but it is not clear whether these substantial buildings were constructed before the directors, their credit exhausted, reluctantly voted to abandon all production in 1796.[22] Nearly two decades would pass before the brick mill at Waltham and a comparable stone textile mill in Rhode Island came into being: some nineteen years after stonemasons finished Paterson and eighteen after bricklayers completed the Ellicotts' first mill at Gwnn's Falls.[23]

Mid-Atlantic laborers brought under roof another early textile mill in masonry the year after the Paterson facility opened, 1795, on the banks of Little Elk Creek, where the northern reaches of the Chesapeake Bay project almost to the northeastern corner of Maryland. These waters beyond the Susquehanna separate the state's eastern and western shores. The Cecil Manufacturing Company organized the interests of a group of private investors from the regional corridor extending southwesterly from Philadelphia and Wilmington into Maryland at the head of the Bay. Perhaps originally—but certainly as rebuilt after a fire in 1796—the company erected a three-story stone structure, thirty-six by sixty feet long, where operatives spun woolen yarn that they also wove into fabrics. Unlike the ambitious project at Paterson, which collapsed under the weight of its own precocious grandiosity, the Cecil Company continued in business for twenty years.

After the Treaty of Ghent brought the War of 1812 to a close, Britain loosed a flood of inexpensive textiles into the American market, undermining many of the more powerful nation's smaller overseas competitors. Cecil was among this unfortunate group.[24]

The rapid demise of these operations at Paterson and Little Elk—and perhaps more pointedly, their presence beyond the paled scholarly terrain of New England—has left their history, like the noiseless fall of a limb in a deep and distant forest, unobserved. Nevertheless, an even more significant industrial branch grew to maturity farther south, on the wooded slopes at Ellicotts' Mills, where both the thriving factory village and the large stone mill form favored corresponding development. In 1794, the year after Slater's frame textile mill went into production and the same year the much more substantial stone factory at Patterson began spinning yarn, another capacious masonry industrial building began to take shape.

This structure, a paper mill organized by Philadelphia merchant Thomas Mendenhall, shadowed the east bank of the Patapsco below the coopers' shop and dwellings on the Baltimore road. In 1808, four years before the Boston Associates cleared the ground for Waltham, yet another extensive factory complex in masonry, the Union Manufacturing Company of Maryland, closely modeled on Hamilton's "National Manufactory" at Paterson, rose on the steeper valley grade above the bend in the falls

The falls of the Passaic River, near the site of Alexander Hamilton's "National Manufactory" of 1791 at Paterson, New Jersey.
New York Public Library.

upstream of Ellicotts' Mills. Patapsco waterpower also came to drive the machinery of yet two more cotton textile mills in this early period, the Patapsco and the Thistle, erected in 1813 and 1822 on the Union Manufacturing Company model, concurrent with the first factory buildings at Waltham and at Lowell. These Maryland installations trace a branch of America's industrialization story begun by their mid-Atlantic brethren, the merchant flour mills—and all improperly pruned from the family tree.

New York Public Library.

Thomas Mendenhall's paper mill on the Patapsco was similar in scale and materials to this paper mill in Germantown, Pennsylvania: three story stone construction with eight bays of windows (the Germantown mill, slightly smaller, had seven bays).
Library of Congress.

CHAPTER NINE

The Maryland Branch

THE SUMMER AIR that settled heavily into the Patapsco valley the days the Duke de la Rochefoucauld wiped the sweat from his brow as he explored the village lanes and buildings also accompanied a period of change for Ellicotts' Mills. By the time of la Rochefoucauld's July 1796 visit, the third incarnation of the family company had been in operation for just over a year, subsequent to the death of founding partner John Elliott in 1795. The company's development of the Gwynn's Falls site was then underway, with the first of the two large brick flour mills nearing completion, and Philadelphia merchant Thomas Mendenhall was preparing to press out sheets of paper in a large new mill below the village. In 1790, the first federal census takers had listed forty-seven people residing at Ellicotts' Mills.[1]

Since the Ellicotts' original property purchases in the early 1770s, the brothers had reorganized the company ownership and gradually extended their control of real estate. Nathaniel Ellicott, who evidently had remained in the brothers' native Bucks County as a silent partner, sold his quarter share of the company to Joseph in 1777, who in turn withdrew from the partnership himself the next year, trading his shares in the Lower Mill tract for those of John and Andrew in that of the Upper Mill (Hood's mill, its village named "Fountainvale").[2] It was after Joseph's unsuccessful bid to subdivide and develop the Upper Mill tract by an auction sale of lots, and his decease some months later in 1780 at age forty-eight, that the "John & Andrew Ellicott Company" embarked on a campaign of significant expansion.[3] As the clouds of the Revolution began to break, the company—and Joseph's sons—undertook the initial development of Ellicotts' Dock on the Baltimore waterfront.[4] The General Assembly of the new state of Maryland moved to expedite the flow of commerce to the wharves of this flourishing port by authorizing "several turnpike roads in Baltimore County," and the Ellicott Company surveyed and undertook improvements to the highway west from Pratt Street on the inner harbor to the mill seats on Gwynn's Falls, then recast their own road through the valley at Ellicotts' Mills farther west to the wheat-country town of Frederick.[5]

Concurrently, John and Andrew made the first of many additional property acquisitions in the valley, multiplying the extent of the original 135.5-acre tract nearly three times by 1786, when Andrew conveyed his half-share of the company's assets to three of his sons, including Jonathan and George. These young men, with their uncle John, continued to invest capital in real estate, and by the mid-nineties the company owned or controlled through leases some 1,300 acres in the valley, occupying the greater part of the seven miles meandering down the stream from the Upper Mill tract to and including the land and facilities of Pierpoint's successor, John Cornthwait, this site renamed "Ilchester."[6]

In this manner—through access to waterpower, a vital adjunct to land holding—the "John & Andrew Ellicott Company" and its immediate successor, "Ellicott & Company," managed to influence each of the major non-family industrial enterprises that sought advantageous locations on the Patapsco at Ellicotts' Mills. Here individual negotiations concerning permissible degrees of water use and the purposes to which waterpower could be directed attained legal force in real-estate indentures transcribed into the courthouse deed books, rather than through the legislation and judicial verdicts that accompanied the competing claims of New England's corporations later in the nineteenth century.[7]

More significant is the early and explicit recognition of waterpower as a legal entity. Since facilities of increased scale required greater motive force to drive the machinery, investors came to understand that energy was as important as locale in calculating the worth and use of a site and its potential for profit. Yet it was not only the waterpower that proved attractive to these investors, but also the proximity of the falls to a prosperous industrial village and its well-traveled thoroughfare. In a very real sense,

these new establishments extended the margins of the Ellicotts' own urbanistic imagination in a calculated and natural way, giving the sinuous form of the village other supple branches.

The idea for the first of these belonged to Thomas Mendenhall, a paper-maker who approached the Ellicott brothers in early 1794 with plans to erect a paper mill on land immediately downstream from the Baltimore County portion of the mill village. The terrain fell more sharply to the river here, below the Baltimore road's ascent to the eastern plateau, and the 21-acre tract Mendenhall bought from another individual did not include sufficient river frontage to contain the mill pool required to power his equipment.[8] The John & Andrew Ellicott Company consequently opened an account with Mendenhall and advanced him possession of an adjacent 14.25-acre tract, recording its value as a balance due the company with interest—essentially a mortgage.[9] The property came with a condition, though, reiterated in a later deed. The Ellicotts specified the allowable height of the mill pool and the activity it was permitted to power: "provided always and it is to be understood that the said . . . [owner] his heirs or assigns shall not at any time apply the water for the purposes of grinding wheat Rye or Indian Corn but may be for any other purpose whatsoever."[10] So the Ellicott company sought to ensure complementary, not competitive development.

Two views of Thomas Mendenhall's paper mill after its transformation into workers' housing for the Patapsco Manufacturing Company cotton factory. To the left in each image. ABOVE, a detail from Ellicotts' Mills, Md., Chromolithograph by E. Sachse & Co. (1854) and BELOW, a detail from *View of Ellicotts Mills*, E. Sachse & Co., Baltimore.
Maryland Historical Society.

In August and December accountings of 1794, Mendenhall obtained from the Ellicotts the labor of "Billy sawing" and a substantial amount of plank, perhaps for the construction of his dam, and by October 1795 earned a credit on his account "By Ball[ance] on Bill of Paper," an indication that some level of production was going forward.[11] Prospective paper makers called for the positions Mendenhall advertised in the *Federal Gazette* in January 1796, and that summer, shortly after la Rochefoucauld's visit, the Philadelphian sold a half-share in the 21-acre mill tract to another merchant colleague from the Quaker city, John Field.[12] La Rochefoucauld's failure to mention the paper factory suggests that the structure may have been unfinished in July 1796, and the half-share sale to Field that August likely raised sufficient funds to bring the project to term.[13]

Certainly construction of the complex proceeded in stages, but Mendenhall's builders also followed design ideas that were clearly influenced by the Ellicotts, since the configuration of the paper factory corresponds so well to that of the merchant mill. Like the Ellicotts, Mendenhall thought big. The relative narrowness of the valley below the Baltimore road compelled the paper maker to site his factory parallel to the river, rather than perpendicular, as the Ellicotts had done, yet the building overspread every bit as much space as the merchant flour mill—and then some. Laborers cut a deep foundation trench into the hillside sloping to the water's edge, and masons set stone footings for walls of thirty-eight by one hundred feet, two feet greater in breadth than the Ellicotts' mill. The stone walls laid up from these foundations rose three stories over ground level on the riverside and two stories over the sloping bank above. In a mid-nineteenth-century chromolithograph, eight bays of windows overlooking the river were presumably mirrored on the two stories facing uphill. Their identical ranks made for a clear expression of the classic factory form, though Mendenhall may have originally configured the upper story openings differently, as will be seen. A long gable brought the structure under roof.[14]

Mendenhall's builders had raised an exceptional structure, almost as capacious as the contemporaneous yarn-spinning mill at Paterson, New Jersey, that stood one story taller than the paper mill.[15] Yet certainly Mendenhall's factory also found a model in the Ellicotts' building, and not only in its size and materials—a slightly larger footprint with a one-

story increase in elevation, all in stone—but also in its conceptual scale, in the endeavor to build larger than necessary from the beginning so that anticipated growth could be more easily accommodated.

The situation of the paper factory doubtless made for some difficulty in laying out the millrace, a canal that had to run a course parallel to the long axis of the building and thus possibly perpendicular to the wheel. The manner in which the mechanics solved the approach problem—which may have involved a covered trunk line under or beside the river road before sharply angling ninety degrees into the wheel pit, as at the Ellicotts' mill—is no longer known. Nor do we know whether the wheel was interior or exterior, yet Mendenhall boasted that the flow in even low-water periods could drive twice the number of engines than the three originally installed.[16]

These engines cleaned, shredded, and pulverized cotton and linen rags into the fibers that laborers would shape into a sheet in a vat, then press, dry, and treat with non-absorbent sizing to make finished paper. Before the introduction of more fully mechanized production methods in the second quarter of the nineteenth century these engines, or beaters, were the only water-powered element of the process. The fineness of their operation determined the quality of the paper.[17] As the Ellicotts did by extending the drive train to increase grinding capacity within their own already exceptionally large mill, so Mendenhall projected sufficient "room for two more vats," as well as an increase in the noisy reverberations of three more engines to fill the voids in his own extensive building.[18]

Anticipation of greater production volume not only meant that space be provided for additional engines, but that sufficient capacity must exist under roof for drying large numbers of pressed paper sheets. Instead of the classic factory's steady cadence of window bays, some turn-of-the-eighteenth-century paper mills contained upper-story rooms open to the exterior and fitted with jalousies or sliding shutters in place of exterior walls. These permitted as much air circulation as possible while protecting the fragile sheets from inclement weather.[19] When a new owner modified the building for residential use in the 1810s, the eight regular bays of fenestration depicted in the mid-nineteenth-century prints had probably replaced wide, upper-story openings.

The paper mill's ancillary structures included an attached stone extension to the east end for "sizing houses and vat houses," and the complex provided laborers' housing in a single-story "small log dwelling house near the mills."[20] Other structures listed in a 1797 sale advertisement, were a two-story frame dwelling with a kitchen, a smokehouse, a log stable, and a stone springhouse—a standard domestic collection certainly occupied by the owner. Of this domestic group, only the springhouse was stone, and though its position "not more than ten yards away" from the owner's dwelling could well have been determined by a pre-existent spring, the Ellicotts piped water to their houses from sources higher on the valley slopes.[21] Perhaps the same occurred here. At the paper mill, in addition to supplying potable water, the springhouse would have served as a reservoir of clear water necessary for the beating engines to shred rags into fibers and for the laborers to form clean sheets of those fibers in the vats. The structure was thus in some measure an industrial building, and may have been solidly built and intentionally sited near the owner's residence to ensure control of the essential resource it contained. At the very least, the architecture of the paper mill complex clearly pronounced the social distinction between worker and owner.

Two successive owners undertook further additions to the complex, for which one early-nineteenth-century author claimed the greatest productive capacity in the nation.[22] These improvements included a "large stone barn and stables . . . six small houses for the accommodation of workmen, [and a] saw mill."[23] Although the enlarged and more solidly constructed barn and stables must have served the needs of the itinerant rag pickers, who would have ridden out over the byways of an extensive territory to collect disintegrated clothing and linens, one is tempted to read here as well a conceptual organization of ancillary services analogous—on a smaller scale—to those at Ellicotts' Mills. The paper mill's draft horses could well have served as supplemental teams for hire when demand for hauling at the merchant mill village exceeded capacity, while the operation of a competing saw mill testifies to increasing demand for lumber as the city of Baltimore and its shipbuilding industry continued in rapid development. Of course the teams also hauled timber and delivered lumber and reams of paper.

Conditions at Ellicotts' Mills seem also to have influenced the architectural hierarchy of labor at the paper factory and may be discerned in modifications to the sizing house extension to the east end of the mill: this wing housed the lower classes of workmen, "journeymen and apprentices."[24] Could these younger employees have shared rooms here in a boarding-house arrangement, more closely supervised until reaching the age and skill level to be called "workmen," the men who took shelter in the separate row of six small dwellings? That kind of paternalistic labor organization also occurred at the Ellicotts' senior miller's dwelling and at Jonathan Ellicott's house a short walk up the dusty river road.

The local influence of Ellicotts' Mills on Mendenhall's factory was not simply a case of emulation, but more importantly, a function of globalizing economic processes. These work as follows: economic historians argue that successful and geographically extensive industrial production spurs further industrial growth, especially in an environment of rapid urban expansion. The availability of capital, credit, and technological advances, combined with the capacity for organization, and the presence of well-suited natural and human resources, effectively set in motion a self-perpetuating system. Economic transactions extend up and down the supply chain, fostering expansive and steadily enlarging networks of commercial activity.[25]

In the mid-Atlantic, the geographic, economic, and political conditions that initiated the agricultural ascendancy of wheat also served to develop and maintain the urban networks that wheat engendered. Once successfully established, these networks themselves came to generate their own expansion and diversification. A critical factor in the growth of the Baltimore region, then, derived from its own momentum. Although the concentration of industry in the mid-Atlantic never matched that which developed in New England as the first and second quarters of the nineteenth century progressed, it is clear that the same cultural and economic forces that drove New England to become such a nationally dominant industrial region in that period also proved influential elsewhere, and even at the smaller scale of the discrete community.

The Ellicott Company's gain in production efficiency from use of Oliver Evans's flow-technology mechanisms, the company's highway improvements and investments in port facilities, the structure of wage labor, interrelated company-owned and contracted services, and the local and international exchange of flour and other commodities—along with the availability of land, credit, and the criti-

As at the Ellicotts' mill village, the paper mill facility also included a large stable and sawmill. Its teams of draft horses, like these prize Percherons at work on an Indiana farm, would have hauled timber and lumber, as well as supply wagons of rags and finished paper. Probably the teams were hired out to the Ellicotts' nearby merchant mill, too. New York Public Library.

cal geographic reality of waterpower—generated a remarkably powerful dynamic. These commercial links through Ellicotts' Mills produced the first significant, non-family extension of the village in a natural, almost inevitable way. Ellicotts' Mills readily encompassed the installation Thomas Mendenhall and his successors constructed along the eastern extension of the river road. Others would follow, and the result would be a vernacular industrial town extended along the course of the river, as distinct in form from the densely populated mercantile city of Baltimore as from the earlier, planned towns of the colonial Chesapeake, which lacked the economic support networks and incentives for growth that flour production and marketing initiated.

Certainly the Ellicotts used their control of resources to shape development to their own advantage, but they also recognized the reciprocal benefits

urbanization brought to them and to new project investors alike. The reverse had occurred earlier in the century at Elk Ridge Landing, on a mercantile rather than industrial basis, when the petitioners of 1762 failed in their appeal to the colonial authorities to obtain "ground on any Tolerable Terms for building Warehouses and other Conveniences" for the rising trade in grain.[26] The long-standing intransigence of the landowners had forestalled development over a period of such duration as to fatally weaken its potential for success. None of that occurred here, with the new mentality of a new generation. After the completion of Mendenhall's paper factory at Ellicotts' Mills, another even more ambitious industrial facility, the Union Manufacturing Company of Maryland, extended the boundaries on the opposite end of town, and it, too, obtained the Ellicotts' cooperation and support.

Panoramic View of the Scenery on the Patapsco.
Chromolithograph by E. Sachse & Co.
Maryland Historical Society.

CHAPTER TEN

The Republican Industrialist's Dream

Over the decade before 1808—when Maryland granted the Union Manufacturing Company the state's first incorporation charter for a commercial entity—the Ellicott Company hastened its own industrial expansion of the factory village on Patapsco falls.[1] Having completed their second large, brick merchant mill on Gwynn's Falls shortly after 1798, the Ellicotts refocused attention on the Patapsco with two major capital projects: a mill to grind plaster of Paris for agricultural fertilizer, undertaken by 1803, and an iron rolling and slitting mill, including a nail manufactory, by 1807.[2]

Advocates of scientific farming, among them President Jefferson, aimed to increase agricultural production through the application of Enlightenment principles over traditional agricultural methods. Utilization of "plaister," or lime, on cultivated land greatly increased yields and must have helped Baltimore maintain its quarter-share of the nation's total exports of wheat and flour in the first quarter of the nineteenth century.[3] The nail manufactory also aimed to bring greater efficiency to volume production. Demand in Baltimore—where the population had more than doubled in the 1790s and would double again within the next two decades—must have continually outstripped the quantities small-scale suppliers could generate, an incentive that would have motivated regional sawmill operations, quarries, and brickyards, as well.

Ellicott & Company constructed the plaster mill within the existing architectural framework of the village industrial zone; it occupied an extension to the east end of the saw mill and shared the existing race with the sawmill and merchant mill.

The ironworks required a new dam and millrace, set upriver to the north, on the Baltimore County side of the Patapsco beyond the bridge and tannery. This facility rolled out "hoop iron for cut nails," and produced "spike and nail rod," as well as cut and wrought nails in a full range of sizes.[4]

Concurrent with these, other improvements to the village included a linseed oil mill that entered operation as a contracted enterprise using the waterpower in the branch on the Anne Arundel side of the village. In addition, Jonathan Ellicott took a county appointment in 1802 as "a supervisor on the Frederick, turnpike road." Jonathan's section ran "from Ellicott's Mills to Baltimore, and [he was] allowed 120 dollars, to keep the same in repair."[5] Soon state-funded laborers made even more extensive improvements to the turnpike road, including beautifully arched stone bridges and stone retaining walls at the riverbanks, a result of the thoroughfare being linked in 1806 to the nation's first federally funded highway.[6] With this "National Road," President Jefferson's administration intended to draw the wide new lands of the Ohio and upper Louisiana to the Atlantic rim, securing them across the Alleghenies to the port of Baltimore, the new nation's coastal mid-point. This politically charged concept of unity—present but unarticulated in the maturing urban networks centered on the merchant flour mills—would be much more explicitly reprised with the formation of the Union Manufacturing Company.

International political and economic conditions had long played a critical role in the success or failure of American mercantile and industrial development, as la Rochefoucauld had observed in the mid-1790s, and would again in the first decade of the

Private Armed Schooner Patapsco of Baltimore Rich. Moon Com. Making her Escape from an 18 Gun Brig after Receiving three Broad Sides off Lanzrote 21.th September 1814

The War of 1812 disrupted Atlantic trade for the new nation, and beginning with President Jefferson's trade embargo of 1807, provided a powerful impetus for the development of domestic manufacturing capacity. Maryland Historical Society.

new century. By those years, conditions had become so sharpened on the international scene as to provoke a major crisis for the new nation, answered by an embargo on trade to Europe and by multiplied efforts to root manufacturing enterprises in American soil.

Napoleon Bonaparte's ambitions for French dominion in Europe had unleashed a series of wars that at first benefited American mercantile neutrality through disruption of European-based shipping, then led to British and French interceptions of American traders. When the British warship *Leopard* fired on the American naval vessel *Chesapeake* off Cape Henry, Virginia, in June 1807, President Jefferson mobilized action not for what likely would have been a disastrous war, but for another kind of national sacrifice: an economic embargo. Enacted on December 17, 1807, the embargo was intended to induce the British to acknowledge American sovereignty.

Over the next year, American mercantile interests endured the blow as national export values dropped 76 percent, and Baltimore's by more than eighty, yet the restrictions held in place through the remainder of Jefferson's presidency, to March 4, 1809. Then his partisans, fearing severe erosion of political support, terminated the embargo three months earlier than the president

had desired. Ultimately, the policy failed to affect the desired attitudinal change, in large part the result of fortuitous new trading opportunities for the British in South America and the West Indies. Increasing tensions culminated in the war of 1812. Yet the embargo did serve to increase demand for local industrial production and gave an incentive to shift capital from mercantile to manufacturing ventures. Investors organized as many as 170 cotton mills nationwide during the fifteen-month period.[7]

It was in January 1808, a matter of weeks after the embargo legislation became law, that Baltimore merchant and Bank of Maryland president William Patterson organized a series of public meetings to engage support for just such a manufacturing venture. Patterson backed Jefferson and the embargo, yet the industrial vision that Federalist Alexander Hamilton had crafted for Paterson, New Jersey, seventeen years earlier must have impressed the energetic Baltimore Republican.[8] "The establishment of Manufactures in the United States," Hamilton had written in the prospectus for the 1791 venture,

when maturely considered will be fo[und] to be of the highest importance to their prosperity. It [is] an almost self-evident proposition that the com[muni]ty which can most completely supply its own w[ants] is in a state of the highest political perfection.[9]

"Political and economic perfection!" William Patterson proclaimed in his own prospectus, and the race was on as American industrialists bolted from the starting block. Patterson threw down the gauntlet in clear and emphatic language. "The time will come when the United States *must* and *ought* to *manufacture* her own supplies of clothing and other necessary articles, if she is ever to become completely an *independent nation.*"[10]

Hamilton's project had begun with cotton yarn spinning and fabric weaving, set within a much larger planned installation of thirteen factory production lines. So, too, did the Baltimore committee that Patterson chaired envisage cotton textiles as but the heart of a much more extensive emplacement of mills, a union of manufacturing interests.[11] The joint stock corporation the committee formed to raise sufficient capital for these expansive ambitions opened its books on March 7, 1808 with twenty thousand shares for sale at fifty dollars each—a one-million-dollar capitalization, like Hamilton's project. Yet here purchase was payable in increments of $2.50 every sixty days, or as ordered by the directors, to make shareholding accessible even to persons of moderate means. One thousand shares were reserved for a public subvention from the state of Maryland, ten thousand for residents of Baltimore City and County, and the remainder to be offered in all other counties of the state, "so shall we insure to the establishment, *Customers* for its fabrications from every quarter, by interesting a large number in the success of our experiment."[12]

Recognizing that there was no time to waste, both to fulfill accumulating demand and to leap ahead of potential competitors, Patterson moved quickly and expansively. Once subscriptions had reached a threshold of five thousand shares, the company was authorized to begin production. Seventy-four-year-old Andrew Ellicott lent his family's stature to the project by joining other Baltimore capitalists to oversee stock enrollment in the city; the clerks recorded 5,093 share sales in Baltimore the first day, and the company entered operations with coffers holding somewhat more than a third of its total sanctioned funding. Shareholders elected Andrew's son Benjamin to the board of directors at the first corporate meeting on April 7.[13]

Baltimore merchant William Patterson organized the Union Manufacturing Company of Maryland, given the state's first commercial incorporation charter in 1808. Maryland Historical Society.

To this union of manufacturing and citizen-customer-investors, Patterson also proposed an investment of labor, to be enlisted from the region's able-bodied poor: "these, whatever may have been their follies, are still human beings . . . . [and] are yet entitled to the protection of the community; but this, alas! is too frequently denied them," Patterson lamented, his communitarian viewpoint coming earnestly to the fore.[14] Bad conditions, he elaborated, bred depravity more so than did bad character. Productive occupation would offer a vital inducement for self-improvement.

Although large-scale industrial development of the kind that Patterson and Hamilton before him had envisaged remained fundamentally a trial of American economic strength, Patterson also regarded industrialization as a social experiment, analogous to the political one that had unified citizens and states into the federal system in 1787. Here the persuasive industrial advocate constructed his proposition with careful attention to ennoble what was, fundamentally, a profit-making enterprise. The project would serve the public interest by employing the able-bodied poor and dispensing public relief as efficiently as possible, as well as offering practical education, he argued. For the most disadvantaged, industrial employment could break the cycle of poverty; for others, technical education could offer an attractive alternative to the professions. In "less than seven years," he predicted, our wealthy merchants and farmers should find this a very desirable school of industry and useful information, where they may be anxious to send their sons, for the acquisition of a knowledge far more useful in common life than tedious counting house calculations, dry studies of the law, or medical disquisitions . . .

necessary activities all, but oversubscribed, he stated flatly.[15] Modern readers will recognize these arguments on the nature of poverty and the value of vocational education as having echoed through the years to our own era.

As a guiding concept, Patterson's theoretical framework was not too dissimilar from the utopian paternalism promoted later at the Waltham and Lowell textile mills. There the celebrated labor force of "Lowell girls" consisted of educated, morally uplifted farmers' daughters who cycled through the factories for a few years before returning home to marry, enabling mill owners to avoid the development of a permanent and restive underclass, as had happened in Britain.[16] But, in fact, the Lowell gleam began to tarnish as soon as that elaborate system was exposed to air, for "the Irish day laborers, who had dug the canals, built the dams and mill structures, and continued at menial jobs . . . [found housing in an adjacent] shantytown . . . not part of the famous landscape" of carefully supervised propriety and culture.[17] Moreover, in the 1830s the women themselves began to engage in labor actions, and in the next decade, mill owners increasingly supplanted their transient local charges with a greater and more permanent population of Irish immigrants, unsupervised outside of the factories. By the 1850s they constituted half the workforce.[18]

Although mid-century mill owners conveniently liberated themselves from the social reform responsibilities of their fathers, in part by abandoning the theory of environmental causation of poverty for one of inherent moral failure, Patterson's early-nineteenth-century civic advocacy aligned well with the views of his reformist contemporaries in the century's first decades. Industry in this period validated its own expansion—indeed, even existence—by promoting republicanism.[19] Thus, concluding his "Address to the People of Maryland," Patterson intoned: "for this laudable and patriotic purpose" the Union Manufacturing Company will operate "under the influence (as we trust) of that expanded Philanthropy, which would cement us together as members of one common family."[20] Both Patterson and Francis Cabot Lowell—founder of the Waltham-Lowell labor system—recognized the economic value inherent in the nation's move to large-scale industrial production, yet these far-sighted men also demonstrated that on the American stage, the factory system first had to be viewed as serving self-consciously altruistic, practical, and political ends.

Patterson's themes of self-interest and the public good, of national sovereignty through economic as well as political union, justified not only the general place of industry in the new Republic but also a level of industrial production and coordination raised to what had been until then a visionary scale. A letter writer to the *Federal Gazette*, who called himself "A Native of Baltimore," did object to Patterson's ambitious plans, reprinting Jefferson's famous query XIX from *Notes on the State of Virginia*—"let our workshops remain in Europe"—yet the basis of the writer's argument was not the now familiar lament for the loss of an agrarian republic, but instead a fear of monopoly.[21]

> Mr. Jefferson was far from supposing such gigantic efforts would be made in the United States, as the accumulation of this enormous capital implies, well knowing that where encouraged, the manufactures are employed at their own uses by individual capitalists, a system which afford[s] the greatest advantage to both, and much more commendable than a monopoly, which must reduce every private workman to the company's terms, or to absolute idleness and want.[22]

"Baltimore Native's" commentary quite plainly assumes the value of industry, as the work of "individual capitalists," and in so doing bears out historian Joyce Appleby's perceptive contention that the romantic view of the Jeffersonian Republicans as anti-capitalist agrarians is mistaken. That public good developed out of the new nation's philosophy of individual political freedom gave rise, she argued, to an analogous rationale for individual economic freedom. "Adam Smith's invisible hand"—the conception of a natural law by which the collective operation of self-interest coincides with the greatest public welfare—"was warmly clasped by the Republicans."[23]

This political-economic philosophy animated the ideas of both Patterson and "Baltimore Native," but recognition of the expansive geographical reach of the Republic enabled Patterson—and Jefferson, it seems—to chart a different, more hopeful course for manufacturing than that which "Native" feared. Appleby elaborated:

The prosperity that began in 1789 affected all but the most destitute in the United States. Western lands drew off wage earners from both rural and urban areas, and wages rose as the work force grew smaller. It was a relationship well understood by the Republicans in Congress who voted to reduce the minimum size of land purchases, extend credit to buyers, and place land offices in the areas where ordinary men and women lived. Nor were benefits confined to farmers. "As yet our manufacturers are as much at their ease, as independent and moral as our agricultural inhabitants," Jefferson explained in a letter of 1805, and "they will continue so as long as there are vacant lands for them to resort to; because whenever it shall be attempted by the other classes to reduce them to the minimum of subsistence, they will quit their trades and go to labouring in the earth."[24]

Where "Native" saw a threat in the potentially monopolistic reach of the Union Manufacturing Company, William Patterson doubtless viewed the grand experiment as part of a still greater national system of manufacturing and capital accumulation, a system that would produce benefits for Jefferson's future nation, itself far more extensive than "Native" was able to imagine. The issue of the day, then, was not manufacturing, per se, but the appropriateness of its scale.

And that scale was gigantic. In mid-March 1808, Patterson advertised for "the owners of mills or mill seats within twenty miles of Baltimore" to offer proposals to him for the directors' consideration, and in just over two months after April 7, the first meeting of the board, the directors assembled a nine-hundred-acre tract running along both banks of the Patapsco for almost two miles, some half of this acreage purchased from the Ellicotts.[25] "This estate," company president Robert McKim reported, ". . . may be viewed as one of the most valuable, and for the purposes intended, among the most ap-propriate to be found on this side of the Alleghany mountains."[26] The flow of commerce along the National Road would answer the stream of waterpower through a site rich in timber and stone.

At the northern extremity of the tract, the company built a heavy wooden dam sustained by stone piers, and the impounded waters flooded a canal twenty feet broad, extending at a nearly level grade along the Baltimore County side of the valley for a mile and a quarter. The length was sufficient to attain a fifty-foot elevation from the rapids falling away among the shoals below.[27] This waterpower, descending to the riverbed in a succession of parallel channels, could drive the wheels of sixteen proposed mills, two ranges of eight buildings each, upper and lower, aligned between the canal and the river.

Chief mechanic Samuel Hopkins organized and directed work crews on site beginning in July—masons, carpenters, and lime-burners; machinists skilled in fabricating cotton textile equipment; quarrymen, masons' attendants, and laborers to excavate and clear the race and roadway. Sub-contracted crews handled discrete portions of the long canal. The first factory building these mechanics raised over the next twenty-two months stood in stone five stories tall, 106 by 44 feet, a footprint enlarging that of Mendenhall's paper mill by an even six feet in both dimensions. Its precise con-figuration survives in a drawing by Baltimore artist and architect Maximilian Godefroy: twelve bays of

Photographed in 1904, this dam was similar to the one constructed for the Union Manu-facturing Company: a wooden frame braced between two large stone abutments.
Enoch Pratt Free Library.

The Union Manufacturing Company's millrace extended for more than a mile and brought enough water to power sixteen mills.
Enoch Pratt Free Library.

"The Union Manufactories of Maryland on Patapsco Falls, Baltimore County," as drawn by Maximilian Godefroy, depicted "the Republican industrialist's dream."
Maryland Historical Society.

1. Thread mill.
2. Superintendent's dwelling.
3. Weaving mill.
4. Double boarding house.
5. Row houses.
6. Cabins at the river.

windows with sober jack-arched lintels filled out the new building's flanks. Above, six skylights set into each pent of the gable roof lighted a sixth useable floor, and a classical balustrade ran the length of the gable's apex, from a chimney above a gable-end demi-lune window at one extreme to a belfry cupola presiding over the entry at the other. It was to date the largest textile mill in the country.[28] Downriver, at the opposite end of the village, a successor to Thomas Mendenhall employed as many as nine adult men and women at the paper factory, while the Ellicotts probably retained for the merchant mill and ironworks no more than twenty-five to thirty men and ten boys.[29] When Matthew Waddell, an English immigrant hired to superintend at Union,

threw open the new factory doors in May 1810, 150 wage earners crossed the threshold, a workforce that dwarfed those of his neighbors, just as those neighbors' mill buildings dwarfed the nation's supposed first factory.[30]

"Upwards of 70" of these first 150 operatives were "boys indentured to the Company," said Sir Augustus Foster, a British traveler who visited a year or two after 1810, observing that "the work was principally done by apprentices, Boys and Girls." He calculated a "Population of 300 Persons, in all, kept together by the establishment," doubtless including some workers' family members.[31] The presence of such numbers begs the question of factory housing, and here the initial configuration of the mill and mill village is partially known, like that at Ellicotts' Mills, from a remarkable drawing.

In 1811 or 1812, the company directors commissioned Maximilian Godefroy to draw a perspective representation of the complex arrayed across the valley slope to the steep bank at the river's edge. Godefroy's polished but incomplete drawing—evidently intended to be the basis of an engraving never executed—depicts the first factory building with exceptional clarity and detail, as related above, in addition to five other substantial masonry structures and several smaller ones, of wood, above the river in the foreground.[32] The contrast between the wooden and masonry structures reflects not only a literal distinction in type but also represents the improving values of large-scale industry, a reading enhanced by an allegory Godefroy centered with the title in the lower border of the drawing.

The Union Manufacteries of Maryland   on Patapsco Falls

Maximilian Godefroy.
Maryland Historical Society.

This complex image appears in a cartouche of clouds, revealing its visionary nature as against the precise and literal details in the drawing above, yet the allegory recites with as great a degree of clarity the heroic themes of William Patterson's discourse. *Home-based production, Commerce, Labor, Agriculture,* and *International trade* together pull a barque holding the infant *Industry* in a cradle, soon to be crowned by a cherub holding a victor's laurel wreath. Rays from the eye of Providence illumine the infant as well as a mirror held by *Destiny,* in the far left of the image, who reflects a shaft of light back onto the face of a rustic settler asleep against a boulder, inspiring him to wake to this new world. Above these images, *Columbia,* holding a spear with a billowing American flag, is seated in a rich landscape with a powerful waterfall—the natural and industrial promise of the American continent—and at her left hand *Victory* extends a laurel crown to a colonizer at the shore. "A pull," runs the motto in a banner, "a strong pull and a pull altogether."

This fluid and prophetic union of recent past and future promise blends well with the portentous moment depicted in the drawing above, where lives of material deprivation will be transformed by the fine industrial buildings standing above the hovels at the river. It is an apt representation of the era's remarkable optimism. One might justifiably entitle the whole picture not its actual and pedestrian "Union Manufactories of Maryland on Patapsco Falls Baltimore County," but "The Republican Industrialist's Dream."[33]

Descending now to a less exalted plain, the two principal industrial buildings took pride of place in the center of the drawing, and though the thread mill actually stood perpendicular to the river at the end of the canal, Godefroy repositioned the building for a better view of its long flank, to emphasize the structure's exceptional size and to show the two large waterwheels that drove the yarn spinners inside. Immediately behind the factory to the left stood a smaller-scale structure with similar attri-

butes—simple gable roof with skylights, a gable end terminating in a chimney, and abundant windows capped with jack arches—all drawn with the same dark line-weights as the factory equated with it. This well-lighted, three-story stone structure had been designed, certainly, to contain the hand looms on which the adult male weavers—"a few Englishmen," Foster observed—produced fabrics of the graded yarns spun in the adjacent mill. By 1813 the company advertised at its Baltimore offices "a constant supply of COTTON YARN. . . . [and] *Cotton Shirtings, Sheetings, Twilled Goods,* and a number of other articles of Cotton cloth, all of their own manufacture."[34]

The road to these buildings, which the company's surveyors had grafted onto the new lane to the ironworks in Ellicotts' Mills, led north from the Baltimore-Frederick turnpike by the tannery

Although the Union Manufacturing Company employed the Slater system of "putting out" yarn to be woven into fabric in homes, the company, from the beginning, operated a separate weaving mill that centralized fabric production and enabled closer supervision of labor.

and the iron rolling and slitting mill, thence up the steep incline to a narrow, level cut that proceeded to the textile factory site. Here the valley slope opened out to a degree into a kind of bowl, permitting the factory and adjacent buildings to stand together in a centralized grouping, and where the lane continued farther along the high bank, the building sites narrowed again. As with the Ellicotts' eighteenth-century mill village, the terrain dictated a sinuous, linear form, and although a large factory building served as the fulcrum for each village plan, the more populous Union community lacked the transcendent architectural expressions of knowledge and religious faith so carefully juxtaposed with the mundane commercial and industrial activities arrayed below at Ellicotts' Mills. When the directors applied to the state land office to patent the Union land, they christened the tract—and the village—"Oella . . . in commemoration of the name of the first Woman who applied herself to the spinning of Cotton on the Continent."[35] As the name implies, all focused here on productive labor, embodied in the factories. These bold new systems and architecture nevertheless found deep roots in earlier ideas and experiences, just as the large-scale merchant flour mills were heirs of the local country grist mill.

Godefroy's drawing shows Oella's first residential buildings facing the industrial center in a rough semi-circle—or aligned on the up-hill side of the lane, where terracing could be cut into the slope. Two three-and-a-half-story dwellings flanked the factory and weaving house, and the artist rendered these in a lighter wash to indicate distance as well as a lower status. These four-bay, gable-roofed stone structures, probably both with rear wings, were double houses, and their side-by-side entrances occupied the two center bays on the ground floor. Their larger-than-usual domestic scale suggests that they were intended to be boarding houses for the company's young charges.[36] On the hillside to the left, prominently sited above the industrial buildings and boarding houses, the superintendent's dwelling also faced the center, and Godefroy gave it, too, a lighter wash than the factory and weaving house, reinforcing the importance of the two principal buildings. This two-story, five-bay stone dwelling with a rear wing recalls the configuration of George Ellicott's house below at Ellicotts' Mills, the most prominent residence in the village, and in Oella the company designated this structure for their senior supervisory employee. A frame smith's shop and two stables stood in view of the superintendent nearby, and where the lane continued beyond them farther across the valley slope, the company constructed six attached rowhouses, two-and-a-half story stone dwellings, doubtless for workers with families, perhaps initially the adult weavers.[37]

The company's builders also erected a number of structures Godefroy did not depict, possibly out of view behind the industrial buildings or not yet sketched out when he left the drawing unfinished, including a schoolhouse and five possibly temporary wooden dwellings for the construction crews. These dwellings indicate a further distinction between employees—so evident among the superintendent, weavers, and boarding-house children—and calls to mind the possibility of a precursor to the construction/menial-laborer "shantytown" beyond the city limits of Lowell, which came into existence more than a decade later.[38]

Most important of the unillustrated buildings—here because its location was too far away, and its activities ancillary to the industrial center—was a machine shop fitted out in an existing grist mill on the Anne Arundel side of the Patapsco about a mile upstream from the factory site. This thirty-foot square, two-story frame structure had been standing beside the river most likely since 1796, and though it does not appear to have functioned with great success as a country grist mill, it became the busy center of the construction staging area for the Union complex, where the company builders sited dwellings, a saw mill and smith's shop, in addition to transforming the grist mill itself into the first incarnation of the facility for making machines and parts. From here a sturdy bridge "thrown over the River, admitting the passage of horses" enabled building materials and equipment to be hauled to the canal, finished in April 1809, a year before the first factory, "affording a good boat navigation" to the industrial center.[39]

In the summer of 1808, the company purchased cotton yarn-spinning apparatus from a Providence, Rhode Island, machinist, who had coincidentally maintained a workshop in the lower floor of the old Paterson textile mill until that exceptional building burned in 1807. Then the Union machinists proceeded to use these as models for their own self-made inventory of textile equipment. Later in the fall the company purchased and insured a large supply of cotton stored in a Baltimore warehouse. The company's first experiments with machine fabrica-

tion and textile production took place in the former grist-mill facility, just as Thomas Mendenhall had produced reams of paper before his factory building was completed and the Ellicotts flour before construction of their great merchant mill commenced.[40]

The trials in this smaller facility proved successful, and operations soon got underway in the first factory.[41] At this point in the development of the American textile industry, only two of the three stages of cotton fabric production were automated: the preparatory processes of picking, carding, and roving, in which cotton fibers were pulled apart, combed and drafted into a sliver, or slightly turned shape; and the processes of spinning, in which these slivers were drawn into tighter lengths, then twisted, and finally wound into different grades of yarn. Weaving yarns into fabric on a loom remained a hand-powered operation in America until Francis Cabot Lowell integrated power-driven looms

The Union Manufacturing Company Weaving Mill, photographed in 1936.
Library of Congress.

with the pickers, carders, and throstle spinners at Waltham in 1814.[42] For the moment, though, in 1810, "upwards of fifty looms, owned by individuals" in Baltimore took in home-based weaving from cotton yarn manufacturers, the author of a "Domestic Manufactures Report" wrote, "and as soon as our large spinning factories get into full operation, there is no doubt but the number will rapidly encrease."[43]

The Union company did purchase and rent looms to individuals in Baltimore, and in this respect adopted the organizational methods Samuel Slater had established in Rhode Island in the 1790s, in which factory-produced yarns were "put-out" to home weavers. Yet their modifications to Slater's system of family-based production indicate how the Maryland directors imagined the American textile industry would develop in the new century.[44] Where the "Union system" varied was in its push toward greater centralization: a larger scale of facility and production, use of employees who were not all members of families resident on the premises, and incorporation of weaving on site in a specific structure, where the full range of work could be more carefully and efficiently monitored.

In this period, the relative scale of cotton textile production facilities was most typically indicated by the number of spindles on which yarn would be wound. Union's experimental facility contained eight hundred spindles, and a contemporaneous small mill on Jones' Falls in Baltimore operated a thousand; when the first Union factory opened in 1810, it turned an impressive 5,500.[45] During the war years of 1813 to 1815, lack of competition from cheap British imports enabled this large facility to report a profitable annual return of 8 percent on the company's capital investment, and prospects appeared so promising that soon after the first factory opened, the directors made plans for a second, equally large building, probably brought to completion in late 1813 or early 1814.[46] Like the first building, this factory rose five stories in stone, its interior sheltered by a simple gable roof with a balustrade running the apex between gable-end chimneys, themselves projecting above gable-end demi-lune windows. Skylights probably rendered the garret useable, as a mid-century engraving shows less leaky dormers installed on both mills. The mechanics extended the footprint of this second factory slightly longer than the first, to 110 feet over 106, sufficient to add another bay of windows, thirteen in all, along the

flanks of the building. The width remained forty-four feet.[47]

As the first mill building terminated the canal at the elevation of the proposed upper range of factories, so the second set the alignment of the proposed lower range, and the shear wall of its flank rose from a narrow set-back at the river's edge, the wheels turning on the gable end instead of the center of the side. Whether or not these differing drive-train configurations indicated a distinction to be maintained between the upper and lower ranges of mills or reflected an engineering refinement in the mechanics of power distribution for such a large building is no longer known. In any case, the Union site was extensive enough to have been able to accommodate either the right-angle placement the first two factory buildings possessed or two lines of parallel structures. A single, stone-channeled race, descending the slope from the canal could thus have powered four mills, two in the upper range immediately below the canal, configured as mirror images to each side of the descending race, and two similar mirror images in the lower range, at the river's edge. Four such races could have powered the sixteen projected mills. The second factory opened with four thousand spindles instead of 5,500, despite its slight increase in size and probably accommodated other processes. Four hundred employees kept the two factory's 9,500 spindles and associated hand looms functioning.

All was going splendidly. For one brief, shining moment, the Union Manufacturing Company of Maryland attained the highest productive capacity of cotton textiles in the nation during the 1814 and 1815 production years.[48]

It would be only a moment. On a December night in 1815, a tuft of raw cotton thrown into the air while being beaten clean caught fire at a lamp and descended on "the *flowings* at a rough partition inclosing a quantity of picked cotton."[49] The mass flared, then smoldered over the next hour. Three times flames emerged from the cotton stores, and three times the flames were extinguished. When the fourth flared, the water tanks were dry. But for its high stone walls, the first great Union mill, its equipment and cotton and yarn, fell to ash, and with it vanished $192,000 of the company's invested capital.[50] To be sure, the flames made for a devastating loss, but the seed of the company's diminishment was present instead at its birth, and that baleful

speck was not an ember but a piece of equipment. When Augustus Foster visited the works three years earlier, the skilled English weavers he saw could produce three or four yards of fabric per man per day, which sold for fifty to seventy-five cents per yard; with a water-powered loom, one individual—and not necessarily an adult—could oversee the generation of as much as forty yards of cloth, at retail prices of ten to twelve or twenty cents a yard.[51]

It was Francis Cabot Lowell's successful replication of the mechanisms of British power-loom technology and his prescient incorporation of the power loom into the processes of cotton textile manufacture at Waltham that made the factory there so remarkably profitable and so resilient to the onslaught

of British machine-woven cloth that arrived with the peace in 1816.[52] It was ultimately the power loom that made the second much larger, 150-foot factory building at Waltham practicable when it entered service in 1818. And it was the power loom, the larger factory form, and the much greater potential waterpower of the Merrimack that gave birth to the town of Lowell. Lowell's dramatic expansion from one corporation in 1822 to ten giants within its first nine years of existence derived from the capacity of these independent mill owners to mobilize capital for each factory company individually, to negotiate linkage to the financially separate canal entity, and finally to undertake sales through a unified marketing concern.[53] William Patterson's grand vision

The Union Manufacturing Company as it looked after the Civil War.

Charles Wagandt.

The Union cotton factories in 1855, showing the dormer windows that replaced the original rooftop skylights.

From Eli Bowen, *Rambles in the Path of a Steam Horse: A General & Descriptive View of the Scenery and Prominent Features of the Traveled Route from Baltimore to Harper's Ferry, Cumberland, Wheeling, Cincinnati & Louisville* (Philadelphia, 1855).

Edward Gray.
Maryland Historical Society.

The Patapsco Manufacturing Company factory, as rebuilt on a smaller scale after the 1820 fire, and Edward Gray's home in 1860.
Maryland Historical Society.

of multiple factories along a single, lengthy canal was correct, partially. But it took the power loom, the innovative financial arrangements of the multi-corporate Lowell agglomeration, and, concurrently, the institution of protective tariffs to realize the Republican industrialist's dream.[54]

So here the Maryland branch of the American factory and factory-town origination story diverges from the heroic Massachusetts line of ever larger buildings and corporations, organized into a fully planned and carefully gridded city. Yet the much-reduced "Union system" did adopt the critical technological modification of power weaving in 1817 — doubtless a result of the successes at Waltham — and set a local standard that continued to influence other Patapsco investors.[55] One of these was Edward Gray, one of four Baltimore and Philadelphia merchants and booksellers who held the mortgage for the paper mill downstream. When the last owner of this facility defaulted on his debts in 1812, the court-ordered sale awarded ownership

to his creditors. The Philadelphia bookmen divested and a new group of owners reorganized under Gray's leadership to build a cotton textile mill on the site. These four investors ultimately obtained a state charter for a privately held corporation, the Patapsco Manufacturing Company.[56] Laborers began excavations for the factory, aligned about 150 feet downstream from the paper mill, in July 1813. Masons assembled on site in August, and by February 1814 Gray was advertising for bids on "the plaistering work of the *Cotton Factory* now erecting near Ellicott's Mill, and of Thirteen Dwelling Houses contiguous to said Factory."[57] Newly spun varieties of cotton yarn filled the Patapsco Manufacturing Company's Baltimore warehouse shelves a year later.[58]

In conjunction with new construction, Gray had engaged in an economical remodeling of the paper mill structures for factory housing, most notably the old mill building itself, where his carpenters and masons installed wooden partitions and interior chimneys to make a set of six rowhouses — essentially a multiplication of the Union three-story, boarding-house duplex form—then very likely proceeded to renovate the owner's residence and the six small dwellings originally constructed for the paper mill workmen. These modifications yielded the "Thirteen Dwelling Houses" that required plasterwork in 1814.[59] The new cotton factory building itself filled a footprint of approximately forty by one-hundred feet, a variation of the local model, and contained thirteen bays of fenestration on the long river elevation, as at the second Union mill. Gray's masons had laid up the stone walls sufficiently high to complete the building with five stories. After the now tragically familiar story of a disastrous fire, this one in 1820, the form the structure took—"rebuilding on the same plan but on a much smaller scale"—gave it a three-story elevation with a gambrel roof sheltering a full fourth floor and a low garret above, brightened by skylights.[60] In its five-story version, the Patapsco factory must have echoed the scale and configuration of the two Union cotton mills, and all three exceeded the size of the first factory at Waltham, under construction the same year as the Patapsco, 1813.[61]

Over its first year of operations, 1815, the Patapsco factory only wound and sold yarn, yet Gray's eyes must have been attentive to the two principal features of the groundbreaking work at Waltham—staffing and equipment—as he advertised that year not only

Gearing and belt drives on the interior of a nineteenth-century cotton mill.

The Miriam and Ira D. Wallach Division of Art, Prints and Photographs: Photography Collection, The New York Public Library.

for "two or three families . . . . [or] widows who have large families" but also for the kind of worker associated with the Waltham system: "Young Women, who can produce good recommendations, can get lucrative situations, and be accommodated with

Ilchester, 1936, superintendent's house at center, factory building at left.

Enoch Pratt Free Library.

The Thistle Mill at Ilchester in the 1930s, after the original gable roof had been removed.
Enoch Pratt Free Library.

boarding in a moral and well regulated family."[62]

Just as the Union company built a schoolhouse for its child workers, so Patapsco "provide[d] a competent teacher to instruct the children employed in their service, in reading, writing and arithmetic."[63] These young Patapsco laborers soon began to monitor power looms in addition to spindles, perhaps in 1817 with the first Union outlays for this critical equipment, and the company clerks inventoried fabrics in Patapsco's Baltimore warehouse at least by 1818. Gray later stated of these early years that "the proprietors had introduced at a great expense the plan of weaving by water and at the time the factory was burned they had 80 looms in operation which were worked by 40 girls."[64] Some forty more girls and boys handled spinning, ten men worked about the factory, and thirty others wove more complicated fabrics—"plaids, stripes, Denims & c"—on hand looms.[65]

At this same time, 1820, the Union operatives worked thirty-two power looms, a number augmented to fifty in 1822, the year the Union directors authorized rebuilding the first factory within its charred original walls. This facility entered operations in 1825 and within two years some 7,000 spindles turned yarn, and 150 power looms rolled out yards of fabric from the two mills.[66] Gray began to rebuild the Patapsco factory in 1823, and when his new mill opened in 1825, 2,200 spindles of a 4,000-spindle capacity spun yarn for twenty-four power looms.[67] When the next partnership of Baltimore merchants organized the third early cotton-mill installation in the Patapsco valley, the Thistle factory, they demonstrated careful attention to their predecessor's experiences.

Alexander Fridge and William Morris, specialists in British textile imports since before the embargo, pursued economical cloth inventories from the very beginning of their manufacturing venture by investing heavily in power looms. The two Baltimore partners initiated factory operations in 1824 with one hundred water-driven looms in a building designed like the second Union and the first Patapsco mills, that is, a gable-roofed stone structure with thirteen bays of fenestration on its flanks, the windows capped with trimmed jack arches. Unlike its taller peers, the Thistle mill rose only four stories, but had a 6,000-spindle capacity.[68] Its mill seat, like the Mendenhall-Patapsco parcel and the Union-Oella tract, had originally belonged to the Ellicotts.

Jonathan Ellicott & Sons, the fourth incarnation of the family enterprise, had advertised the sale of "WATER WORKS, on the main Falls of the Patapsco river" in 1821. The sixty-eight-acre tract on the river next below the Patapsco cotton factory, conveyed to Fridge and Morris in 1822, lay just above the right-angled turn in the river, opposite the "Stony Hillside" where Charles Pierpoint had built the Patapsco's first colonial grist mill.[69] The location was not of antiquarian interest only. The Ellicotts had acquired and operated the successor flour mill on Pierpoint's site at the turn of the century, and, though John Cornthwait's "old dismal mill" was no longer functioning, the company exacted concessions in the deed of sale, not only excluding use of the Thistle mill seat for "grinding Wheat, rye, or Indian corn unless that grain shall have been purchased in Baltimore City," but much more importantly, reserving a right-of-way for a road.[70]

Fridge and Morris petitioned the justices of the Baltimore County Levy Court to lay out a road ascending the valley slope to join the Baltimore-Frederick turnpike some miles east of Ellicotts' Mills, while the Ellicotts' reserve extended the river road from the Patapsco factory by the Thistle works to a ford or bridge leading to the Pierpoint-Cornthwait site on the river's opposite bank. This river road ran between the Thistle factory and its own mill village, a group of stone two- and three-story, four-bay double houses lining the switchback lane that climbed the slope to the turnpike. Facing the factory across the river road, a two-story, five-bay structure likely served as the dwelling for the factory superintendent, as it recalls the form of the Union director's house and that of George Ellicott's.[71]

In 1825, one hundred individuals populated the Thistle village, 150 next door at Patapsco, and six hundred farther up the river road in Oella. Perhaps three hundred lived at Ellicotts' Mills.[72] In total, 1,200 individuals populated a multiplicity of large-scale mills and villages, joined by the river and the river road to the first national turnpike west, the national highway of commerce. It was a meandering but purposeful new kind of community, just then coming into its own. The most important of the nineteenth-century New England mill towns were larger and more densely populated—Lowell began its existence with a population of 2,500, and by the time of its incorporation as a city in 1836, housed 17,633 individuals—yet the trajectory and form of the Ellicotts' industrial town discredits the old assertion that New England's developmental experience, however successful, populous, and long-lived, can stand in its entirety for the nation's.[73] Architectural form cannot and does not originate in a single entity, and in terms of the story of American industrialization, that means neither the small wooden mill on Pawtucket's Blackstone for the industrial building nor the great associated mills of Lowell for the industrial town. "There is no first factory," the Maryland branch says clearly, "only first factories," and that realization is where the richness and interest in history reside, in the multiplicity of complementary and conflicting narratives that reach back differently into the past and together are present in the future.

Workers' cottages at the Thistle Mill.
Enoch Pratt Free Library.

The fury of the flood of July 24 was graphically depicted in *Harper's Weekly*, August 15, 1868.
Enoch Pratt Free Library.

Coda

A Dangerous River

Long before the factory town of Ellicotts' Mills reached maturity, the Duke de la Rochefoucauld admired the scale and engineering of a great merchant flour mill, heart of a small village already a generation old, where the Baltimore road crossed the Patapsco. The conditions for its success la Rochefoucauld readily grasped, and his conversations there with the Ellicott sons of their fathers' ambitions must have turned on the points he later presented to European readers curious about this new America:

> The land is, in general, good, and produces wheat, rye, barley, and Indian corn, in considerable quantities for the export trade of Baltimore, and also some hemp and flax. Much flour is likewise sent to Baltimore out of the country, where the number of mills is very considerable. . . .
>
> Tobacco was formerly cultivated in great quantities; but this species of culture, which has as much decreased in Maryland as in all the other Southern States, is here almost reduced to nothing. It has been superseded every-where by the culture of wheat."[1]

In a day the French visitor followed the Baltimore road out of the village, eastbound, and as the well-traveled turnpike climbed towards the plateau, one wonders if he noted the new crossing, a lane falling back down the slope, the new river road. Were the walls visible then, through the dense and humid summer foliage? What we know is that la Rochefoucauld did not remark on them, and with the lament he gave for the serial collapses of the stumbling American textile industry, perhaps the shell of an unfinished paper mill represented something not only untried, but not yet real, not worthy of mention.

But the river road and the rising walls of the paper factory were real, would become real. They were natural extensions of the small village and the great mill, as securely joined to them as the conditions of economic culture and architectural influence can be. And joined not just in the specific formal attributes we have seen, but more importantly in the attitudes of aspiration and imagination, pooled into an architectural wellspring running out of the past. The Ellicott brothers and their heirs drew inspiration from that pool, and the factory village they created grew into a thriving industrial town along the course of the Patapsco, a key element in the story of America's industrial origins.

La Rochefoucauld did not witness the full extent of those waters of inspiration along the Patapsco, pressed as he was for other more distant and promising destinations. He never returned to Maryland. But if we were to return ourselves to that moment on a summer morning in the early 1790s, to ride beside him to the crossroads, and to take the turn that he did not, what would lie before us in time and place is not only the fulfillment of the potential set in motion by the Ellicott brothers, but also its denouement, in the form of a horrific flood.

The falling terrain of the river valley yielded the waterpower that drove the development of Ellicotts'

This chapter is largely reproduced from: Henry K. Sharp, *The Patapsco River Valley: Cradle of the Industrial Revolution in Maryland* (Baltimore: Maryland Historical Society, 2001), with generous permission from the Society.

Elizabeth Gray.
Historic Hudson Valley,
Tarrytown, New York.

John Pendleton Kennedy.
Maryland Historical Society.

Mills. It produced the picturesque cascades that la Rochefoucauld admired. It also made possible an easy grade west when, a generation later, at the end of the 1820s, another group of ambitious Maryland investors chose to build a parallel river road — ultimately of steel and steam — from the port of Baltimore to the Ohio. The nation's first commercial railroad reached Ellicotts' Mills in May of 1830, and in another decade the system bounded from twenty-three miles to twenty-eight hundred. By 1869 it spanned the continent.

Only a few years before that transcontinental link was made, William Howard Russell "took the cars" of the Baltimore and Ohio along the river's edge and kept a diary of his observations. "The Patapsco," he wrote:

> by the bank of which the rail is carried for some miles, has all the character of a mountain torrent, rushing through gorges or carving out its way at the base of granite hills, or boldly cutting a path for itself through the softer slate. Bridges, viaducts, remarkable archways, and great spans of timber trestle work leaping from hill to hill, enable the rail to creep onwards and upwards by the mountain side.[2]

Russell's romantic language is of a piece with that of Thomas Scharf, who displayed a similar poetic sensibility for the natural landscape in his 1881 history of Baltimore. For both authors, though, the natural world was principally a frame for the deployment of human genius: engineering and economic progress. But nature never stood by deferentially in silent collaboration. Along with the falls' conspicuous capacity for benefit came the threat of devastating destruction.

Floods on the region's rivers had been reported almost as soon as newspapers began to circulate among colonial readers. In 1766, not long after Joseph Ellicott began working with William Moore at the Jones' Falls mills, the *Maryland Gazette* gave notice of a mid-summer flood in the western counties, and in 1786 the *Gazette*'s editor wrote of an inundation during a cold October night on Jones' Falls in Baltimore.[3] Presumably these eighteenth-century floods also struck the Patapsco, but it was not until 1817 that a local newspaper reported directly of damage along the river. Two days of heavy rains in August that year washed the banks of the Patapsco and other streams so severely that "hardly a single bridge remains," *Niles' Register* stated.[4] In fact this memorable freshet, as rivers in flood stage were then called, rose so high against the walls of the Ellicott's Patapsco Mill — which had replaced their original mill building, burned in 1809 — that the workmen inscribed the water's elevation on the facade, and made the mark a reference point from which to gauge the severity of all future floods.[5]

The various surviving newspaper accounts from the mid-eighteenth century to the late nineteenth indicate that almost every decade or two residents witnessed floods severe enough to cause significant damage. In addition to the freshet of 1817, high waters swept the region's river valleys in 1837, again in 1847, and most violently of all in 1866 and 1868, when two successive floods so thoroughly ravaged the communities along the edge of the Patapsco that the valley never fully regained its former industrial prominence.[6]

Few first-person accounts of these dramatic events are preserved outside of the newspaper stories, though one very important collection of manuscripts does survive. John Pendleton Kennedy, the noted nineteenth-century author and politician,

Etching showing the front of the Gray/Kennedy house before the addition of Kennedy's tower and library, which were attached to the right. Only the two-story section with the step gables on the left survived the 1868 flood.

Henry T. Tuckerman, *The Life of John Pendleton Kennedy* (New York: G. P. Putnam & Sons, 1871).

kept a series of journals, and his many entries concerning life on the Patapsco often include references to the river. Kennedy had joined the Patapsco community by marrying Elizabeth Gray, daughter of cotton mill owner Edward Gray, in 1829. The family spent many summer and fall seasons in a residence beside Gray's Factory, and Kennedy went so far as to construct a substantial and stylish Italianate addition to this house in 1854, a romantic suburban villa of the type then fashionable. When the builders had finished the stair tower and library wing, Kennedy explained the design to the essayist and novelist Washington Irving. "The proximity of the river . . . suggested a Venetian fancy, and this will explain my campanile turret, my round arched windows, and the hanging balconies," he began, then added wryly, "if you could send me a gondola, and a guitar man, in cloak and feather, with a dark mustache, I should take it as a friendly contribution to the intended architectural conceit. In the mean time," he conceded, "we shall use our village organ-grinder, and the little skiff of the dam which will carry one man and two boys."[7] Kennedy spent much time writing in his new library beside the river, and his family and many guests enjoyed the "beautiful lookout on the waterfall" through the willows at the water's edge.[8]

A wealthy and widely traveled man, Kennedy's experience of the Patapsco was idyllic compared to that of the men and women who moved at the call of the factory watchman's bell. Nevertheless, his observations demonstrate how central the river was to the region's identity.[9] His journal entries reveal something of the mentality shared by all of the residents of the valley, regardless of social standing, and show how quickly the Patapsco's changing condition could transform serenity into apprehension. "The day after the election — Oct. 7. it rained very hard," Kennedy noted in 1847, "as it did, in fact, all the night of the 6th." On the eighth, Kennedy and his wife drove in a carriage from Baltimore to the Patapsco, intending to eat dinner, but instead "found the family in the greatest confusion from the rise of the waters." The night had been harrowing, he concluded. "It appears that about 2 oclock a.m. the river had swollen into a great freshet, which by daylight increased into the heaviest inundation ever known here." The roiling water undermined the mill dam, pulled up fences and destroyed every bridge but the one linking the complex with the

B&O Railroad, across the river. This one "had an extraordinary escape," Kennedy marveled, but of the buildings along the river, all were to some degree damaged. "The Factory office was nearly carried away," he noted, a machine shop and packing house left standing in several feet of water, and the cellar of his own house filled to the brim. "Twenty-eight bales of goods were damaged — two of them lost" — swept downstream in the current. Kennedy estimated a loss of at least "five or six thousand dollars," plus many days' labor to build a false dam and to dismantle and rebuild half of the principal mill dam. Workers also had to wade out into the river to dredge sand filling the channel and tail race so that the mill wheels might again turn properly.[10]

Barely three years later, in early September 1850, drenching downpours again alarmed the household: "At day light this morning we are awakened by the severity of the rain and the roar of the river," which spilled over into the mill yard before retreating later in the day.[11] Kennedy's notes of another late-summer storm, this time in 1859, give a strong sense of the immediacy of these periodic threats. Every few hours on a September Saturday he dashed off a few descriptive lines, and a reader can almost feel the crescendo of rushing water and anxiety:

[Rainfall] nearly all night with a violent gale of wind. This morning the river begins to rise.

The rain pours down furiously all day. The river in a freshet, rising all the time. . . .

At night the waters very high, threatening mischief to our works.

Mr. Bone [the factory manager] very anxious. Makes preparations to remove every thing of value from the reach of the waters. The men are ready to watch all night.

At 10 O'clock the water is two feet deep in the dyeing house, and on a level with the side wall at the buttress of the bridge.

At 11 O'clock stationary.

The sky is becoming clear — the wind has changed — stars are out, and by 12 the water begins to sink.

A long and trying day until that midnight reprieve, and on the following morning Kennedy was grateful to find "[n]o great damage done, although much mud is thrown into the lower parts of the Factory." He also noted the loss of one bridge, and a great deal of erosion at the river bank.[12]

What Kennedy's observations establish is that floods were not an uncharacteristic occurrence on the Patapsco. The surviving newspaper accounts, in recording only the most extensive and damaging, give an incomplete picture of the totality, the periodic rise and fall of water that were part of the daily pattern of life along the river. Who could know which freshet might grow to fully disastrous proportions, which threatened inundation would prove to be real?

John and Elizabeth Kennedy left the Patapsco in June 1866 for an extended sojourn in Europe, and by their return two years and three months later, the landscape had been permanently changed. After settling into their house in Baltimore, the Kennedys made a reluctant visit to the valley. "Here we witness the terrible desolation of the great flood of last July," Kennedy began. Over the next hours they assessed the damage. Their own house stood largely "in ruins . . . the porches carried away — my library entirely taken off leaving no vestige of books, prints, busts and other articles with which it was furnished." All of the smaller support buildings at the complex were gone, and Kennedy reported incredulously that factory manager Hugh Bone's house had been "lifted up from its foundation and borne bodily away upon the flood." Drifts of white sand several feet deep and jumbled stone blocks covered the ground where tall trees and other vegetation had grown. Indeed, he concluded: "The devastation has so completely altered the aspect of the place that I should not know it."[13]

The Gray cotton factory still stood but was "shockingly injured," he declared, "requiring some fifty thousand dollars of repairs." This was an extraordinary financial loss, but Kennedy was not insensitive to the human suffering wrought by the flood as well. On the road up to Ellicott's Mills, he observed "the same kind of ruin is visible all the way. — It has been an overwhelming affliction to many families here. The loss of life extended to forty two persons." The Kennedys boarded an afternoon train for Baltimore at the Ellicott's Mills station, and as the cars passed down the ruined valley by the remains of Gray's Factory and turned to the east at Relay, he and Elizabeth mused over what they had experienced. "It was very sad to us to see our old home and all that beautiful scene of rural content and happy abode which the valley presented when we left it, to make our visit across the Atlantic, so

disastrously changed."[14] Kennedy never returned to live on the Patapsco, though in the just under two years left him, he oversaw the reconstruction of the factory complex.[15]

The full extent of the desolation John and Elizabeth Kennedy witnessed that November afternoon was actually the result of two very different floods. Several days of sustained and heavy rainfall made a torrent of the river in October 1866, while a single terrific cloudburst in July 1868 drove a wall of water down the valley. The truly extraordinary magnitude of the 1868 flood has colored all subsequent views of earlier inundations in the valley, so although the 1866 flood was soon overshadowed by its later and more destructive peer, at the time it occurred a correspondent for the *Baltimore County Union* characterized the '66 flood as "the greatest and most disastrous ever known" on the Patapsco.[16] He did not exaggerate.

It began with an ordinary thunderstorm. Wirt Shriver, traveling through the region from New York City, arrived in Baltimore on October 10, 1866. On the eleventh, he directed a letter home with information on his journey: "We got here [yesterday] in a thunderstorm with the rain pouring down — but by the time we had secured our baggage and a carriage it had stopped." The prolonged downpour started later, he noted: "It rained last night incessantly & bids fair to keep on today."[17] In fact the rain fell so heavily overnight that destruction began in the early morning hours while Shriver slept; persistent rainfall for three more days kept the waters at flood stage and increased the injury already done.

The earliest newspaper reports suggested that the fall of a dam at Elysville, upstream of Ellicotts' Mills, initiated a succession of damaging incidents downstream. This dam belonging to the Alberton Cotton Factory had been undergoing repairs and was likely in a weakened condition when the Patapsco began to rise. On the morning of the twelfth, the *Baltimore Sun* reported, "The wreck of this structure caused the destruction of the bridge upon the Frederick turnpike road, at Ellicott's Mills. These wrecks, with the water swollen to a prodigious extent, caused the destruction of the heavy stone arch bridge at Ilchester . . . upon the Baltimore and Ohio railroad."[18]

This stone bridge was the widely admired Patterson Viaduct, a "splendid rail road bridge" that had been constructed in 1829 where the original line of

The Patterson Viaduct.
Maryland Historical Society.

the B&O crossed the Patapsco. Though it had "resisted all former floods without any damage," the battering it now suffered finally brought down the two wide and graceful arches spanning the stream.[19]

Almost every enterprise along the river, from the Union Factory down to Relay, suffered damage. Richard Townsend, a manager for the Union Manufacturing Company, catalogued in his own diary a list of Union property carried off: the "Dam, and the Bridge, connecting the Mills with the Railroad — the stone stable — the Wagoner's house — & quantities of Wood, Coal & Hay."[20] Just downstream from the Union Works, the dam of the Granite Manufacturing Company and its substantial stone foundry, a one-story building eighty-

five by seventy-five feet, were totally destroyed.[21] At the time of the flood, the factory building—originally constructed in the 1840s on the land of the Ellicott iron rolling and slitting mill—was undergoing reconstruction from a fire. Three thousand dollars worth of lumber and other building materials vanished in the current. Water eroded the race of the Patapsco Flour Mill and swept away four houses and a machine shop positioned at the edge of the turnpike road, between the millrace and the river bank, in the area where the Ellicotts' original large stone stable and principal miller's residence had once stood. Three of the structures the flood destroyed were stone and two frame. In addition, half of a large brick building containing a store and

In this detail from E. Sachse and Co.'s *View of Ellicotts Mills,* a B&O train crosses the Patterson Viaduct at Ilchester. The large house in the center is George Ellicott Jr.'s residence. To the right is the Ilchester Flour Mill at a sharp bend in the river, where Pierpoint's flour mill had stood in the eighteenth century.
Maryland Historical Society.

The Union Manufacturing Company as shown in Sachse, *Ellicotts Mills.*

Maryland Historical Society.

residence collapsed. Parts of the dams at Gray's and the Thistle Factory came down, as did the bridges linking Gray's Factory to the railroad and the county road crossing the Patapsco at Ilchester.

If in fact the tumbling pieces of the dam at Elysville brought down the turnpike bridge at Ellicott's Mills and the Patterson Viaduct as first reported, surely these other disintegrating structures augmented the mix of gravel and stones, timbers, trees, and the very force of the water itself to destroy.

Alex Porter, a blacksmith at Ilchester, and his friend, a Mr. White, walked out on the Patterson Viaduct to watch the dramatic scene. The two men probably had no idea of the destructive forces bearing down upon them. Porter went down with the bridge, and White barely escaped with his life. Farther downstream, the rushing waters undermined a tall chimney stack and walls of a nail factory at the Avalon Ironworks, the dam, and workers' dwellings.[22] Avalon stood at the site of Dorsey's forge, purchased by the Ellicott family in 1815.

Remarkably, Porter's death was the only one reported to have occurred on the Patapsco during those days of flooding; even the residents of the houses destroyed by the Patapsco Mill race escaped to safety in the hour after midnight when the damage began.[23] Such was not the case in 1868. Then the river rose so quickly and with so little warning that many people found themselves trapped in buildings that fell to pieces around them. In an irony of nature, that devastating flood began with a severe drought.

The first three weeks of July 1868 were dreadfully hot and dry all over the mid-Atlantic. Even northern cities sweltered under temperatures as high as 105 degrees. In Baltimore, Mrs. L. F. Ryan wrote to an acquaintance, then away on a retreat to the mountains of Virginia: "[I] am almost sorry that I did not join your party [at Allegheny Springs], for we have had a most unpleasant time in the City, & have been closely confined to the house" by the extreme heat. Searing temperatures had baked the ground so hard that virtually any rainfall would wash into runoff. That is exactly what happened. As Mrs. Ryan stated, "The water came on like a sudden torrent, & swept all before it; giving no time scarsely, for escaping."[24]

Witnesses in Ellicott City remarked on how inconsequential the rainfall had been there on July 24, the morning of the flood.[25] George Ellicott, mayor of the community (and son of the young man who had drafted the detailed surveyor's sketch of Ellicotts' Mills in the 1780s), attorney George Sands, and others related their experiences to Mr. Fulton, a reporter for the *Baltimore American.* A "brisk shower" had fallen that morning along with a little rain the night before, though by nine a.m. "the Patapsco had risen but slightly, and as there was no cause for a flood none was anticipated," Fulton explained. Soon, however, a heavy black cloud gathered on the western horizon and grew into an enormous thunderhead darkening the sky. Shopkeepers lit lamps in their stores. Laborers at the Granite Cotton Factory stepped away from the mule spinners and looms, unable to see their work in the sudden darkness. Many walked out of the building to the hillside above. At 9:30, a witness on the Howard County side of the Patapsco noticed that the river had risen to the level of the turnpike bridge. It was to the point of spilling over the retaining wall that extended from the bridge downstream to the Patapsco flour mill and its immediate neighbor, the Chesapeake mill, built along with the Patapsco after the Ellicotts' original merchant mill had burned. Intending to warn the occupants of the houses beyond the floodbreak, the observer set out for the crossing but discovered before he even got to the bridge that the waters had surpassed it, "rising at the rate of a foot a minute." The current being too swift for him, "he beat a hasty retreat," Fulton stated, and in the space of half an hour the river rose twenty-five feet.[26]

A tremendous volume of water had fallen somewhere upstream. Twenty-five miles west, a morning express train bound for Baltimore chanced to pass under the billowing storm clouds as the deluge commenced, and two passengers later wrote descriptive accounts of the flood's genesis. The express

The railroad tracks just above the river in an early twentieth-century photograph.
Enoch Pratt Free Library.

had pulled out of the Mt. Airy station at 5:45 a.m., and had traveled about two miles down the tracks along the east bank of the Patapsco when the rain began, or rather, in the words of one witness, "It did not rain — it poured in a solid volume, as if a lake had fallen, in mass, upon us." Mud and water streamed from the high hills beside the railroad. "In three minutes" the speeding engine had plowed the cars into a mire covering the rails, "and we were completely anchored. This proved our salvation," the passenger asserted, "for the flood could not sweep us off." Quickly the conductor herded all the passengers into the lead car, which with the engine was most deeply fixed in the mud. Here nearly sixty terrified people endured the storm, unable to move for hours.[27]

Peals of thunder broke all around "at intervals of only a few seconds," and lightning, seared in "red and blue streaks," splintered trees and telegraph poles. Rainwater descended the vales opening to the river gorge with such speed that it shot out over the edge of the "high rocky clifs . . . dashed through the tops of the dark pine trees, and then plunged like cataracts . . . to the other shore — forming a bridge of waters clear across the river." A great downdraft of cold air struck the ground, and with it came hail "in blocks of two or three inches in diameter." From 6 to 7:10 a.m. hail pummeled the valley, shattering the windows and the glass panels in the doors of the passenger cars, even killing a cow and calf and other animals near the train. The explosions of thunder and lightning, wind-whipped rain, battering hail, and the increasing roar of the hugely swollen river, together resounded through the valley like nothing else "but the noise of battle."[28]

The train was embedded at a point about twenty feet above the ordinary level of the stream, which had so expanded that at its highest "the edge of the river was really flowing under the car," one observer reported. For another, the accumulation of waters submerging the valley seemed "almost as large as the Potomac is at Washington." Before the freshet ultimately receded some hours later, all manner of debris washed past the soaked and trembling passengers. "Houses, barns, hay stacks, logs and cattle" careened with the current downstream, the pressure of the contents forcing a wave before it, augmented by the succession of pools loosed with each falling dam. The narrow river bed above Ellicott's Mills thus served only to magnify the destructive power of the current that annihilated so much that day. In perhaps the most vivid account of the event, the editor of the *Ellicott City Common Sense* characterized the flood as a single ferocious entity, vengeful and malevolent, a conventionalized literary device to be sure, but an effective one to portray the all too human incomprehension of the sheer magnitude of the disaster.[29]

The Granite Factory as it appeared in 1854, before its 1867 rebuilding, in Sachse, *Ellicotts Mills.* Maryland Historical Society.

Just north of Ellicott City, another B&O train was heading westbound past the Union Manufacturing Company dam when the engineer noticed water swelling over the rail bed. He brought the engine to a stop and reversed the pistons in an attempt to back the train down the track to the station at Ellicott's, not quite two miles distant, but the river rose too quickly. The crew made a bridge of planks "hastily thrown from a platform of the cars," and all escaped up into the wooded hillside. Soon the current was tossing the coaches "to and fro like toys" until it finally shoved them all back against a tree.[30] Remarkably, the newly rebuilt Union dam adjacent to the train withstood the flood, though the raging water so injured the millrace that two months of repair work passed before the channel could again conduct water to the wheels. The new dam of the Granite Manufacturing Company at Ellicott City also resisted the flood for some time, and the waters thrown back on themselves upstream poured into the second story of the Union mill building closest to the river. Union also lost its reconstructed stables, wagoneer's house, and "every thing that would float away" along the

river bank, though the generally higher elevation of the complex spared it from any more serious damage.[31] The circumstances at nearby Granite, however, could not have been more different.

The Granite factory had been built right at the edge of the river, and a portion of its lower story walls were twenty feet thick, designed to incorporate an abutment for its large wooden dam crossing the Patapsco. Both the building and the dam stood as a floodbreak for the community that had collected beside the Patapsco and Chesapeake flour mills just downstream. The quickly rising waters that morning slammed full force into the mill building and dam, where the rebounding spray surged twenty feet into the air. Swirling water blasted through the lower story windows and began pouring into the building. All but eight of the Granite workers had left the factory after 9 a.m., when the growing darkness made work at the textile machines impossible. Seven of those who had remained inside now climbed out upper story windows and escaped to the bank by swimming or catching ropes held by the men on the hillside.

Fifty-six-year-old Mathias McCauley stood alone in the building, unable to make himself jump to safety. Seeking refuge above the waves, McCauley climbed up and up through the buffeted structure and emerged on top of an adjacent stone tower that probably incorporated a flue for a steam engine. As he reached this high point, cracks appeared and grew along the mortar joints of the masonry, opening into fissures: the rebuilt mill, barely a year finished, was going to come down. Witnesses saw it move with the pounding flow. Then the factory's "water wall . . . gave way, carrying with it the roof," and the great stone mill building emptied out its four floors of brand-new machinery into the river and toppled "with a crash that drowned the roar of the elements." The tower remained for a "few moments . . . swaying . . . like a reed," then collapsed with McCauley still inside.[32]

Instantly the water overspread the site of the factory and rebounded off the hillsides at the edge of the river. The surge engulfed, then crushed all the nearby buildings already undermined by the heavy current. Five dwellings and a substantial machine shop at the Granite complex disintegrated, plus six structures and a lumber yard across the river at the foot of the railroad embankment. Also destroyed was a frame house opposite the factory on a level with the railroad bed, some thirty feet above the normal height of the river. The turnpike bridge fell. All the houses beside the Patapsco and Chesapeake flour mills now lay fully exposed.

These structures on the Baltimore County side of the Patapsco occupied a sliver of land separating the river from the millrace. The Baltimore and Fredericktown turnpike ran between the parallel waterways alongside this row of buildings, then ascended a ramped embankment and made a ninety-degree turn to the bridge across the Patapsco. Just above this right-angle turn, the millrace split off from the river, and the flood waters likewise split here, quickly isolating the row of houses, shops, and mills. The five buildings destroyed in the flood of 1866 had stood at the head of this row, beginning just below the turnpike bridge. They had not been rebuilt since the earlier flood because their lots "were a great deal more exposed than any of [the others] . . . and [were] threatened even by floods of very inferior dimensions," the editor of the *Common Sense*, Mr. Unger, explained. No other building here had ever been "washed away," he continued, so "at

first, no steps were taken to quit the houses, and when, a very few minutes later, the situation became threatening and fearful, the water had risen to such a height that both escape and assistance had become utterly impossible."[33]

Dr. Thomas B. Owings lived with his family and three servants in the middle of the row. Six structures stood upstream of his new three-story frame house, and six below, then came the Patapsco Mill with its bridge crossing to the railroad, the Chesapeake Mill, and a "row of frame cottages, attached, built out over the river." As the dark cloud began expanding overhead that morning, Owings received a call to attend a patient, but the young physician demurred; his wife, Margaretta, urged him not to expose himself to the threatening weather. Again the call came, and again he declined. A third time, more urgent, the message reached him, and he could not refuse. The doctor hurried out, and some minutes later the river began to rise. Perhaps he saw his patient briefly or perhaps he was called back on his way by the sounds of chaos, but like the observer's experience on the Howard County side of the Patapsco, by the time Owings returned, the rushing waters had submerged the millrace bridges so deeply he could not cross.[34]

Owings stopped in the lane, facing the millrace and the river. On his right, just uphill from the millrace bridge, stood a house opposite his own, one of the group of substantial stone dwellings that had formed the upper-level residential quarter of the Ellicotts' eighteenth-century mill village. He dashed inside, and from this vantage point called out to his wife to gather the household and climb to the top floor. When the Granite factory fell, the first building of the row across from him — a brick store partially injured in the flood two years before — immediately washed apart. Next below stood a row of four attached dwellings. Together these proved a more substantial impediment, withstanding the current long enough for a resident of the second dwelling to clamber out onto the roof. Young George Reese, son of the family in that second house, scrambled along the ridge of the gable and managed to hang on to the shuddering structure as the flood beat each house to pieces beneath him one by one, killing seven people. Once in the water, Reese swam for a rope thrown from the Patapsco Mill bridge, caught hold of it, and pulled himself to safety.[35]

Before the last collapsing roof cast Reese into the water, the next lower dwelling, a freestanding frame structure, drifted against the Owings' house. John and Mary Gabriel carried their one-month-old daughter through a second-story window into the Owings' house and climbed upstairs. Soon the waves shook even this sizable structure from its foundation and, toppling the chimney, shoved the three-story frame house across a twelve-foot-wide alley into the next structure, an attached row of three stone and brick dwellings. Again, the refugees made an escape through an upper story window: the Gabriels, Margaretta Owings and six of her children—none over ten years old—and the Owings' servants, an African American family whose first names only were reported—William, Louisa, and their daughter Martha.

Doctor Owings shouted for them all to go to the roof, correctly surmising from Reese's experience that their chances of survival were greater should the structure fail. The wreckage of a collapsing building would certainly pin them under the water if they remained inside, as had just happened in the block of dwellings above. William climbed into the garret and took an axe to the sheathing planks and shingles, opening a hole large enough to crawl through. Soon he emerged with the Owings' youngest child in one arm, and with the river

raging around him, helped Margaretta Owings and the others onto the roof, then led them across the slope to the peak of the gable. Below them, inside the building, William Fountain wielded his own axe against the frame party walls separating the three dwellings, then led his wife Mary and their eight-year-old daughter up onto the roof through the hole William had cut. At least sixteen, and perhaps as many as nineteen, people now gripped the roof above the attached dwellings. Seven structures had fallen upstream, three remained below them: a stone double house directly adjacent and a solidly built brick dwelling at the end of the row.

Still the relentless current and its cargo of debris battered the houses. For a while the masonry held, but as the turbulent water undermined the foundations, weakened walls buckled and fell one by one. Doubtless Owings and others joining him along the river bank urged their neighbors and relatives to keep moving, moving down the slippery gables. But for this repeated advice, witnesses and refugees, each horrified person was powerless to do more. William led his charges from roof to roof, and steadily behind him always the same circumstance, collapse after collapse, until one last trembling frame held them from the flood. Then it, too, was gone. The men at the bank struggled to hold Owings back from the water.[36]

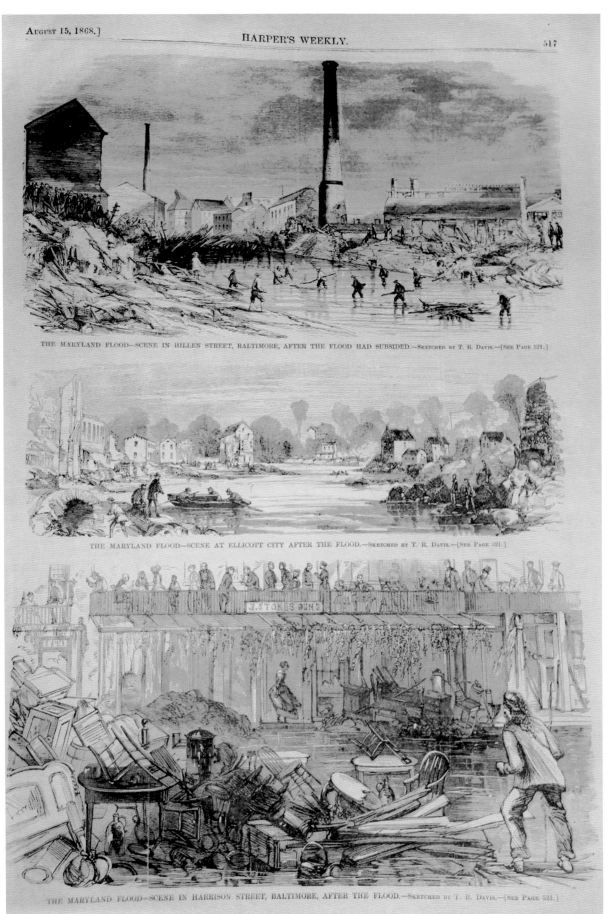

THE MARYLAND FLOOD—SCENE IN HILLEN STREET, BALTIMORE, AFTER THE FLOOD HAD SUBSIDED.—Sketched by T. R. Davis.—[See Page 521.]

THE MARYLAND FLOOD—SCENE AT ELLICOTT CITY AFTER THE FLOOD.—Sketched by T. R. Davis.—[See Page 521.]

THE MARYLAND FLOOD—SCENE IN HARRISON STREET, BALTIMORE, AFTER THE FLOOD.—Sketched by T. R. Davis.—[See Page 521.]

The aftermath
of the flood.
Harper's Weekly,
August 15, 1868.
Enoch Pratt Free
Library.

The ruin to the left is all that remained of the Granite Factory after the flood waters receded.
Maryland Historical Society.

Of those who had climbed to the roofs, only three were saved: George Reese and two other young men, probably boarders in one of the dwellings. All the others who were plunged into the swift current perished: Margaretta Owings and her six children, William and his family, the Gabriels, the Fountains, and twenty others trapped inside the houses, thirty-six in all.[37]

"Every body is speaking of the bravery and devotion of Dr. Owings' man William," Mr. Fulton of

the *Baltimore American* wrote later. Both Fulton and editor Unger of the *Common Sense* singled out William as a man of exemplary character, who could have saved himself yet did not.[38] Such high-minded and public praise of an African American man was exceptional at a time when bitter animosities of the war just ended were still fresh. A brief and less reliable narration of the same event, published in two versions a day after Fulton's story, pointedly makes no mention of William. Instead this account attributes all credit for heroism to William Fountain by making the implausible claim that Fountain chopped "through the walls of seven houses" to escape the flood.[39] Were even the number of buildings correct, several of these walls would have been stone and brick. Certainly Fountain did behave heroically, too, in this tragic circumstance, but as a white man and the head miller at the Patapsco flour mill, he made for that observer a more socially appropriate model.

Indeed, a number of authors shaped narratives to political or social ends unrelated to the incidents portrayed. One of the witnesses of the deluge at Mount Airy, for example, was most likely a Union veteran. He concluded his account with a diatribe against the secessionist sympathies of the residents in that community, played out, he alleged, with inhospitality and racial epithets. Exasperated with the many unverifiable claims and stories circulating, editor Unger stated, "The contradictions in the reports were so palpable, that in many instances it was impossible to sift out the truth. I would therefore request those who can give correct statements, to be so kind as to make them to me for future publication." Unger was a local resident who knew the community well. This fact combined with his acknowledged efforts at verification strongly suggest that his account of the flood is the most accurate of those published in the succeeding days. Fulton's

Ellicott's Patapsco Flour Mill, built in 1809, as it appeared shortly after the flood of 1868. What appears to be a rocky lane is actually the valley floor after floodwaters receded. Most of the rocks are debris from the Granite Manufacturing Company upstream and other buidings destroyed by the flood. The view is roughly south from where the road today meets the bridge crossing the river from the Baltimore County side. Enoch Pratt Free Library.

story, too, seems fundamentally correct. Though his article for the *American* lacks the level of detail given in the *Common Sense,* the interviews he made corroborate Unger's composite narrative.[40]

Both Fulton and Unger noted additional acts of heroism during the crisis. When George Reese pulled himself up from the violent waters to the Patapsco mill bridge, he found Charles Koehl, a lieutenant in the US Navy, and Adam Scott securing the rope. These two men had run out onto the bridge from the Howard County side of the Patapsco when it became clear that the floodwaters were going to bring down buildings still occupied. Koehl and Scott uncoiled ropes and knotted them to grappling hooks, then threw them out toward the persons in the water, hoping to snag their clothing or to give a handhold to the more agile. They succeeded with Reese and two other young men from the row of dwellings: Edgar Parrish and Charles Cramblet. Together these five tried to save the others, but to no avail, as the span supporting them soon became unstable. Just before the bridge was torn from its moorings, they raced into the mill building.

Now alone in the Patapsco Flour mill, and no doubt fearing a repetition of the fall of the Granite Factory, the five gathered barrels and fashioned them into life preservers. Witnesses on the river bank saw them emerge on a gallery at the peak of the roof, where they waited for the inevitable. "From their elevated stand, they saw the dreadful work of destruction going on all around them," Unger wrote. The Chesapeake mill, a building of almost equal size just downstream was dashed to fragments under their eyes, with two men still inside, and the row of frame dwellings beyond that mill was undermined. Beside and above them on the lower slopes of the Baltimore County river bank, they saw porches ripped from the five substantial stone dwellings across the millrace, including the one Doctor Owings had first entered when he returned from his medical call. Two of these houses lost outbuildings positioned close to the turnpike road. Other buildings at a nearby pair of cooper's and wheelwright's shops were either severely damaged or washed away, and of at least ten other structures lining the turnpike down to the river road turnoff to the Gray and Thistle factories, all but one were damaged, and two utterly destroyed.[41]

"They found themselves alone in the midst of a raging element, on a shaking and crumbling structure," ran Unger's vivid prose, all the while compelled to see "the implements of their ruin borne down against their tower by the dashing billows." The upstream corner of the Patapsco Mill received blow upon blow. Suddenly this portion of the building fell out into the current, and the five braced themselves for the expected collapse. It never came. Remarkably, the damaged structure held, and for hours the five young men kept to the gallery. They chanced a crossing about six p.m., when the water had fallen, and managed to reach the hillside successfully.[42]

Had they walked down the riverbank in the waning light that evening, beside the terrible gash the flood waters had gouged into the landscape, the survivors would have seen a path of destruction all the way to Elkridge, as the landing had then come to be known. Now John Pendleton Kennedy's observations of the "shocking injuries" sustained at Gray's mill communicate how thorough the devastation actually was, for Kennedy did not see the valley until three months after the flood occurred. Beyond Gray's, the water had poured into the lower stories of the Thistle Factory, and washed out the millrace and part of the dam. One of the men who had gone down with the Chesapeake Mill survived in the current to this point—the sharp bend of the river at Ilchester, where the first colonial flour mill on the Patapsco had stood. Here he climbed onto a floating roof, but when this unstable raft was crushed against a boulder, he did not reemerge from the water. The accumulation of debris at the river bend took down the county road bridge, replaced since 1866, and then "struck the new iron railroad bridge of the Baltimore and Ohio," successor span to the Patterson Viaduct.[43] The strength of the current wrenched and twisted the girders off the granite abutments.

Between this point and Elkridge a number of industrial facilities had been constructed or expanded over the nineteenth century. On the site of Charles Pierpoint's colonial grist mill, a third-generation structure called the Ilchester Flour Mill had opened about 1833. Since the 1866 flood, this mill had burned, and the "charred walls" of masonry likely fell with the adjacent bridges.[44] At the Orange Grove Flour Mill, built next below Ilchester in the late 1850s, the waters damaged all the structures that stood by the river, though as at the Union Works, the relatively high elevation of the mill building by the railroad spared it from collapse. In contrast, the Avalon Iron works, at the site of Dorsey's forge, lay entirely in the flood plain. Still reeling from the damage done two years before, the works faced near total destruction. This second blow took down almost every other building; the "Nail Factory," Unger stated, "was completely washed away." Hockley Mills, the flour-mill complex at the site of the old Hockley Forge, suffered water damage to the height of its second floor. Hockley stood beside the imposing, and uninjured, multi-arched Thomas Viaduct, completed for the Washington branch of the B&O in 1835. Just beyond the viaduct, where the valley finally opened to the broad lowlands at Elkridge, a structure at the river's edge housing the steam-driven pump for the railroad water station at Relay was destroyed.[45]

With the drenching rain and high water came further loss of life beyond the valley and considerable damage within the city of Baltimore. Precise totals are difficult to come by. Unger had counted thirty-nine people drowned at Ellicott City and perhaps as many as five others elsewhere on the Patapsco. An unknown number of deaths occurred in Baltimore. Nor was a full tabulation of the damages published, though the final accounting must have exceeded a million dollars. At any event, perhaps such numbers are misleading. This storm of such sudden and unprecedented fury "brought desolation & misery to a great many persons, who were near the neighborhood of the flood," Mrs. Ryan of Baltimore aptly concluded to her Virginia correspondent. "The papers will tell you what a terrible scene it presented, & how much property has been destroyed," she said, then added to reassure him, "none of our friends were injured."[46]

Long after the scattered and broken fragments of the buildings and ruined lives had been cleared from the river bed, the Patapsco still resonated with the memory of that horrific July day, as it might yet for anyone who recalls the story. Dawson Lawrence recognized it on a November afternoon nine years later, as he walked to the top of the heights above Ellicott City. Stopping just below the stairs ascending to the Patapsco Female Institute, Lawrence stood at the edge of the winding lane, put his hands on the railing, and looked down into the valley. "It was a clear, calm, pleasantly cool, fall day," he observed. Ancient trees descended the hills all around, clothed in the "variegated robes of . . . sea and mine," the varied hues of green and brown old hardwoods take in the autumn. Children played in the leaves nearby, and over the whole landscape he sensed the suffusing calm of a Saturday evening near sunset, the lovely, quiet blending of a week of work into the day of rest.

Lawrence had been busy composing a history of Howard County, an essay to be included in an atlas published the following year as an aid to economic recovery and development in the region. *Common Sense* editor Unger's account of the flood had stayed with him. It took only "a glance at the dark water, far down the rocky hillside, discolored by the rainfall and wash of the previous day" to cue his recollection. How troubling must it be to live beside the constant stream, "perplexed at every approach of the gentle rain, and prepared, each time, to escape to the hills?" he pondered. "Asleep or awake, they hear the hiss, and beat, of the swelling waters, and see the mangled forms of the drifting swimmers floating before them," a vision of sorrow as ineffaceable as the sound of the falls.[47]

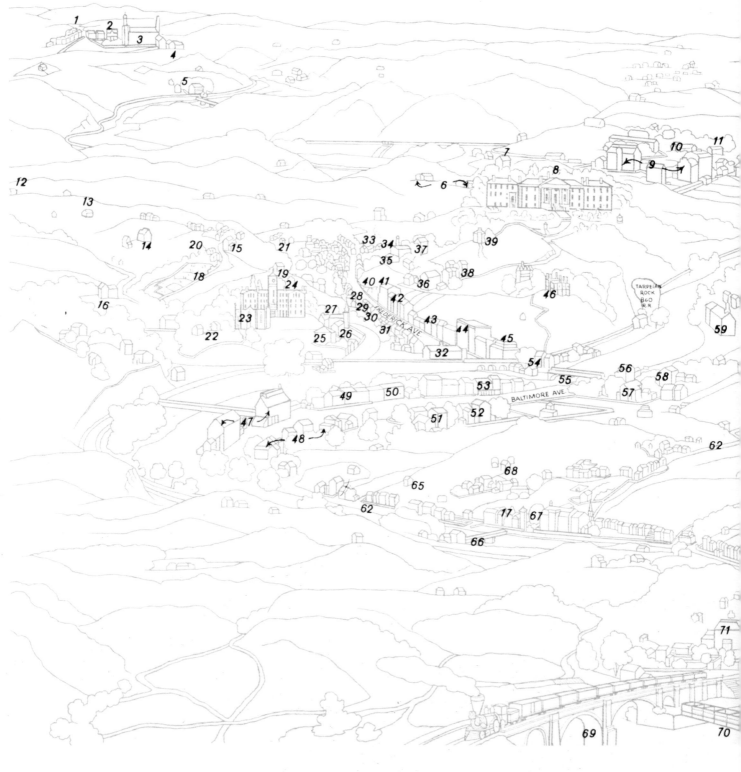

1. Bollman's Patent Iron R.R. Bridges over Patapsco at Elysville
2. Residence of James A. Gary, Esq.
3. Alberton Factory, Elysville, property of Alberton Manufacturing Co.
4. Alberton Store
5. Ellicott's Upper Mills, built by Jos. Ellicott 1775, and graveyard
6. County residence of R. H. Hare, Esq.
7. Mansion of Major G. W. Peter

8. Patapsco Female Institute, built 1837
9. Union Manufacturing Company Works, built 1809, and Railroad bridge across Patapsco built 1856
10. Residence of Jas. Thompson, Esq. Manager of Union Works
11. Union Company's Store and School and Meeting House
12. Dr. Jas. Rowland's Residence, Columbia Turnpike
13. Wm. Hughes' Residence, Columbia Turnpike

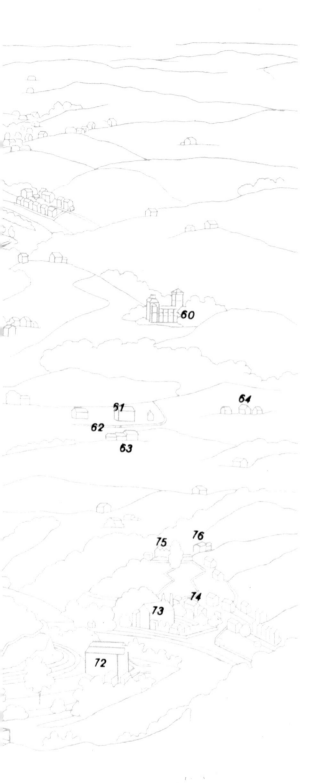

21. W. J. Timanus Residence and Property
22. Prof. J. Veith's Residence and Property
23. St. Peter's Prot. Episcopal Church — built 1844
24. Rock Hill Academy, built 1857
25. Patapsco Bank Building
26. Howard Swain's Residence
27. St. Paul's (Roman Catholic) Church, built 1838, enlarged 1850
28. Junction of Frederick and Montgomery turnpikes
29. David Feelemeyer's Store and Residence
30. Thos. Jenkins' Store and Residence
31. Thos. McCrea's Residence and Depot Mill
32. Railroad Station of Baltimore and Ohio Railroad
33. Union Hotel, Mrs. Dorsey's
34. Howard County Courthouse built 1843
35. Presbyterian Church, built 1844
36. Methodist Episcopal Church, built 1837
37. Oak Lawn Female Seminary
38. Presbyterian Parsonage and Parsonage School
39. Mount Ida, built by Wm. Ellicott
40. Junction of Frederick Avenue and Ellicott Street; to Patapsco Female Institute
41. Howard House. J. Groves
42. O. Tazewell's Residence
43. Mrs. Hunt's Store and Residence
44. New Town Hall and Odd Fellow's Hall and Meeting House of First Baptist Church, erected 1857
45. Patapsco Hotel, built by Andrew McLaughlin, Esq.
46. Angelo Cottage, built by Andrew McLaughlin
47. Patapsco Flour Mills, built by the Ellicotts
48. House and Store of John Ellicott Sr., built 1772, and Patapsco Mill Office
49. Residence and shops of Wm. Partridge
50. Palmer's Row, Residence of Dr. Owings and Dr. Burns
51. George Ellicott's House, built 1789
52. Jonathan Ellicott's House, built 1782
53. Leisher's Store
54. Granite Store, Renehan & Co.
55. Proposed new iron bridge across Patapsco at Ellicott's Mills
56. John Collier's Residence and Stores
57. House built by Andrew Ellicott Sr.
58. Residence of David Barnum McLaughlin
59. Granite Factory, Foundery and Machine Shop, built 1846 on site of Ellicott's Rolling Mill
60. The Alhambra, residence of John Ellicott, Esq.
61. Residence of Mrs. Palmer, Frederick Turnpike
62. Turnpike Road to Baltimore
63. Residence and Farm of Mrs. Geo. W. Waring
64. Residence and Farm of Thos. C. Miller, Esq.
65. Patapsco Store
66. Residence of Hugh Bone Esq., Manager of Patapsco Factory. The New Bridge and Patpasco Falls
67. Patapsco Factory, built by Edward Gray, Esq., 1820
68. Residence and Farm of P. W. Gibbons, Esq.
69. Patterson Bridge and Viaduct, B&O R.R. at Ilchester
70. Bollman's Pat. Suspension Bridge over Patapsco, erected 1858
71. "Ilchester" Residence of George Ellicott
72. Ilchester Flour Mills, built by Geo. Ellicott 1831
73. Thistle Factory, built by Mr. George Morris 1821
74. Thistle Store and Meeting House
75. Summer Villa of the Misses Morris at Thistle
76. Residence of George Kerr, Esq.

14. Dr. Wm. Denny's Residence
15. Chas. McKenzie's Residence and Property
16. Villa of H. R. Hazlehurst, Esq. Built 1857
17. Summer Villa of Hon. Jno. P. Kennedy
18. Ellicott's Grave Yard
19. Friend's Meeting House (built 1798), and Grave Yard
20. Misses Nowland's Cottage

Envoi

ONE YEAR EXACTLY after the devastating flood of 1868, the Parisian railroad station with which we began this story opened to the public. That same year in America, 1869, the first transcontinental railroad opened to unite the nation like never before. The modern world was on the move, and technological innovation inspired unprecedented accomplishments—from the exceptionally wide span of an urban railroad shed to the spanning of an entire continent. Increasingly sophisticated processes and systems opened new avenues for development. Territorial expansion opened new lands for exploitation, supplanting centuries-old native cultures. Progress has its price, always.

The prescient innovations the Ellicott brothers brought to the Patapsco Valley played a significant role in a continuum of transformation for the entire region, supplanting one cultural and economic system in the Chesapeake with another. It should not be surprising, then—or lamentable—that the remarkably advanced position their factory town held in the eighteenth century would be itself superseded by further development elsewhere, in Baltimore, in New England, and farther west as the continental United States expanded . . . and indeed overseas, as Agriculture and Industry, hand in hand, swept the developing world. In this sense, the great flood of 1868 only accelerated change that was already underway.

On the Patapsco, some industrialists chose to rebuild after that memorable July day, while others could not return. The community has always worked tirelessly to recreate itself, as it still does after the July flood of 2016. The Union Manufacturing Company resumed operations until it entered default in the 1880s. William J. Dickey bought the complex and modernized the facilities, switching over to woolen production. The Dickey Company supplied uniform fabric for doughboys in World War One and survived another devastating fire, closing only in the 1970s with the onslaught of polyesters. The Granite textile mill was never rebuilt, but Edward Gray's heirs kept his mill in operation to the end of the nineteenth century. Ultimately this facility was sold to a regional electric power generating company, the next new thing, while power plants were also installed at the Dickey Mills, on the site of the old linseed oil mill in Ellicott City, and on Bonnie Branch at Ilchester—perhaps here to power the street railway system of Baltimore City—and, most impressively at Bloede Dam, which contained dynamos within the structure of the dam itself. Thistle mill produced fibers for automobile tires before switching to cardboard, and, ultimately, recycling. Its mill building, last of the early-nineteenth-century group, was only recently taken down. The Gambrill Company reopened the Orange Grove flour mill. When a fire devastated that site in the early 1900s, Gambrill consolidated milling operations at Ellicott City, where the Ellicotts' 1809 building had been repaired and expanded, and a steam plant added to supplement power generation. A portion of the boiler house and the stone base of the tall stack are still visible at one end of the towering mill structures that replaced the nineteenth-century buildings in the early decades of the 1900s.

It is perhaps most appropriate of all that customers can still buy brands of meal and flours from Wilkins Rogers, Incorporated, Ellicott City, Maryland. These seemingly ordinary products are heirs of a grand regional transformation, and—we know now—that transformation was a significant landmark in the history of the Industrial Revolution in America.

REFERENCES

PART I: Tobacco and Iron

CHAPTER ONE

1. J. Thomas Scharf, *The History of Baltimore City and County from the Earliest Period to the Present Day, Including Biographical Sketches of Their Representative Men* (Philadelphia: L. H. Everts, 1881), 17.

2. Lois Green Carr, "'The Metropolis of Maryland': A Comment on Town Development Along the Tobacco Coast," *Maryland Historical Magazine* 69 (1974): 124–45; Paul G. E. Clemens, *The Atlantic Economy and Colonial Maryland's Eastern Shore: From Tobacco to Grain* (Ithaca: Cornell University Press, 1980); D. W. Meinig, *The Shaping of America: A Geographical Perspective on 500 Years of History*, vol. 1, *Atlantic America, 1492–1800* (New Haven: Yale University Press, 1986); John W. Reps, *Tidewater Towns: City Planning in Colonial Virginia and Maryland* (Williamsburg: Colonial Williamsburg Foundation, 1972); Stephen Salsbury, "American Business Institutions Before the Railroad," in Glenn Porter, ed., *Encyclopedia of American Economic History*, vol. 2 (New York: Scribner's, 1980); Charles G. Steffen, *From Gentlemen to Townsmen: The Gentry of Baltimore County, Maryland, 1660–1776* (Lexington: The University Press of Kentucky, 1993).

3. Scharf, *History of Baltimore City and County*, 15.

4. Benjamin Sparks, "Baltimore," *North American Review*, January 1825, p. 126; corrected in "Notes," *North American Review*, April 1825, p. 461.

5. Dolores Greenberg, "Reassessing the Power Patterns of the Industrial Revolution: An Anglo-American Comparison," *American Historical Review* 87 (1982): 1258–59, 1261; Jeremy Atack, Fred Bateman, and Thomas Weiss, "The Regional Diffusion and Adoption of the Steam Engine in American Manufacturing," *Journal of Economic History* 40 (1980): 282.

CHAPTER TWO

1. Meinig, *Atlantic America*, 151.

2. Carr, "The Metropolis," 139–41; Clemens, *Atlantic Economy*, 21, 22, 36; Salsbury, "American Business," 603–4; Steffen, *Gentlemen*, 137, 152; William Byrd, *A Journey to the Land of Eden and Other Papers, by William Byrd* (New York: Macy-Masius, 1928), 359–60.

3. Clemens, *Atlantic Economy*, 35, 39, 111–13.

4. T. H. Breen, *Tobacco Culture: The Mentality of the Great Tidewater Planters on the Eve of Revolution* (Princeton: Princeton University Press, 1985), 36; Carr, "The Metropolis," 142; Clemens, *Atlantic Economy*, 115–18; Carl R. Lounsbury, ed., *An Illustrated Glossary of Early Southern Architecture and Landscape* (New York: Oxford University Press, 1994), 189; Meinig, *Atlantic America*, 157; Salsbury, "American Business," 604–5; Steffen, *Gentlemen*, 152.

5. Carr, "The Metropolis," 124, 142; Steffen, *Gentlemen*, 137, 152.

6. Reps, *Tidewater Towns*, 92–114.

7. Ibid., 232.

8. Cary Carson, Norman F. Barka, William M. Kelso, Garry Wheeler Stone, and Dell Upton, "Impermanent Architecture in the Southern American Colonies," *Winterthur PortFolio* 16 (Summer/Autumn 1981): 135–96; Cary Carson, "The 'Virginia House' in Maryland," *Maryland Historical Magazine* 69 (1974): 185–96; William M. Kelso, *Kingsmill Plantations, 1619–1800: Archaeology of Country Life in Colonial Virginia* (Orlando: Academic Press, 1984); James Deetz, *Flowerdew Hundred: The Archaeology of a Virginia Plantation, 1619–1864* (Charlottesville: University Press of Virginia, 1993); Lounsbury, *Glossary*, 136, 393; Frazer D. Neiman and Alonzo D. Dill, *The "Manner House" Before Stratford: Discovering the Clifts Plantation* (Stratford, Va.:

Stratford Hall, 1980); Dell Upton, *Holy Things and Profane: Anglican Parish Churches in Colonial Virginia* (Cambridge: MIT Press, 1986); Dell Upton, "Vernacular Domestic Architecture in Eighteenth-Century Virginia," in Dell Upton and John Michael Vlatch, eds. *Common Places: Readings in American Vernacular Architecture* (Athens: University of Georgia Press, 1986); Camille Wells, "The Planter's Prospect," *Winterthur Portfolio* 28 (January 1993): 1–31.

9. Carson, "Impermanent," 158, 163, 168–69.

10. Anne Arundel County unpatented certificate no. 400, Talbott's Vineyard, S1189, Maryland State Archives, Annapolis [hereinafter MSA]; Anne Arundel County unpatented certificate no. 400, Talbott's Vineyard, 1689, S1212, MSA; Anne Arundel County patented certificate no. 1011, Moore's Morning Choice, 1695; Anne Arundel County patented certificate no. 662, Hanover, 1737 (mentioning three earlier patents: Cusack's Forest, 1685, Cusack's Welfare, 1687, and Foster's Fancy, 1670); and Anne Arundel County patented certificate no. 173 , Barran Hills, 1748 (mentioning Hockley, 1669), S1189, MSA.

11. Book of Genesis, 9:20

12. Anne Arundel County patented certificate no. 1533A, Talbott's Last Shift, S1189, MSA.

13. Ibid.

14. See Lounsbury, *Glossary,* 309.

15. Anne Arundel County Deed Book RB 2, p. 313.

16. Anne Arundel County patented certificate no. 662, Hanover, S1189, MSA.

17. Carson, "Impermanent," 181, 190. Wells, "Planters' Prospect," 18.

18. Anne Arundel County patented certificate no. 662, Hanover, S1189, MSA.

19. *Archives of Maryland Online,* 39:125, hereinafter cited as *Arch.Md.Online.*

20. *Arch.Md.Online,* 46:158.

21. Keach Johnson, "Genesis of the Baltimore Ironworks," *Journal of Southern History* 19 (1953): 162; Ronald L. Lewis, *Coal, Iron, and Slaves: Industrial Slavery in Maryland and Virginia, 1715–1865* (Westport, Conn.: Greenwood Press, 1979), 21–23; Michael W. Robbins, *The Principio Company: Iron-Making in Colonial Maryland, 1720–1781* (New York: Garland Publishing, Inc., 1986), 300–301.

22. Another nearby site of ore was "Iron Hill," see Anne Arundel County Deed Book RB 2, p. 534.

23. Anne Arundel County Deed Book RB 1, 257, and RB 2, 502; Anne Arundel County Deed Book RB 2, p. 534; "An Act to prevent injuring the Navigation to Baltimore-Town, and to the Inspecting House at Elk Ridge Landing, on Patapsco River," November 16, 1753, *Arch. Md.Online,* 50:374; Anne Arundel County Deed Book RB 2, p. 502.

24. Anne Arundel County Deed Book BB 3, 193; Anne Arundel County Deed Book NH 2, 322; Anne Arundel County Deed Book NH 8, p. 592; and Anne Arundel County Deed Book NH 9, p. 40.

25. Anne Arundel County Deed Book BB 3, p. 193. Other pertinent leases in: Anne Arundel County Deed Book BB 3, pp. 223, 372, 374, 381, 679; JB & IB 1, pp. 137, 140, 419; and IB 2, p. 25. Anne Arundel County Deed Book BB 3, p. 679 identifies Shipley as draughtsman of the plan.

26. Anne Arundel County Deed Book NH 3, pp. 47, 432.

27. Anne Arundel County Deed Book NH 4, p. 200; *1798 Federal Direct Tax–Maryland*: 729:144, *Arch.Md.Online,* Anne Arundel County, Elk Ridge and Elk Ridge Landing Hundred, "B-List, Lands," Charles Carroll of Carrollton, MSA.

28. Anne Arundel County Deed Book IB 2, p. 216; *1798 Federal Direct Tax–Maryland*: 729:152, *Arch.Md.Online,* Anne Arundel County, Elk Ridge and Elk Ridge Landing Hundred, "B-List, Lands," James French, MSA.

29. *1798 Federal Direct Tax–Maryland*: 729:144, *Arch.Md.Online,* Anne Arundel County, Elk Ridge and Elk Ridge Landing Hundred, "B-List, Lands," Nicholas Carroll, MSA; Anne Arundel County Deed Book RB 3, p. 268.

30. The most notable examples were the colonial capitals, Annapolis, Maryland, and Williamsburg, Virginia.

31. Tobacco warehouse advertisements: *Maryland Journal,* June 20, 1788, and August 26, 1791.

Chapter Three

1. Arthur Cecil Bining, *British Regulation of the Colonial Iron Industry* (Philadelphia: University of Pennsylvania Press, 1933), 15–16, 24–31. Lewis, *Coal, Iron and Slaves,* 22 and Johnson, "Genesis of the Baltimore Ironworks," 159 give 1718 as the Principio company's founding date; Robbins, *Principio,* 190, indicates March 4, 1720.

2. Robbins, *Principio,* 6–7; Bining, *Regulation,* 10–15.

3. Paul F. Paskoff, *Industrial Evolution: Organization, Structure, and Growth of the Pennsylvania Iron Industry, 1750–1860* (Baltimore: The Johns Hopkins University Press, 1983), 7–8; Robbins, *Principio,* 6–9, 174–75, 187, 190; Bining, *Regulation,* 15–16, 29.

4. Robbins, *Principio,* 133–34, 160, 162–63.

5. Salsbury, "American Business," 609; Robbins, *Principio,* 18, 88; Bining, *Regulation,* 19; Breen, *Tobacco Culture,* 118–20; Lorena S. Walsh, "Slave Life, Slave Society, and Tobacco Production in the Tidewater Chesapeake, 1620–1820," in Ira Berlin and Philip D. Morgan, eds., *Cultivation and Culture: Labor and the Shaping of Slave Life in the Americas* (Charlottesville: University Press of Virginia, 1993), 170; Lewis, *Coal, Iron, and Slaves,* 11–35; Johnson, "Genesis of the Baltimore Ironworks," 175.

6. Bining, *Regulation,* 36–38; Robbins, *Principio,* 11–12.

7. Bining, *Regulation,* 39–40, and Appendix B, 128; *Arch.Md.Online,* 33:467–69.

8. Bining, *Regulation,* Appendix B; *Arch. Md.Online,* 37:589; Johnson, "Genesis of the Baltimore Ironworks," 160n10; Robbins, *Principio,* 16 and 19–20.

9. Bining, *Regulation,* 71–72, 76.

10. Robbins, *Principio,* 209; Bining, *Regulation,* 98–99, 110; Salsbury, "American Business," 608–9.

11. Bining, *Regulation,* Appendices B, C, and D, and loss of records mentioned in Bining's note p. 132; Robbins, *Principio,* 19–20.

2. Anne Arundel County patented certificate no. 1011, Moore's Morning Choice Enlarged, S1189, MSA.

3. Anne Arundel County Deed Book IHT 1, p. 382. Other tracts include: Anne Arundel County patented certificate no. 260, Caleb and Edward's Friendship; no. 262, Caleb's Pasture; no. 263 Caleb's Vineyard, S1189, MSA; see also: Provincial Court Land Record Deed Book EI 9B, pp. 617, 619, 620. Maxwell J. Dorsey, et al., *The Dorsey Family: Descendants of Edward Darcy-Dorsey of Virginia and Maryland for Five Generations and Allied Families* (s.l.: Genealogical Publishing Company, 1997) and Joshua Dorsey Warfield, *The Founders of Anne Arundel and Howard Counties, Maryland: A Genealogical and Biographical Review from Wills, Deeds, and Church Records* (Baltimore: Kohn and Pollock, 1905).

14. Anne Arundel County patented certificate no. 1011, Moore's Morning Choice Enlarged, S1189, MSA.

15. "Hockley" on the Patapsco, as opposed to "Hockley-in-the-Hole," the Dorsey Family plantation on the Severn, was patented by a William Edden (or Ebden) in 1669, as related in a later patent for a larger tract incorporating it called "Barran Hills" (Anne Arundel County patented certificate no. 173, Barran Hills, S1189, MSA). By 1717, "Hockley" on the Patapsco was in the hands of Caleb Sr.'s, first cousin, Samuel Dorsey, who mortgaged it that year to Charles Carroll, Esq. (1660–1720), perhaps to raise funds for the construction of the house called "Foster's Fancy," mentioned below (Provincial Court Land Records Deed Book TP 4, 453). The Patapsco tract has been conflated with the "Hockley-in-the-Hole" tract on the Severn. See, for example, the Maryland Historical Trust survey inventory HO-387 for the Chittick House,

also called "Foster's Fancy," and, mistakenly, "Hockley-in-the-Hole." "Foster's Fancy" is an eighteenth-century house on the Patapsco River adjacent the "Hockley" patent. See also the Charles Carroll of Carrollton Papers, Microfilm Series, items 5219 and 5220, MdHS, for surveys placing "Hockley-in-the-Hole" on the Severn River. [Hereinafter Charles Carroll of Carrollton Papers.]

16. John W. McGrain and Ronald W. Fuchs both provide a reference to Chancery Records liber IR 5, folio 91, for the recorded *ad quod damnum* writ, condemning 100 acres of Moore's Morning Choice Enlarged for the Elk Ridge Furnace, and Fuchs supplies the date of July 29, 1755 (McGrain Collection, Molinography of Maryland, Howard County Notebook, Elk Ridge Furnace, MSA SC 4300, MSA; and Ronald W. Fuchs Jr., " 'At Elk Ridge Furneis As You See, William Williams He Mad Me,' The Story of an Eighteenth-Century Maryland Iron Furnace," *The Journal of Early Southern Decorative Arts* 22 (Winter 1996): 43n10. However, I was not able to locate the writ in the stated volume of Chancery records, catalogued as MSA S 520-3, at the MSA.

17. Provincial Court Land Record Deed Book EI 9B, pp. 617, 619, 620; Anne Arundel County Deed Book IB 3, p. 293.

18. Alexander Lawson correspondence, Carroll-Maccubbin Papers (1644–1888), MS 219, Maryland Historical Society [hereinafter MdHS]; Baltimore Company Papers (1703–1737), MS 65, MdHS; Robbins, *Principio*, 303; John W. McGrain, *From Pig Iron to Cotton Duck: A History of Manufacturing Villages in Baltimore County* (Towson, Md.: Baltimore County Public Library, 1985), 189.

19. Advertisement, *Maryland Journal*, June 15, 1779, p. 2; ibid., June 22, 1779, p. 4; William B. Marye, «The Baltimore County 'Garrison,' and the Old Garrison Roads,» *Maryland Historical Magazine* 16 (September 1921): 238, 239n52.

20. Samuel Gustaf Hermelin, *Report About the Mines in the United States of America, 1783* (Philadelphia: The John Morton Memorial Museum, 1931), 39–40; Robbins, *Principio*, 150–51.

21. Robbins, *Principio*, 304, gives the date of the Curtis Creek Works, 1759.

22. As quoted in Johnson, "Genesis of the Baltimore Ironworks," 170, 172–73.

23. Paskoff, *Industrial Evolution*, 25.

24. Johnson, "Genesis of the Baltimore Ironworks," 170, 175–76, and note 51.

25. Robbins, *Principio*, 180–83.

26. Joshua Hempstead, quoted in "Notes and Queries: Cecil County in 1749," *Maryland Historical Magazine* 49 (1954): 348; also rendered with corrections in Robbins, *Principio*, 182.

27. Caleb Dorsey Accounts, 1757–1766, Alexander Contee Hanson Papers (1737–1877, 1900), MS 408, MdHS [hereinafter Hanson Papers]. Chancery Case 4549, folder 7, account dated October 15, 1766, MSA S512-6–4718, MSA.

28. Caleb Dorsey Account Book, letter draft, October 5, 1754, Margaretta Howard Ridgeley Papers (1733–1885), MS 717, MdHS [hereinafter Margaretta Ridgeley Papers].

29. Caleb Dorsey correspondence, February 1, 1757 and March 12, 1757, Hanson Papers.

30. Caleb Dorsey Account Book, entries for White and Johnson, September 1757, Margaretta Ridgeley Papers.

31. In 1895, the *Ellicott City Times* reported that pigs stamped "Elkridge, 1755," "Elkridge, 1769," and "Principio [date lost]" had been purchased by the owner of a Baltimore iron foundry ("Elkridge Iron," *Ellicott City Times,* June 8, 1895, p. 3, also cited in Fuchs, "Elk Ridge," 43, and 57n11). It is highly unlikely that the 1755 date is correct, as the furnace construction probably did not begin until after the site had been condemned (July 29, 1755) and with the funds raised by issuance of security (September 20, 1755). Furthermore, the Elk Ridge Company partnership was not formalized until April 5, 1756. The Caleb Dorsey Account Book contains occasional entries from 1739 to 1760 without mention of iron until 1757 (Margaretta Ridgeley Papers).

32. Caleb Dorsey correspondence, April 7, 1762, Hanson Papers; Caleb Dorsey Account Book, account entries for White and Johnson, 1757–1759, Margaretta Ridgeley Papers.

33. Store Accounts, 1766, entry for February 26, 1767, Hanson Papers.

34. Fuchs, "Elk Ridge," 46–49.

35. *Maryland Gazette,* October 7, 1756.

36. Fuchs, "Elk Ridge," 46; Lewis, *Coal, Iron and Slaves,* 120 ff.

37. See Jillian Elizabeth Galle, "Strategic Consumption: Archaeological Evidence for Costly Signaling Among Enslaved Men and Women in the Eighteenth-Century Chesapeake" (Ph.D. diss., University of Virginia, 2006).

38. "100 a. in Anne Arundel County for a Forge Condemned June 17th 1760," Charles Carroll of Carrollton Papers.

39. Letter of Charles Carroll of Annapolis (1702–1782) to Walter Dulany, December 6, 1760, Charles Carroll of Carrollton Papers; Maxwell Dorsey, *The Dorsey Family,* 155–57.

40. Baltimore Company Minutes, November 2, 1763, Charles Carroll of Carrollton Papers, MdHS; *1798 Federal Direct Tax–Maryland*: 729:156, *Arch.Md.Online,* Anne Arundel County, Elk Ridge and Elk Ridge Landing Hundred, "B-List, Lands," Christopher Johnston & Company, MSA; Assessment Records, Anne Arundel County, Elkridge Hundred (1783), MSA S1437, 1161-1-3, MSA.

41. Provincial Court Land Records Deed Book DD 4, p. 389.

42. Baltimore County Deed Book WG D, 541; *1798 Federal Direct Tax–Maryland,* 729:986, *Arch. Md.Online,* Baltimore County, Patapsco Upper Hundred, "B-List, Lands," Edward Dorsey, MSA.

43. 1762 Store Accounts, Hanson Papers; Provincial Court Land Records Deed Book DD 3, 542.

44. Anne Arundel County Deed Book JB & IB 1, 446; Anne Arundel County Deed Book BB 3, 374; Chancery Case 4549, folder 10, Chancery Papers [1713–1853], MSA S512-6-4718, MSA.

45. Hermelin, *Report,* 75; *Maryland Journal,* August 18, 1778, col. 9; ibid., June 22, 1779, p. 3; ibid., February 22, 1780, p. 2.

46. William Byrd, *A Journey to the Land of Eden and Other Papers by William Byrd* (s.l.: The Vanguard Press, 1928), 356–58. Of course Byrd could have tipped his informants with coins instead of rum.

47. Ibid., 357–58.

48. Letter of December 7, 1776, *Journal and Correspondence of the Maryland Council of Safety, July 7–December 31, 1776,* 12:512, *Arch.Md.Online.*

49. Letter of June 4, 1777, *Journal and Correspondence of the Council of Maryland, March 20, 1777–March 28, 1778,* 16:275, *Arch.Md.Online.*

50. Calendar of Maryland State Papers, No. 4, The Red Book, Part Two, p. 174, as cited in Robbins, *Principio,* 285.

51. *Maryland Journal,* February 22, 1780, p. 2; ibid., August 20, 1782; ibid., June 22, 1779, p. 3. The individuals named in these advertisements were probably lessees, so the ultimate sale of the property must have taken place later. Walter W. Ristow, *A Survey of the Roads of the United States of America, 1789, by Christopher Colles* (Cambridge, Mass.: The Belknap Press, 1961), 177; 1798 Federal Direct Tax Records, Anne Arundel County, Elkridge and Elkridge Landing Hundred, MSA M3468-4, MSA.

PART II: Wheat

Chapter Four

1. Reps, *Tidewater Towns,* 52, 64, 65, 92ff.

2. John F. Hart, "The Maryland Mill Act, 1669–1766: Economic Policy and the Confiscatory Redistribution of Private Property," *American Journal of Legal History* 39 (1995): 8n36.

3. Ibid., 7.

4. Ibid., 2, 3, 8, 9, 15.

5. Ibid., 17n96.

6. Meinig, *Atlantic America*, 132–35.

7. Clemens, *Atlantic Economy*, 176–77.

8. Joyce Appleby, *Capitalism and a New Social Order: The Republican Vision of the 1790s* (New York: New York University Press, 1984), 41; Steffen, *Gentlemen*, 140–41; Clemens, *Atlantic Economy*, 119; Brooke Hunter, "Rage for Grain" (Ph.D. diss., University of Delaware, 2001), 64.

9. Clemens, *Atlantic Economy*, 177.

10. Ibid., 176–77; Steffen, *Gentlemen*, 140–41.

11. Geoffrey Gilbert, *Baltimore's Flour Trade to the Caribbean, 1750–1815* (New York: Garland Publishing, 1986), 27–28; Steffen, *Gentlemen*, 140–41; Reps, *Tidewater Towns*, 287.

12. James F. Shepherd, "Commodity Exports from the British North American Colonies to Overseas Areas, 1768–1772: Magnitudes and Patterns of Trade," *Explorations in Economic History* 8 (1970): 18, 27, 34, 43; Sparks, "Baltimore," 119.

13. "Elkridge Landing: Petition for a Town" [1762], MS 2018, MdHS; *Arch. Md. Online*, 58:xxxiii.

14. Steffen, *Gentlemen*, 141.

15. Walsh, "Slave Life," 181.

16. Anne Arundel County patented certificate no. 150, A Stony Hillside, S1189, MSA. This locale came to be known as "Ilchester" after the Ellicott Family purchased the tract in 1802 (General Court Land Records Deed Book JG 6, p. 254; Anne Arundel County patented certificate no. 779, Ilchester, S1189, MSA).

17. Anne Arundel County patented certificate no. 1156 , Pierpoint's Pleasure, S1189, MSA.

18. Prerogative Court, Inventory for Charles Pierpoint, Anne Arundel County, liber 39, p. 168, MSA SM11-39, MSA.

19. Anne Arundel County Deed Book IB 3, p. 216.

20. Prerogative Court, Inventory for James Hood, Anne Arundel County, liber 100, p. 221, MSA SM11-101, MSA.

21. Francis Blackburn advertisement, *Maryland Gazette*, August 7, 1772.

22. The plural "mills" is legal boilerplate; Hood's heirs sold a single mill. In addition, the clerk appears to have transposed words in the deed, which I have corrected in the text in brackets (Anne Arundel County Deed Book IB 5, pp. 137, 141).

23. Baltimore County Deed Book AL C, 680, 683; Anne Arundel County Deed Book IB 3, p. 216.

Chapter Five

1. Baltimore County Deed Book L, pp. 297, 301, and 362; Baltimore County Deed Book BG, p. 209; Anne Arundel County patented certificate no. 742, Hoods Haven, and no. 61, Addition to Hoods Haven, S1189, MSA.

2. Baltimore County Deed Book TR A, p. 138.

3. Baltimore County Deed Book TB A, p. 101; Baltimore County Deed Book BG, p. 292; Baltimore County Deed Book BK, p. 398.

4. Baltimore County Deed Book BK, p. 398.

5. These are likely indicated on a 1797 map of Baltimore, in Reps, *Tidewater Towns*, 291, figure 203. Sherry H. Olson, *Baltimore: The Building of an American City* (Baltimore: Johns Hopkins University Press, 1997), 12; and J. Thomas Scharf, *The Chronicles of Baltimore: Being a Complete History of "Baltimore Town" and Baltimore City from the Earliest Period to the Present Time* (Baltimore: Turnbull Brothers, 1874), 53, 76, 77.

6. Baltimore County Deed Book L, p. 297.

7. Baltimore County Deed Book L, pp. 301, 362; Baltimore County Deed Book AL A, p. 44; Baltimore County Deed Book WG X, p. 590; Baltimore County Deed Book WG BB, p. 125; William Moore Insolvent Estate, Chancery Papers [1799–1800], MSA S512-4-3427, MSA.

8. Baltimore County Deed Book AL D, p. 301; Baltimore County Deed Book AL I, p. 270.

9. Thomas Ellicott essay in: Oliver Evans, *The Young Mill-Wright & Miller's Guide [1795]* (Wallingford, Pa.: The Oliver Evans Press, 1990), part five, p. 75 and plate VII.

10. Reps, *Tidewater Towns*, 284–89; Steffen, *Gentlemen*, 139–42; *First Records of Baltimore Town and Jonestown, 1729–1797* (Baltimore: s.n., 1905), 37; Baltimore County Deed Book TB D, p. 325. Moale's drawing was used as the basis for an engraving printed in 1817, reproduced in Reps, *Tidewater Towns*, 285, figure 199; and also in Laura Rice, *Maryland History in Prints, 1743–1900* (Baltimore: Maryland Historical Society, 2002), 16. The crude original sketch—or a more faithful copy of it—is reproduced in Rice, *Maryland History in Prints*, 15.

11. Reps, *Tidewater Towns*, 287–89.

12. Scharf, *Chronicles*, 141.

13. Joseph Alibone Diary (1772), leaves 6 and 7 [pages unnumbered], Collection 3047, (PHi) AM .00607, Pennsylvania Historical Society.

14. James F. Shepherd, "Commodity Exports from the British North American Colonies to Overseas Areas, 1768–1772, Magnitudes and Patterns of Trade," *Explorations in Economic History* 8 (Fall, 1970): 18, 24–28, 34, 43; and Gilbert, *Flour Trade*, 31–37, 125, 156, 185–86. Total grain exports for 1768 were 12,853 tons, while total tobacco exports amounted to 12,192 tons. Gilbert's careful analysis of ships' clearances, contemporary statistical reports, and secondary literature inspires confidence in the figures he presents concerning Baltimore's export trade. In consequence, a total tonnage of flour and bread exports for 1769 reported in Scharf, *History of Baltimore*, 374, must be a mistake. Scharf stated that the total quantity of flour and bread exported from Baltimore that year was 45,868 tons, a volume not reached—as suggested by Scharf's own tables, p. 376—until the second quarter of the nineteenth century. Terry Sharrer repeated Scharf's error in a journal article, and I repeated Sharrer's in my *Patapsco* (G. Terry Sharrer, "Flour Milling and the Growth of Baltimore," *Maryland Historical Magazine* 71 [1976]: 324; and Sharp, *The Patapsco River Valley*, 6).

15. Scharf, *History of Baltimore*, 376; Sparks, "Baltimore," 109.

16. Gilbert, *Flour Trade*, note 14; Sparks, "Baltimore," 119.

17. Appleby, *Capitalism*, 39, 40.

18. Barry Levy, *Quakers and the American Family: British Settlement in the Delaware Valley* (New York: Oxford University Press, 1988), 124–27, 152; James T. Lemon, *The Best Poor Man's Country: A Geographical Study of Early Southeastern Pennsylvania* (Baltimore: The Johns Hopkins Press, 1972), 219–24.

19. Meinig, *Atlantic America*, 267–70, 284–95.

20. Appleby, *Capitalism*, 43.

21. Gilbert, *Flour Trade*, 27–39.

22. Steffen, *Gentlemen*, 152, 172–73; Reps, *Tidewater Towns*, 289; Meinig, *Atlantic America*, 294; Baltimore County Deed Book WG X, p. 590; Steffen, *Gentlemen*, 173; Baltimore County Deed Book WG X, p. 590; Baltimore County Deed Book WG BB, p. 125.

CHAPTER SIX

1. Charles W. Evans, *Biographical and Historical Accounts of the Fox, Ellicott, and Evans Families* (1882), reprinted in Harry Lee Hoffman Jr. and Charlotte Feast Hoffman, eds., *American Family History* (Cockeysville, Md.: Fox, Ellicott, Evans Fund, 1976); Baltimore County Deed Book AL C, pp. 680, 683; Baltimore County Deed Book AL K, p. 394; Stephen G. Del Sordo, "Work in Progress: Eighteenth-Century Grist Mills: Some Chester County, Pennsylvania Examples," *Perspectives in Vernacular Architecture* 1 (1982): 67 and 77n5.

2. Levy, *Quakers*, 127.

3. Ibid., 126–29, 144–45, 152.

4. Frederick B. Tolles, *Meeting House and Counting House: The Quaker Merchants of Colonial Philadelphia, 1682–1763* (New York: W. W. Norton & Co., Inc., 1963), 53.

5. Ibid., 49–53.

6. Evans, *Young Millwright*, part five, v.

7. Baltimore County Deed Book L, p. 301.

8. Ellicott Ledger, p. 306, Henry Maynadier Fitzhugh Family Collection [1698-1902], MSA SC 4688, MSA, hereinafter cited as John Ellicott & Company, Ledger D.

9. Anne Arundel County Deed Book IB 5, pp. 134, 138; John Ellicott & Company, Ledger D, pp. 305, 502, 519, 711; John Ellicott, Mill Ledger Accounts, p. 79, Maryland Manuscripts Collection, Series 4, Business and Other Financial Records, Item 1347, hereinafter cited as John Ellicott & Company, Ledger E; and Ellicott's Mills, Mill Ledger, p. 384, Maryland Manuscripts Collection, Series 4, Business and Other Financial Records, Item 1348, hereinafter cited as John & Andrew Ellicott Company, Ledger B, both at the University of Maryland at College Park, Special Collections Division.

10. See Alfred D. Chandler, *The Visible Hand: The Managerial Revolution in American Business* (Cambridge: Belknap Press, 1977); and for an opposing view, Philip Scranton, *Proprietary Capitalism: The Textile Manufacture at Philadelphia, 1800–1885* (Philadelphia: Temple University Press, 1987), 9.

11. Baltimore County Deed Book AL K, p. 394 [online 404]; Baltimore County Deed Book AL L, p. 158; John Ellicott & Company, Ledger D, p. 565; John Ellicott & Company, Ledger E, p. 48 and unnumbered pages after p. 109; Ellicott's Mills, Mill Ledger, initial page unnumbered, Maryland Manuscripts Collection, Series 4, Business and Other Financial Records, Item 1347, University of Maryland at College Park, Special Collections Division, hereinafter cited as John & Andrew Ellicott Company, Ledger A; Agreement of Charles Carroll with John Ellicott, February 3, 1777, Charles Carroll of Carrollton Papers, Microfilm Series, item 725, MdHS; John Ellicott & Company, Ledger D, p. 199; John Ellicott & Company, Ledger E, p. 17.

12. Baltimore County Deed Book AL C, pp. 680, 683.

13. Anne Arundel County patented certificate no. 1220, Prestdige's Folly, S1189, MSA. The stream is known today as Tiber Branch.

14. Anne Arundel County patented certificate no. 1027, Mount Unity, S1189, MSA. The warrant for resurvey was issued May 19, 1773, and the tract surveyed November 4, 1773, but the patent was not granted until February 16, 1784. Anne Arundel County Deed Book IB 5, p. 134.

15. Anne Arundel County patented certificate no. 150, A Stony Hillside, S1189; Baltimore County patented certificate no. 1259, Cragged Hills; and no. 1606, The Escheat, S1190, MSA. See also Anne Arundel County patented certificate no. 1220, Prestidge's Folly; no. 571, Good Neighborhood; and no. 263, Caleb's Vineyard, S1189; Anne Arundel County unpatented certificate no. 346, Rebecca's Lot, S1212; Baltimore County patented certificate no. 3372, Mount Gilboa; and no. 4833, Teals Search, S1190; Baltimore County patent for Stout, now subsumed into Anne Arundel County patented certificate no. 1027, Mount Unity, S1189, MSA.

15. John W. McGrain, ed. *The Founders of Ellicotts' Mills, by John S. Tyson* (Baltimore: privately printed, 1994), 6–9, PAM 10,872, MdHS.

17. Anne Arundel County Court Minutes, 1772, Judgment Record contained in series C91, as quoted in Pat Melville, "Roads in Anne Arundel County, 1765–1794," *The Archivists' Bulldog, Newsletter of the Maryland State Archives* 18 (October 15, 2004): 2, 3.

18. Andrew Ellicott, Letter, May 17, 1771, Society Collection, Pennsylvania Historical Society.

19. John Ellicott & Company, Ledger D, general analysis.

20. List of Taxables for Patapsco Upper Hundred, 1773, Baltimore County Court (Tax List) 1773, Patapsco Upper Hundred, MSA CM918-25, MSA; Henry C. Peden Jr. *Inhabitants of Baltimore County 1763–1774* (Westminster, Md.: Willow Bend Books, 2000), 80, 89, 103; John Ellicott & Company, Ledger D, pp. 62, 268, 305, 542; Anne Arundel County Deed Book IB 5, p. 134; Baltimore County Deed Book AL K, p. 394 [online 404]; Baltimore County Deed Book WG A, p. 289; Baltimore County Deed Book WG C, p. 144; Baltimore County Deed Book WG C, p. 171.

21. John Ellicott & Company, Ledger D, p. 306; List of Taxables for Patapsco Upper Hundred, 1773, Baltimore County Court (Tax List) 1773, Patapsco Upper Hundred, MSA CM918-25, MSA; Peden, *Inhabitants of Baltimore County 1763–1774*, 80, 89, 103.

22. The initial three volumes for John Ellicott & Company—"Journal A," recording mill and general company accounts; "Ledger B," registering activities in the blacksmith's shop; and "Ledger C," probably concerning wholesale mercantile accounts—appear to have been lost, however the surviving series does include entries from various dates near the initiation of the Patapsco venture and projects into the early nineteenth century. These volumes take up with "Ledger D" and successors, which continue Journal A's mill and company accounts, and also include one independent store ledger; line items identify the numerous other books no longer extant.

23. The Smith's book was Ledger B; it is referenced in later account entries recorded in John Ellicott & Company, Ledger D, pp. 73, 542.

24. John Ellicott & Company, Ledger D, pp. 81, 255; Anne Arundel County patented certificate no. 1220, Prestidge's Folley, S1189, MSA; Anne Arundel County Deed Book IB 5, p. 134.

25. John Ellicott & Company, Ledger D, pp. 2, 7, 11, 77, 104, 178, 226, 285, 339.

26. Ibid., pp. 2, 96, 125; Anne Arundel County Deed Book IB 5, p. 139, 141.

27. John Ellicott & Company Ledger E, pp. 79, 106–9 and succeeding pages, unnumbered.

28. John Ellicott & Company, Ledger D, pp. 255, 306.

29. Anne Arundel County Deed Book WSG 2, p. 119.

30. John Reubens Smith Collection, box F, American Landscape, Maryland, unprocessed accession numbers PR 13 CN 1995, 140.436 and PR 13 CN 1995, 140.437, Prints and Photographs Division, Library of Congress, hereinafter cited as Smith Collection, 436 or 437. I am grateful to Lance Humphries for sharing his knowledge of the Smith drawings with me. See also: Allison Ellicott Mylander, *The Ellicotts: Striving for a Holy Community* (Ellicott City: Historic Ellicott City, 1991).

31. Jeremy Markowitz, "Jay T. Snider Collection: Featuring the History of Philadelphia and Important Americana, New York, Wednesday, 19 November 2008, 1 pm" (s.l.: Bloomsbury Auctions, [2008]), lot 327, image 45; Robert F. Looney, *Old Philadelphia in Early Photographs, 1839–1914: 215 Prints from the Collection of the Free Library of Philadelphia* (New York: Dover Publications, Inc., 1976), 35, 36.

32. Ellicott insurance declaration, Policy 3018, March 16, 1811, Record of Policies C, Baltimore Equitable Society Collection (1729–1996), box 2, MS 3020, MdHS; Smith Collection, 437; Anne Arundel County Deed WSG 2, p. 119; Griffith Morgan Hopkins, *Atlas of Baltimore County, Maryland* (Philadelphia: G. M. Hopkins, 1877), 31.

33. Dell Upton, ed., *America's Architectural Roots: Ethnic Groups that Built America* (Washington, D.C.: The Preservation Press, 1986), see the essays by Cary Carson, "English," p. 55; Jay Edwards, "French," p. 62; Edward A. Chappell, "German and Swiss," p. 69; and Henry Glassie, "Irish," p. 75.

34. Baltimore County patented certificate no. 3372, Mount Gilboa, S1190, MSA; Anne Arundel County patented certificate no. 1220, Prestidge's Folley, S1189, MSA. The 1798 Federal Direct Tax documents inventory all of the Ellicott structures in several lists: *1798 Federal Direct Tax – Maryland, Arch.Md.Online,* 729:987, Baltimore County, Patapsco Upper Hundred, "B-List, Lands," Ellicott & Company, MSA.

35. The three buildings of the eighteenth-century village still standing are: 1) George Ellicott's dwelling, 1791, John & Andrew Ellicott Company, Ledger C, p. 70, Maryland Manuscripts Collection, Series 4, Business and Other Financial Records, Item 1349, University of Maryland at College Park, Special Collections Division, hereinafter cited as John & Andrew Ellicott Company Ledger C; 2) the Quaker meeting house, ca. 1796, Anne Arundel Deed Book NH 8, 257, 300; and 3) the school house, in existence as early as 1798, *1798 Federal Direct Tax – Maryland, Arch.Md.Online,* 729:151, Anne Arundel County, Elk Ridge and Elk Ridge Landing Hundred, "B-List, Lands," Ellicott & Company, MSA. A fourth building may encompass parts of the tanner's dwelling or his shop (Samuel Smith).

36. Evans, *Biographical and Historical Accounts*, 65–68.

37. Mylander, *Holy Community*; Silvio A. Bedini, *The Life of Benjamin Banneker: The First African-American Man of Science,* 2nd ed. rev. (Baltimore: Maryland Historical Society, 1999), 70–71; and Sharp, *Patapsco*, 10–11.

38. "View of Ellicotts' Mills, Md." (Baltimore: E. Sachse & Company, 1854), Library of Congress, Prints and Photographs Division, digital I.D. http://hdl.loc.gov/loc.pnp/pga.02596; "Panoramic View of the Scenery on the Patapsco," ca. 1860, uncatalogued, MdHS; Mylander, *Holy Community*; John W. McGrain, *From Pig Iron to Cotton Duck: A History of Manufacturing Villages in Baltimore County* (Towson, Md.: Baltimore County Public Library, 1985), 192; Smith Collection, 436 and 437; Hopkins, *Baltimore County*, 31; Sanborn Fire Insurance Maps, Maryland, Ellicott City, June 1887, November 1894, and April 1899, Geography and Maps Division, Library of Congress.

39. This dwelling had a footprint of 30 by 20 feet, while Samuel Godfrey's dwelling had a footprint of 34 by 20 feet (*1798 Federal Direct Tax – Maryland, Arch.Md.Online,* 729:927, Baltimore County, Patapsco Upper Hundred, "A-List, Property," Samuel Smith, MSA; *1798 Federal Direct Tax – Maryland, Arch.Md.Online,* 729:922, Baltimore County, Patapsco Upper Hundred, "A-List, Property," Samuel Godfrey, MSA). Since an estate inventory taken later in Godfrey's dwelling suggests the larger house had no central passage on the first floor, I have assumed that the smaller dwelling also did not. Anne Arundel County Deed Book WSG 2, 119ff; John Ellicott of John, Inventory, 1821, Baltimore County Register of Wills (Inventories), 1819–1821, liber 32, folio 542, MSA CM155-32, MSA.

40. *1798 Federal Direct Tax – Maryland, Arch. Md.Online,* 729:998, Baltimore County, Patapsco Upper Hundred, "B-List, Lands," Samuel Smith, MSA; John Ellicott & Company, Ledger D, pp. 116, 425, 685, 735, 738; Greville Bathe and Dorothy Bathe, *Oliver Evans: A Chronicle of Early American Engineering* (Philadelphia: Historical Society of Pennsylvania, 1935), 23.

41. *Maryland Journal,* January 16, 1779, col. 1; John Ellicott & Company Ledger D, pp. 553, 724.

42. John Ellicott of John, Inventory, 1821, Baltimore County Register of Wills (Inventories), 1819–1821, liber 32, folio 542, MSA CM155-32, MSA.

43. The tanner, Samuel Smith, and Godfrey were listed individually as owners of their houses, not the company, so these buildings did not appear in the sequential list of company property (*1798 Federal Direct Tax – Maryland, Arch.Md.Online,* 729:927, Baltimore County, Patapsco Upper Hundred, "A-List, Property," Samuel Smith, MSA; *1798 Federal Direct Tax – Maryland, Arch.Md.Online,* 729:998, Baltimore County, Patapsco Upper Hundred, "B-List, Lands," Samuel Smith, MSA; *1798 Federal Direct Tax – Maryland, Arch.Md.Online,* 729:927, Baltimore County, Patapsco Upper Hundred, "A-List, Property," Samuel Godfrey, MSA). The same applies to the cooper Thomas Gibbons (*1798 Federal Direct Tax – Maryland, Arch.Md.Online,* 729:922, Baltimore County, Patapsco Upper Hundred, "A-List, Property," Thomas Gibbons, MSA; *1798 Federal Direct Tax – Maryland, Arch.Md.Online,* 729:988, Baltimore County, Patapsco Upper Hundred, "B-List, Lands," Thomas Gibbons, MSA). Yet Smith did not buy his lot and house until 1806 (Baltimore County Deed WG 89, 488), and Godfrey's house, later occupied by Andrew Ellicott, was included in still later company real estate divisions (Anne Arundel County Deed Book WSG 2, p. 119). Gibbons purchased his lots in 1800 and 1804 (Baltimore County Deed Book WG 64, p. 98, and Baltimore WG 82, p. 492). The 1798 assessor must have determined that the legal arrangements granting occupancy were of sufficient durability to constitute ownership.

44. The John & Andrew Ellicott Company Ledger A, p. 160, records a payment of £336.12.60 to Andrew Ellicott on Jonathan's behalf on Octo-

ber 13, 1780; could this large sum have paid for construction of Jonathan's dwelling? The John & Andrew Ellicott Company Ledger C, p. 70, January 1, 1792, records a credit to George's account for board of the carpenters and plasterers at work on his house. George Ellicott, Inventory, 1832, Baltimore County Register of Wills (Inventories), 1831–1832, liber 40, folio 418, MSA CM155-40, MSA.

45. *1798 Federal Direct Tax – Maryland, Arch. Md.Online,* 729:921, Baltimore County, Patapsco Upper Hundred, "A-List, Property," Benjamin Rich, occupant, MSA. Benjamin Rich, Inventory, 1804, Baltimore County Register of Wills (Inventories), 1803–1805, liber 23, folio 309, MSA CM155-23, MSA.

46. No inventory survives for John Ellicott's dwelling, but its dimensions, slightly larger than Jonathan's, suggest a central passage plan as well (*1798 Federal Direct Tax – Maryland, Arch. Md.Online,* 729:921, Baltimore County, Patapsco Upper Hundred, "A-List, Property," Ellicott & Company, MSA).

47. *1798 Federal Direct Tax – Maryland, Arch. Md.Online,* 729:922, Baltimore County, Patapsco Upper Hundred, "A-List, Property," Thomas Gibbons, MSA; *Arch.Md.Online,* volume 729, *1798 Federal Direct Tax – Maryland,* 988, Baltimore County, Patapsco Upper Hundred, "B-List, Lands," Thomas Gibbons, MSA.

48. John Ellicott & Company Ledger D, analysis of laborers, September 1774 to December 1775.

49. Ellicott & Company Ledger A, p. 154.

50. Ibid., p. 242. Because of the designation of lessees from the company as outright owners in 1798, it is possible that Balderson's four dwellings actually belonged to the company. *1798 Federal Direct Tax – Maryland, Arch.Md.Online,* 729:141, 151, Anne Arundel County, Elk Ridge and Elk Ridge Landing Hundred, "B-List, Lands," Ellicott & Company, MSA.

51. Atkinson's Oil Mill, in Isaac Briggs to Thomas Jefferson, June 24, 1808, Briggs-Stabler Papers (1793–1910), MS 147, MdHS; *Federal Gazette,* August 31, 1808.

52. Anne Arundel County Deed Book WSG 9, 365–375; and lot 3 in Anne Arundel County Deed Book WSG 15, p. 531; *1798 Federal Direct Tax – Maryland, Arch.Md.Online,* 729:151, Anne Arundel County, Elk Ridge and Elk Ridge Landing Hundred, "B-List, Lands," Ellicott & Company, MSA; Anne Arundel County Deed Book NH 8, p. 257; John and Andrew Ellicott Company Ledger C, p. 160, possibly this building; Hopkins, *Baltimore County,* 31.

53. "Quaker communalism and especially Quaker domesticity had its uses in North America." Levy, *Quakers,* 152.

54. Margaret Crawford, *Building the Workingman's Paradise: The Design of American Company Towns* (New York: Verso, 1995), 5, 20.

Chapter Seven

1. Charles Pierpoint, Inventory, 1749, Prerogative Court, Inventories, 1749, Anne Arundel County, liber 39, folio 168, MSA SM-11-39, MSA.

2. Baltimore County Deed Book AL I, 270, concerning William Moore's lease.

3. James Hood, Inventory, 1769, Prerogative Court, Inventories, 1769, Anne Arundel County, liber 100, folio 221, MSA SM-11-101, MSA.

4. Recent scholarship has demonstrated that the division of labor was, in fact, the critical component of early industrialization in America, much more so than was the classic New England textile mill. Jonathan Prude, "Capitalism, Industrialism, and the Factory in Post-Revolutionary America," *Journal of the Early Republic* 16 (1996): 242, 243.

5. John Ellicott & Company, Ledger D, pp. 30, 37, 81, 132, 142, 165, 255, 289, 324, 402, 462.

6. *1798 Federal Direct Tax – Maryland, Arch. Md.Online,* 729:987, Baltimore County, Patapsco Upper Hundred, "B-List, Lands," Ellicott & Company, MSA.

7. Policy 3018, March 16, 1811, Record of Policies C, Baltimore Equitable Society Collection (1729–1996), box 2, MS 3020, MdHS.

8. Account with Charles Carroll, John Ellicott & Company Ledger D, p. 199.

9. Thomas Ellicott's mill description appears in Evans, *Young Millwright*, part V, vi–x, 73–77, and plates VI, VII, VIII, IX, and X. John & Andrew Ellicott advertisement for sale of bolting cloths, "grades: superfine, fine, middlings, and shipstuff," *Baltimore Daily Intelligencer* (March 1, 1794): 1.

10. Bathe, *Oliver Evans,* 23.

11. Francois Alexandre Frédéric, Duc de la Roche-foucauld-Liancourt, *Voyage dans les Etats-Unis d'Amerique* (Paris, 1799), 5:114.

12. Anne Arundel Deed Book WSG 2, p. 119.

13. Hunter, *Rage for Grain,* 17–19.

14. Lemon, *Poor Man's Country,* 207.

15. The two rivals were Evans-style mills, taller structures on smaller footprints: a four-story brick flour mill constructed in the 1790s at the Hockley Forge site, sheltering 10,560 square feet on a footprint of 2,640, and elsewhere in Elk Ridge Hundred, a three-story stone structure specifically termed a merchant mill, sheltering 6,864 square feet on a footprint of 2,288. (*1798 Federal Direct Tax – Maryland, Arch.Md.Online,* 729:156, Anne Arundel County, Elk Ridge and Elk Ridge Landing Hundred, "B-List, Lands," Christopher Johnson & Company, MSA; *1798 Federal Direct Tax – Maryland, Arch.Md.Online,* 729:157, Anne Arundel County, Elk Ridge and Elk Ridge Landing Hundred, "B-List, Lands," Benjamin Lawrence, MSA). A calculation of the total number of flour mills assessed in 1798 for Baltimore County is not possible, since some of the returns have been lost, see McGrain, *Grist Mills,* 1, 2.

16. Bathe, *Oliver Evans,* 289, 325.

17. Ibid., 23, 24.

18. *1798 Federal Direct Tax – Maryland, Arch. Md.Online,* 729:156, Anne Arundel County, Elk Ridge and Elk Ridge Landing Hundred, "B-List, Lands," Christopher Johnson & Company, MSA; Baltimore County Deed Book WG OO, p. 253; *1798 Federal Direct Tax – Maryland,*

Arch.Md.Online, 729:742, Baltimore County, Middlesex Hundred, "B-List, Lands," Ellicott & Company, MSA; Ellicott insurance declarations, policies 1431 and 1432, March 16, 1804, Record of Policies B, Baltimore Equitable Society Collection [1729–1996], box 1; and policies 2353 and 2354, March 15, 1809, Record of Policies C, Baltimore Equitable Society Collection [1729–1996], box 2, MS 3020, MdHS).

19. *1798 Federal Direct Tax – Maryland, Arch. Md.Online,* 729:986, 987, 995, 1001, Baltimore County, Patapsco Upper Hundred, "B-List, Lands," Edward Dorsey, Ellicott & Company, Richard Owings, Martin Tschudy, MSA [I have eliminated as a mistake one 10-by-12-foot building listed as a "mill house" on page 992 for William Lineberger; I believe the assessor intended to write "milk house"]; *1798 Federal Direct Tax – Maryland, Arch.Md.Online,* 729:145, 147, 151, 156, 157, 160, Anne Arundel County, Elk Ridge and Elk Ridge Landing Hundred, "B-List, Lands," Charles Carroll, Charles Carroll (Fox, occupant), Charles Elders, D. J. & B. Ellicott, Christopher Johnson & Company, Benjamin Lawrence, Charles Ridgely, MSA; *1798 Federal Direct Tax – Maryland, Arch.Md.Online,* 729:216, Anne Arundel County, Huntington Hundred, "A-List, Property," John Cornthwait, MSA. The 1798 assessor listed the Hood's mill building as frame, but a print depicting a stone lower story appears in Catharine Van Courtlandt Mathews, *Andrew Ellicott: His Life and Letters* (New York: The Grafton Press, 1908), facing page 6. For a similar variability recorded in twentieth-century survivors, see: Gabrielle M. Lanier and Bernard L. Herman, *Everyday Architecture of the Mid-Atlantic: Looking at Buildings and Landscapes* (Baltimore: The Johns Hopkins University Press, 1997), 247.

20. Lemon, *Poor Man's Country,* 222.

21. Del Sordo, "Chester County," 67.

22. The web site "millpictures.com" indexes mill photographs by state and county; this collection includes thirteen such mills. In addition, the Pennsylvania Historical and Museum Commission, Cultural Resources Geographic Information

System includes at least thirteen more mills of this type, and perhaps as many as twenty-eight. The "Mill Pictures" website (http://www.millpictures.com) includes seven mills in Berks County, five in Bucks County, and one in Delaware County, Pa., a total of thirteen. The Pennsylvania Historical and Museum Commission, Cultural Resources Geographic Information System, http://crgis.state.pa.us, includes one such mill in York County, three in Berks County, five in Chester County, one in Montgomery County, one in Northampton County, and two in Bucks County, a total of thirteen. Probable internal wheel types, not specified in the National Register documentation available on the Pennsylvania Cultural Resources Geographic Information System include one in Berks County, six in Chester County, four in Montgomery County, one in Northampton County, two in Bucks County, and one in Delaware County, for a total of fifteen. For both online collections, caveats apply as to accuracy of dating and identification, and thoroughness of survey.

23. Thomas Ellicott essay, in: Evans, *Young Millwright*, 5:63, and plates vi–ix.

24. Evans, *Young Millwright*, 5:v.

25. Guy identifies the large merchant mill in his paintings as Pennington's mill; John Smith mortgaged Moore's mills to Josiah Pennington, of Baltimore, in 1798 and 1799 (Baltimore County Deed Book WG H, p. 14; and WG 58, p. 107).

26. I am grateful to Anna Marley for sharing her knowledge of Guy's paintings with me.

27. This first mill burned on a January night in 1809, and the mill replacing it was an enlarged version of the internal-wheel type: a three-story stone structure, 45 by 50 feet, with a two-story gable, ca. 10,000 square feet.

28. Evans, *Young Millwright*, 5:65.

29. Frame gables are present on otherwise masonry structures in Bucks and Chester Counties, Pennsylvania; Baltimore County, Maryland; and in Northern Virginia. For Bucks and Chester Counties, Pa., see millpictures.com, http://millpictures.com/mills.php, and follow the links for: USA: Pennsylvania: Bucks County, and Chester County (link verified May 19, 2017). For Baltimore County, see the Baltimore County Public Library online catalog, http://catalog.bcpl.lib.md.us/polaris/, and search for "Hartley's Mill in Glen Arm," "Heathcote Mill in Freeland," and "Keeney's Mill in Freeland" (link verified May 19, 2017). For Virginia, see Silvia Sabadell-Johnson, "Aldie and Chapman/Beverley Mills: Influences that Shaped the Northern Virginia Merchant Mills," Architecture in Virginia Series, no. 94 (Charlottesville: School of Architecture, University of Virginia, 1988), 103–6, Albert and Shirley Small Special Collections Library, University of Virginia.

30. The dormer opening above others on the lateral elevation is present on several mills in Berks, Bucks, Chester, and Montgomery Counties in southeastern Pennsylvania. See millpictures.com, http://millpictures.com/mills.php, and follow the links for: USA: Pennsylvania: Berks County, Bucks County, Chester County, and Montgomery County (link verified May 19, 2017). I have found only one for Baltimore County, Md.: see the Baltimore County Public Library online catalog, http://catalog.bcpl.lib.md.us/polaris/, and search for "Keeney's Mill in Freeland" (link verified May 19, 2017). I have found none in Virginia.

31. This configuration of dormers is visible on Hartley's Mill and on Samuel Owing's Lower Mill, both in Baltimore County, Md. For Hartley, see the Baltimore County Public Library online catalog, http://catalog.bcpl.lib.md.us/polaris/, and search for "Hartley's Mill in Glen Arm" (link verified May 19, 2017). For Owing, see Owings Mills New Town Community Association website, History page, http://owingsmillsnewtown.org/History (link verified May 19, 2017). Neither mill is dated.

32. Baltimore County Deed Book WG K, p. 142; "Deeds & Land Papers" Ledger, Joseph Ellicott Papers (1782–1814), MS 1825, MdHS; Policy 2316, February 15, 1809, Record of Policies C, Baltimore Equitable Society Collection, MS 3020, box 2, MdHS.

33. A free-verse compilation of two advertisements for the Ellicott company: *Maryland Journal* (July 19, 1785): 2; and (December 30, 1785): 4.

PART III: Cotton

CHAPTER EIGHT

1. La Rochefoucauld, *Voyage*, 5:114, 115. The translation is mine.

2. La Rochefoucauld, *Travels* [English edition], 4:445, with translated additions from the French edition, 8:7.

3. La Rochefoucauld, *Voyage*, 5:148. The English edition mistakenly renders "Pawtucket" as "Patuxent," a river in Maryland.

4. Caroline F. Ware, *The Early New England Cotton Manufacture: a Study in Industrial Beginnings* (Boston: Houghton Mifflin Company, 1931), 19–23; William R. Bagnall, *The Textile Industry of the United States, Including Sketches and Notices of Cotton, Woolen, Silk and Linen Manufactures in the Colonial Period [1893]* (New York: Augustus M. Kelley, 1971), 152, 153, 155–59. Bagnall traces out a number of earlier attempts to promote and establish manufactures: see note 13, below.

5. Ware, *Early New England*, 27, 28.

6. David Hounshell, *From the American System to Mass Production, 1800–1932* (Baltimore: Johns Hopkins University Press, 1984), xv, xvi, 1; William H. Pierson, Jr., *Technology and the Picturesque: The Corporate and the Early Gothic Styles (American Buildings and Their Architects, volume 2)* (New York: Oxford University Press, 1978), 40; Kulik, "Beginnings," 96; Richard Candee, "New Towns of the Early New England Textile Industry," *Perspectives in Vernacular Architecture 1* (1982): 31; Brooke Hindle and Steven Lubar, *Engines of Change: The American Industrial Revolution, 1790–1860* (Washington, D.C.: Smithsonian Institution Press, 1986), 185.

7. Barrie Trinder, *The Making of the Industrial Landscape* (London: Phoenix Press, 1997), 62–64; Pierson, *Technology*, 31.

8. Fitch, *American Building*; Pierson, *Technology*; Handlin, *American Architecture*; Bryant Tolles, "Textile Mill Architecture in East Central New England: An Analysis of Pre–Civil War Design," *Essex Institute Historical Collections* 107 (1971): 223–53; Gary Kulik, "The Beginnings of the Industrial Revolution in America: Pawtucket, Rhode Island, 1672–1829" (PhD. diss., Brown University, 1980); Theodore Sande, et al., "American Industrial Architecture from the late Eighteenth to the Mid-Twentieth Century [conference session], *Journal of the Society of Architectural Historians* 35 (1976): 265–71; J. W. Lozier, "Rural Textile Mill Communities and the Transition to Industrialism in America, 1800–1840," *Working Papers from the Regional Economic History Research Center* 4 (1981) 4:78–96.

9. Bagnall, *Textile Industry*, 159, gives the dimensions. Although Pierson, *Technology*, 38, describes with greater precision than Bagnall the succession of additions made to the original structure, the two scholars agree on their general lines. However, the reported overall length of the building in its final form does not agree, Bagnall assigning 190 feet while Pierson gives 144. Bagnall and Pierson do agree that the two additions which extended the length of the original building along the line of its gable roof together consisted of 100 feet. If Bagnall's original building length is correct, 40 feet, then it would appear that Pierson's final length is closer to the actual measurement. Pierson, unfortunately, does not state the dimensions of the original building, though he does give evidence of the original roof configuration, later replaced to make a usable third floor.

10. *1798 Federal Direct Tax – Maryland, Arch. Md.Online*, 729:151, Anne Arundel County, Elk Ridge and Elk Ridge Landing Hundred, "B-List, Lands," D. J. & B. Ellicott, MSA; Mathews, *Andrew Ellicott*, facing page 6.

11. Tolles, "Textile Mill," 229, 230.

12. Ibid., 231; Pierson, *Technology*, 31, 32, 41, 42.

13. Bagnall, *Textile Industry*, 31, 41, 51, 61, 86, 97, 106, 112–34.

14. Ibid., 253.

15. Philip Scranton, *Proprietary Capitalism: The Textile Manufacture at Philadelphia, 1800–1885* (Philadelphia: Temple University Press, 1987), 12–17; John F. Kasson, *Civilizing the Machine: Technology and Republican Values in America, 1776–1900* (New York: Penguin Books, 1977), 73–79; Ware, *Early New England*, 60–61, 77–81; Pierson, *Technology*, 37–63; Lozier, "Rural," 229–36; Sande, "American Industrial," 265–71.

16. Pierson, *Technology*, 63; *1798 Federal Direct Tax – Maryland, Arch.Md.Online*, 729:156, Anne Arundel County, Elk Ridge and Elk Ridge Landing Hundred, "B-List, Lands," Christopher Johnston & Company, MSA; *Maryland Journal*, June 11, 1794, col. 7.

17. Ellicott insurance declarations, policies 1431–1434 (1804), Record of Policies B, Baltimore Equitable Society Collection, MS 3020, box 1; policies 2353, 2354 (1809), and policies 3018–3020 (1811), Record of Policies C, Baltimore Equitable Society Collection, MS 3020, box 2, MdHS; "Evans vs. Ellicott," *Baltimore Patriot*, June 1, 1815, p. 2; "Oliver Evans' Appeal," *Baltimore Patriot*, September 16, 1815, 3; Hezakiah Niles' *The Weekly Register*, addenda to volume 3 (1813), 1–16, second addenda to volume 5 (1814), 1–16, and volume 9 addendum (1816), 1–8. Given the similar configuration of the Hockley mill, I have presumed that it also was built for Evans's machinery.

18. Joseph Alibone Diary (1772), leaf 7 [pages unnumbered], Collection 3047, (PHi) AM .00607, Pennsylvania Historical Society; Baltimore County Deed Book WG EE, p. 480, January 15, 1790; Baltimore County Deed Book WG NN, p. 241, February 24, 1794; Ellicott insurance decorations, policy 16, February 26, 1808; policies 193 and 194, November 25, 1808; policies 198 and 199, November 26, 1808, Baltimore Fire Insurance Company Records, vol. 2, MS 75, MdHS; and policies 2314, 2315, 2316, February 15, 1809, Record of Policies C, Baltimore Equitable Society Collection, MS 3020, box 2, MdHS.

19. Pierson, *Technology*, 62.

20. William Nelson and Charles A. Shriner, *History of Paterson and Its Environs (the Silk City): Historical, Genealogical, Biographical* (New York: Lewis Historical Publishing Company, 1920), 318–20, 326–27; Michael Brewster Folsom and Steven D. Lubar, eds., *The Philosophy of Manufactures: Early Debates over Industrialization in the United States* (Cambridge: MIT Press, 1982), 99–100.

21. Nelson and Shriner, *Paterson*, 326–27.

22. Folsom and Lubar, *Philosophy*, 95; Bagnall, *Textile Industry*, 181–82; Nelson and Shriner, *Paterson*, 326–27.

23. Waltham I opened in 1813, and the Nightingale textile mill in Georgiaville, Rhode Island, in 1812, described by Pierson, *Technology*, 44, 45, figure 14. Pierson states that the Rhode Island textile developers came to favor stone construction, while their Massachusetts neighbors preferred to use brick. For further distinctions, see Richard M. Candee "Early New England Mill Towns of the Piscataqua River Valley, in John S. Garner, ed., *The Company Town, Architecture and Society in the Early Industrial Age* (New York: Oxford University Press, 1992), 111–38.

24. Bagnall, *Textile Industry*, 232–35; Ware, *Early New England*, 57–59.

Chapter Nine

1. "Notice," *Federal Intelligencer*, April 1, 1795, p. 2. U.S. Census, 1790, Maryland, Baltimore County, series M637, roll 3, p. 167, returns for John Ellicott and Jonathan Ellicott, Heritage Quest Online, http://www.heritagequestonline.com/hqoweb/library/do/index.

2. Baltimore County Deed Book WG A, p. 289; Baltimore County Deed Book WG C, p. 144; Baltimore County Deed Book WG C, p. 171; John Ellicott & Company Ledger E, p. 109.

3. Joseph Ellicott advertisement, *Maryland Journal*, April 4, 1780, col. 7; Evans, *Biographical*.

4. Baltimore County Deed Book WG K, pp. 12, 14, 142; Baltimore County Deed Book WG M, pp. 72, 526; Bond of Caleb Hall to John and

Andrew Ellicott, August 9, 1782, and Plat for Ellicotts' Dock, by George Gould Presbury, February 4, 1783, in "Deeds & Land Papers" Ledger, Joseph Ellicott Papers (1782–1814), MS 1825, MdHS; John Ellicott advertisement, *Maryland Journal,* January 28, 1783, p. 3.

5. "Road from Stigers Corner to Rogers Hill to Patapsco Falls," Baltimore County Court (Miscellaneous Plats) 1790, MSA C2042-5 and MSA C2042-6; "Road from Baltimore and Eutaw Sts. to bridge over Patapsco Falls," Baltimore County Court (Miscellaneous Plats) 1791, MSA C2042-8, MSA; John & Andrew Ellicott Company Ledger C, pp. 72, 88.

6. Anne Arundel County Deed Book NH 1, p. 203; Baltimore County Deed Book WG K, p. 145; Anne Arundel County Deed Book NH 2, pp. 67, 74; Baltimore County Deed Book WG X, pp. 535 and 538; Anne Arundel County Patent IC E 53, Mt. Vesuvius, October 20, 1787; Baltimore County Deed Book DD, p. 168; Anne Arundel County Deed Book NH 6, p. 703; Baltimore County Deed Book WG MM, p. 302; John & Andrew Ellicott Company Ledger B, p. 348, account for Oliver Matthews; General Court Land Records Deed Book JG 6, p. 254 ; Anne Arundel County patented certificates no. 779, Ilchester, and no. 1673, West Ilchester, S1189, MSA.

7. See Theodore Steinberg, *Nature Incorporated: Industrialization and the Waters of New England* (New York: Cambridge University Press, 1991); for Delaware, John F. Hart, "Property Rights, Costs, and Welfare: Delaware Water Mill Legislation, 1719–1859," *The Journal of Legal Studies* 27 (June 1998): 455, 461–69.

8. This deed, dated February 18, 1794, was not recorded but referenced and the tract described in Baltimore County Deed Book WG XX, p. 531, and in Baltimore County Deed Book WG 71, p. 593.

9. Ellicott, J. and A. Company Ledger, loose accounts, Maryland Manuscripts Collection, Series 4, Business and Other Financial Records, Item 766c, University of Maryland at College Park, Special Collections Division.

10. Baltimore County Deed Book WG 71, p. 597.

11. John & Andrew Ellicott Company Ledger C, p. 135; Ellicott & Company Ledger A, p. 94.

12. *Federal Gazette,* January 8, 1796, col. 5; Baltimore County Deed Book WG XX, p. 531.

13. *Federal Gazette,* December 18, 1797, col. 17; Baltimore County Deed Book WG 71, p. 593.

14. "View of Ellicotts' Mills, Md." (Baltimore: E. Sachse & Company, 1854), Library of Congress, Prints and Photographs Division, digital I.D. http://hdl.loc.gov/loc.pnp/pga.02596; and "Panoramic View of the Scenery on the Patapsco," ca. 1860, uncatalogued, MdHS; *Federal Gazette,* December 18, 1797, col. 17; Edward Gray insurance declaration, policy 4982, November 8, 1825, Pennsylvania Fire Insurance Company Records, Historical Society of Pennsylvania.

15. Judith A. McGaw, *Most Wonderful Machine: Mechanization and Social Change in Berkshire Paper Making, 1801–1885* (Princeton: Princeton University Press, 1987), 59; Lyman Horace Weeks, *History of Paper Manufacturing in the United States* (New York: The Lockwood Trade Journal Company, 1916), 58, 59.

16. *Federal Gazette,* December 18, 1797, col. 17.

17. McGaw, *Wonderful Machine:* 39–49, 117, 118; John W. Maxson Jr., "Papermaking in America: From Art to Industry, 1690–1860," *U.S. Library of Congress Quarterly Journal* 25 (1968) 2: 118, 122, 124–127.

18. *Federal Gazette,* December 18, 1797, col. 17; *Federal Gazette,* April ?, 1805, col. 17, as collected in Industrial Notes from Old Newspapers (1727–1805), MS 481, MdHS.

19. Maxson, "Papermaking," 129; Franklin Manufacturing Company insurance declaration, [no policy number] Record of Policies E, p. 368, Baltimore Equitable Society Collection, MS 3020, box 3, MdHS.

20. *Federal Gazette,* December 18, 1797, col. 17.

21. Ibid.; *Maryland Journal,* January 16, 1779, col. 1; Anne Arundel County Deed Book WSG 2, p. 119.

22. Scott, *Geographical Description*, 92, 93. I suspect that Scott's statement is an exaggeration. In 1810, annual production was 12,000 reams, significantly less than the "Levering & Co. on Gwynn's Falls . . . [which] make 40,000 reams per annum" ("Domestic Manufactures, Report," *Republican Star,* June 12, 1810, p. 2).

23. *Baltimore American,* January 6, 1813, col. 14.

24. Ibid.

25. D. W. Meinig, *The Shaping of America: A Geographical Perspective on 500 Years of History,* volume 2, *Continental America, 1800–1867* (New Haven: Yale University Press, 1993), 374–80, 390.

26. Elkridge Landing: Petition for a Town [1762], MS 2018, MdHS.

CHAPTER TEN

1. *Act to Incorporate the Union Manufacturing Company of Maryland* (Baltimore: John D. Toy, 1847), PAM 3182, MdHS.

2. *Maryland Herald,* August 17, 1803, p. 4; Joseph Scott, *Geographical Description of the States of Maryland and Delaware* (Philadelphia, 1807), 92; Advertisement, *Federal Gazette* (June 2, 1807, and March 23, 1808).

3. *Federal Republican,* June 14, 1810, p. 4; Scott, *Geographical Description*, 49, 78, 80, 91–93; Rosalie E. Calvert to H. J. Stier, November 19, 1803, and George Calvert to H. J. Stier, December 25, 1803, in Margaret Law Callcott, ed., *Mistress of Riversdale: The Plantation Letters of Rosalie Stier Calvert, 1795–1821* (Baltimore: Johns Hopkins University Press, 1991), 60, 66.

4. *Federal Gazette* May 24, 1808, col. 16.

5. Letter of Isaac Briggs to Thomas Jefferson, June 24, 1808, Briggs-Stabler Papers (1793–1910), MS 147, MdHS; Anne Arundel County Deed WSG 15, p. 531 (lots 10 and 11); *The [Baltimore] Republican,* February 2, 1802), p. 3.

6. Scott, *Geographical Description*, 49, 78, 80, 91–93.

7. John S. Pancake, "Baltimore and the Embargo, 1807–1809," *Maryland Historical Magazine* 47

(1952): 174–78, 186; Clark, *History of Manufactures*, 536; Bagnall, *Textile Industry,* 488.

8. *Federal Gazette,* January 4, 8, and 29, 1808, as collected in Industrial Notes from Old Newspapers (1727–1805), MS 481, MdHS; Pancake, "Embargo," 182, 183; Richard W. Griffin, "An Origin of the Industrial Revolution in Maryland: The Textile Industry, 1789–1826," *Maryland Historical Magazine* 61 (1966): 26.

9. Folsom and Lubar, *Philosophy,* 97.

10. *Report of the Committee and Constitution of the Union Manufacturing Company of Maryland* (Baltimore: Niles & Frailey, 1808), 10, PAM 3283, MdHS.

11. Folsom and Lubar, *Philosophy,* 99, 100; *Report of the Committee,* 17, PAM 3283, MdHS.

12. *Report of the Committee,* 15, PAM 3283, MdHS.

13. *Report of the Committee,* 18, PAM 3283, MdHS; untitled article, *Republican Star or Eastern Shore General Advertiser* March 15, 1808, p. 3; Bagnall, *Textile Industry,* 491, 492; *The North American* 1 (April 8, 1808): 3.

14. *Report of the Committee,* 14, PAM 3283, MdHS.

15. *Report of the Committee,* 16, PAM 3283, MdHS.

16. Ware, *Early New England,* 64, 65; Kasson, *Civilizing the Machine,* 69–71, 79; Meinig, *Continental America,* 393–96.

17. Meinig, *Continental America,* 395, 396.

18. Kasson, *Civilizing the Machine,* 93, 103.

19. Ibid., 6, 79, 106; Meinig, *Continental America,* 395–99; Anthony F. C. Wallace, *Rockdale: The Growth of an American Village in the Early Industrial Revolution* (New York: Knopf, 1978), xvi.

20. *Report of the Committee,* 16, PAM 3283, MdHS.

21. Thomas Jefferson, *Notes on the State of Virginia,* "Query XIX, Manufactures," in Merrill D. Peterson, ed., *The Portable Thomas Jefferson* (New York: Penguin Books, 1981), 216, 217; Leo Marx, *The Machine in the Garden: Technology and the Pastoral Ideal in America* (London: Oxford University Press, 1977), 141–44, 375–79; Kasson, *Civilizing the Machine,* viii.

22. *Federal Gazette and Baltimore Daily Advertiser,* March 1, 1808, pp. 2, 3.

23. Appleby, *Capitalism,* 88, but see also, 86–88, 94–96, 99, 104, 105.

24. Ibid., 99.

25. *Baltimore American,* March 9, 1808, col. 14; *Federal Gazette,* March 14, 1808, as collected in Industrial Notes from Old Newspapers (1727–1805), MS 481, MdHS; Bagnall, *Textile Industry,* 492, 493; Baltimore County Deed Book WG 99, p. 277; Baltimore County Deed Book WG 109, p. 51, corrected on p. 123, and Anne Arundel County Deed Book NH 16, p. 302; Anne Arundel County patented certificate no. 1102, Oella, S1189, MSA; Baltimore County Deed Book WG 104, p. 274.

25. "Union Manufacturing Company of Maryland," *Baltimore American,* January 4, 1809, p. 2.

27. Union Manufacturing Company Accounting, 1827, Carroll-McTavish Papers, item 3620, MS 220, MdHS [hereinafter Carroll-McTavish Papers]; Bagnall, *Textile Industry,* 495.

28. *North American and Mercantile Daily Advertiser,* July 18, 1808), p. 3; *Federal Gazette,* July 19, 1808; "Union Manufacturing Company of Maryland," *Baltimore American,* January 4, 1809, p. 2; *Records of the 1820 Census of Manufacturers [microform]: Schedules for Maryland* (Washington, D.C.: U.S. Census Office, 1820), 88 (return no. 99, "[Union] Manufacturing Company of Maryland,") MICRO 406, MdHS; Bagnall, *Textile Industry,* 494.

29. Precise figures are difficult to come by, and the ones I have presented are not exact but do have comparative value. Unfortunately the 1800 federal census returns for Baltimore County were lost, "failed" in the words of the census records for Maryland. The 1810 census return page containing the Ellicotts is illegible, though Mendenhall's successor, John Conrad, lists a total of twelve individuals (U.S. Census, 1800, Maryland, Baltimore County, series M32, roll 9, pp. 413, 414; U.S. Census, 1810, Maryland, Baltimore County, series M252, roll 13, pp. 78, 345, Heritage Quest Online, http:// www.heritagequestonline.com/hqoweb/library/do/index). The 1820 manufacturers' census return for the Ellicotts lists twenty adult men at work in the mills plus five adult men and thirteen boys employed in two ironworks: the Ellicotts' Mills rolling mill and another facility by then in operation at Avalon, the site of Dorsey's forge (*Records of the 1820 Census of Manufacturers [microform]: Schedules for Maryland* [Washington, D.C.: U.S. Census Office, 1820], 94, 107 [return no. 105, Ellicotts' Mills, and return no. 118, Ellicotts Ironworks], MICRO 406, MdHS).

30. Bagnall, *Textile Industry,* 493; *Niles Register* 4 (1813): 173.

31. *Records of the 1820 Census of Manufacturers [microform]: Schedules for Maryland* (Washington, D.C.: U.S. Census Office, 1820), 88 (return no. 99, "[Union] Manufacturing Company of Maryland,") MICRO 406, MdHS; Margaret Kinard Latimer, ed., "Sir Augustus Foster in Maryland," *Maryland Historical Magazine* 47 (1952): 291, 292. Foster visited in 1811–1812.

32. Robert L. Alexander, "Drawings and Allegories of Maximilian Godefroy," *Maryland Historical Magazine* 53 (1958): 27–31; "Union Manufacturing Company of Maryland," *Baltimore American,* January 4, 1809), p. 2.

33. Alexander, in "Drawings and Allegories," recognized the allegory of "agriculture, commerce, [and] navigation," but the more detailed reading presented here is mine.

34. John McGrain, "Oella Mill Village Historical Background," copy in the Maryland Historical Trust Office of Survey, Research, and Registration, Vertical Files, Baltimore County, Oella Historic District; Latimer, "Foster," 291; *Baltimore Patriot,* May 26, 1813, p. 3.

35. Anne Arundel County patented certificate no. 1102, Oella, S1189, MSA.

36. *Records of the 1820 Census of Manufacturers [microform]: Schedules for Maryland* [Washington, D.C.: U.S. Census Office, 1820], 88 [return no. 99, "[Union] Manufacturing Company of Maryland,"] MICRO 406, MdHS.

37. "Union Manufacturing Company of Maryland," *Baltimore American,* January 4, 1809, p. 2.

38. Ibid.; Bagnall, *Textile Industry,* 493.

39. "Union Manufacturing Company of Maryland," *Baltimore American,* January 4, 1809, p. 2; *1798 Federal Direct Tax – Maryland,* Arch. Md.Online, 729:160, Anne Arundel County, Elk Ridge and Elk Ridge Landing Hundred, "B-List, Lands," Charles Ridgely Carnan, MSA; Baltimore County Deed Book UU, pp. 320, 322.

40. Bagnall, *Textile Industry,* 183, 184, 492, 493; "Domestic Manufactures, Report," *Republican Star or Eastern Shore General Advertiser,* June 12, 1810, p. 2; *Federal Gazette,* July 19, 1808. I believe that Bagnall conflates the opening of the experimental facility in October 1809 (containing 800 spindles, a number confirmed in the 1810 *Republican Star* story above), with the actual first factory, which opened in May 1810 with a far greater spindle capacity, per company president Robert Miller's statement in the 1820 manufacturers' census. Policy 206, November 29, 1808, Baltimore Fire Insurance Company Records, volume 2, MS 75, MdHS.

41. "Union Manufacturing Company of Maryland," *Republican Star and General Advertiser,* December 10, 1822, p. 1; Bagnall, *Textile Industry,* 492, 493, contradicted by *Niles Register,* November 20, 1813, p. 207.

42. David J. Jeremy, "Innovation in American Textile Technology During the Early Nineteenth Century," *Technology and Culture* 14 (January 1973): 41–45.

43. "Domestic Manufactures, Report," *Republican Star or Eastern Shore General Advertiser,* June 12, 1810, p. 2.

44. Jeremy "Innovation," 44, 45; Bagnall, *Textile Industry,* 494.

45. "Domestic Manufactures, Report," *Republican Star or Eastern Shore General Advertiser,* June 12, 1810, p. 2; "Union Manufacturing Company of Maryland," *Republican Star and General Advertiser,* December 10, 1822, p. 1; Bagnall, *Textile Industry,* 493, 494. Bagnall has reversed the number of spindles operating in the first and second Union Manufacturing Company mills, figures which are correctly given in the published Union Manufacturing Company accounting of 1827 (Carroll-McTavish Papers); Olson, *Baltimore: The Building of an American City,* 42; Scharf, *History of Baltimore,* 407, 408.

46. Bagnall, *Textile Industry,* 494.

47. *Records of the 1820 Census of Manufacturers [microform]: Schedules for Maryland* (Washington, D.C.: U.S. Census Office, 1820), 88 (return no. 99, "[Union] Manufacturing Company of Maryland,") MICRO 406, MdHS; "Union Manufacturing Company of Maryland," *Republican Star and General Advertiser,* December 10, 1822.

48. *Records of the 1820 Census of Manufacturers [microform]: Schedules for Maryland* (Washington, D.C.: U.S. Census Office, 1820), 88 (return no. 99, "[Union] Manufacturing Company of Maryland,") MICRO 406, MdHS.

49. Letter of Isaac Briggs to Hanna Briggs, December 20, 1815, Isaac Briggs Personal Correspondence, Briggs-Stabler Papers (1793–1910), MS 147, MdHS.

50. Union Manufacturing Company Accounting, 1827, Carroll-McTavish Papers.

51. *Records of the 1820 Census of Manufacturers [microform]: Schedules for Maryland* (Washington, D.C.: U.S. Census Office, 1820), 88 (return no. 99, [Union] Manufacturing Company of Maryland), 22 (return no. 27, Patapsco Manufacturing Company), MICRO 406, MdHS; Latimer, "Foster," 291; "Cotton Manufactures in Maryland, January, 1859," *Journal of Mining Manufactures, and Art,* in, *Hunt's Magazine* 40 (January 1859): 374–76. 374; Jeremy, "Innovation," 48.

52. Jeremy, "Innovation," 44–46, 73–76.

53. Kasson, *Civilizing the Machine,* 71–79; Scranton, *Proprietary,* 17, 18; Ware, *Early New England,* 301, 302; Pierson, *Technology,* 64, 65.

54. Bagnall, *Textile Industry,* 120; Letter of William Patterson to Matthew Carey, May 15, 1819, Matthew Carey Section, vol. 1, no. 251, Edward

Carey Gardiner Collection, Collection 227A, Historical Society of Pennsylvania.

55. Union Manufacturing Company Accounting, 1827, Carroll-McTavish Papers; Bagnall, *Textile Industry*, 495, contradicted in, "Cotton Manufacturies in Maryland, January, 1859," *Journal of Mining Manufactures, and Art*, in, *Hunt's Magazine*, January 1859, 374.

56. Anne Arundel County Deed Book WSG 1: 445 and Baltimore County Deed Book WG 116, p. 318; Chancery Court Case 2086, October 19, 1812, Chancery Record 84, p. 205, MSA S512-3-2156, MSA; Baltimore County Deed Book WG 121, pp. 550, 553; Baltimore County Deed Book WG 123, pp. 488, 490; Baltimore County Deed Book WG 129, p. 180; "An Act to Incorporate the Patapsco Manufacturing Company," *Session Laws, 1815, Arch.Md.Online*, 634:151, MSA.

57. *Federal Gazette*, July 3, 1813, August 16, 1813; *Baltimore American*, February 8, 1814.

58. *Federal Gazette* or *American*, February 17, 1815, as collected in Industrial Notes from Old Newspapers (1727–1805), MS 481, MdHS.

59. Edward Gray insurance declaration, policy 4982, November 8, 1825, Pennsylvania Fire Insurance Company Records, Historical Society of Pennsylvania.

60. *Niles Register* 9 (1816) supplement, 183; *Niles Register* 17 (1820): 376; *Records of the 1820 Census of Manufacturers [microform]: Schedules for Maryland* (Washington, D.C.: U.S. Census Office, 1820), 22 (return no. 27, Patapsco Manufacturing Company), MICRO 406, MdHS.

61. Waltham I: 40 x 90, four stories plus gambrel story = 18,000 square feet; Union I: 44 x 106, five stories plus garret = 27,984; Union II: 44 x 110, five stories plus garret = 29,040; Patapsco I: 40 x 100, five stories = 20,000; Patapsco II: three stories plus gambrel story = 16,000. I infer the number of stories in Patapsco I (pre-fire) from a newspaper article that gives the overall dimensions of the building, 40 x 100 x 60 high, (*Niles Register* 9 (1816) supplement, 183). Isaac Briggs made numerous notes in this period relative to cotton manufacturing, and a factory

description he presents gives 11.5 feet elevation per floor; I have rounded this to 12 feet to obtain five stories (Isaac Briggs Notebook 3, no page number, Briggs-Stabler Papers (1793–1910), MS 147).

62. *Federal Gazette* or *American*, February 17, 1815, as collected in, Industrial Notes from Old Newspapers (1727–1805), MS 481, MdHS; *American* April 28, June 23, and August 29, 1815, col. 4.

63. *Session Laws, 1815, Arch.Md.Online*, 634:151, 153, "An Act to Incorporate the Patapsco Manufacturing Company," MSA.

64. *Records of the 1820 Census of Manufacturers [microform]: Schedules for Maryland* (Washington, D.C.: U.S. Census Office, 1820), 22 (return no. 27, Patapsco Manufacturing Company), MICRO 406, MdHS; *Baltimore Patriot & Mercantile Advertiser*, June 15, 1818, p. 2.

65. *Records of the 1820 Census of Manufacturers [microform]: Schedules for Maryland* (Washington, D.C.: U.S. Census Office, 1820), 22 (return no. 27, Patapsco Manufacturing Company), MICRO 406, MdHS.

66. *Records of the 1820 Census of Manufacturers [microform]: Schedules for Maryland* (Washington, D.C.: U.S. Census Office, 1820), 88 (return no. 99, [Union] Manufacturing Company of Maryland), MICRO 406, MdHS; Union Manufacturing Company Accounting, 1827, Carroll-McTavish Papers; "Proposals Wanted," *Baltimore Patriot*, May 16, 1821, p. 2; Sparks, "Baltimore," 128.

67. Sparks, "Baltimore," 128; Baltimore County Deed Book WG 175, p. 50; Baltimore County Deed Book WG 169, p. 770; Chancery Court Case 11452, July 10, 1820, Chancery Court (Chancery Papers) 1713–1853, Chancery Record 116: 347, MSA S512-14-11280, MSA; Baltimore County Deed Book WG 162, p. 299; Baltimore County Deed Book WG 163, p. 747; Baltimore County Deed Book WG 167, p. 60; Anne Arundel County Deed Book WSG 9, p. 205; Anne Arundel County Deed Book WSG 9, p. 294; Baltimore County Deed Book WG 173, p. 714.

68. Alexander Fridge correspondence, 4/80 and 4/81, Emigrants' Letters Collection, British Library of Political and Economic Science, London School of Economics; "Fridge and Morris," *Federal Republican & Commercial Gazette,* May 12, 1809, p. 3, September 12, 1809, p. 1, and II September 15, 1810, p. 3; *Baltimore Patriot,* November 10, 1815, p. 1; Sparks, "Baltimore," 128; "View of Ellicotts' Mills, Md." (Baltimore: E. Sachse & Company, 1854), Library of Congress , Prints and Photographs Division, digital I.D. http://hdl.loc.gov/loc.pnp/pga.02596.

69. "Water Power," *Baltimore Patriot,* September 10, 1821, p. 2; Caleb Dorsey of Caleb and Caleb Dorsey of Thomas vs. Samuel Ellicott, Rachel Ellicott, George Ellicott, Evan T. Ellicott, Nathaniel Ellicott, and William Kenworthy, Estate of John Ellicott, Baltimore City Circuit Court, Equity Papers (in particular the Bond to Fridge and Morris, folder 5, and the Deed to Fridge and Morris, folder 6), MSA C 186-3, MSA; Baltimore County Deed Book 169, p. 29, confirming an unrecorded deed executed February 13, 1822.

70. Baltimore County Deed Book 169, p. 29.

71. "Mr. Fridge, Mr. Morris . . . Petition to lay out a road from Thistle Factory to Baltimore and Frederick town turnpike," August 5, 1823, with endorsement of August 7, 1824, Baltimore County Court, Land Commission Papers Plat, MSA C 349-11, MSA.

72. Sparks, "Baltimore," 128, gives the "number of persons at present employed within the works," but the 1820 Mfg Census returns for the individual textile enterprises report significantly lower numbers of actual employees.

73. Frederick William Coburn, *History of Lowell and Its People* (New York: Lewis Historical Publishing Company, 1920), 1:162, 218.

Coda

1. La Rochefoucauld, *Travels,* English edition, 2:125.

2. William Howard Russell, *My Diary North and South* (London: Bradbury and Evans, 1863), 290.

3. *Maryland Gazette,* July 24, 1766, and October 19, 1786; as noted in the "Milling" folder, Industrial Notes from Old Newspapers, Ms 481, MdHS.

4. "The Late Freshet at Baltimore," *Niles Weekly Register,* August 16, 1817, pp. 191–95.

5. "Destructive Rain Storm," *Baltimore County Union,* October 20, 1866, p. 2. "The water at Ellicott's Mills was two feet higher than during the memorable freshet of 1817. . . ."

6. Henry T. Tuckerman, *The Life of John Pendleton Kennedy* (New York: G. P. Putnam & Sons, 1871), 141, described the valley in this way: "In the palmy days of the township, before flood and fire had marred its prosperity. . . ." For the floods, see: "The Late Freshet at Baltimore," *Niles Weekly Register,* August 16, 1817, pp. 191–95; "Dreadful Inundation," *Baltimore Sun,* June 16,1837, p. 2; "Further Damage by the Storm and Freshet," *Baltimore Sun,* October 12, 1847, p. 4; "Destructive Rain Storm," *Baltimore Sun,* October 12, 1866, p. 1; "The Flood at Ellicott City," *Baltimore Sun,* July 25, 1868, p. 1.

7. Kennedy to Washington Irving, June 19, 1854, as quoted in Tuckerman, *Life of John Pendleton Kennedy,* 386; see also Kennedy's journal entries for May 26–31 and June 30, 1854, in *Journals,* vol. 8, and August 7, 1854, in *Journals,* vol. 9, John Pendleton Kennedy Papers [microform]/editor John B. Boles (Wilmington, Del.: Scholarly Resources, 1972).

8. Kennedy to Washington Irving, August 8, 1854, as quoted in Tuckerman, *Life of John Pendleton Kennedy,* 388. The willows are mentioned in Kennedy to Irving, June 19, 1854, quoted in Tuckerman, *Life,* 386.

9. Kennedy to Irving, August 8, 1854, quoted in Tuckerman, *Life of John Pendleton Kennedy,* 388.

10. *Journals,* vol. 1, October 11, 1847, Kennedy Papers. Most mill dams on the Patapsco were constructed of wood. See also, *Journals,* vol. 4, October 8, 1850: "the Thistle dam, which the owners are now renewing. Saw Mr. Carr there, the manager. Asked him to be particular about the line . . . which regulates the height of that

dam. He tells me he has been very careful in setting the new timbers to adjust the ridge or upper beam."

11. *Journals*, vol. 4, September 2, 1850, Kennedy Papers.

12. Ibid., vol. 11, September 17 and 18, 1859, Kennedy Papers.

13. Ibid., vol. 15, November 4, 1868, Kennedy Papers.

14. Ibid.

15. Tuckerman, *Life of John Pendleton Kennedy*, 144, 490. Kennedy died August 18, 1870.

16. "Destructive Rain Storm," *Baltimore County Union*, October 20, 1866, p. 2.

17. [H.] Wirt [Shriver] to [Frederick] A. [Shriver], October 11, 1866, Shriver Family Papers, Ms 2085, MdHS.

18. "Destructive Rain Storm," *Baltimore Sun*, October 12, 1866, p. 1.

19. *Baltimore Sun*, October 12, 1866; *Baltimore County Union*, October 20, 1866.

20 Richard Townsend, Diary, 2:1020, October 1866, transcription in the possession of Charles Wagandt, Baltimore, Maryland.

21. The foundry perhaps incorporated the former Ellicott Iron Rolling and Slitting Mill. Its description is given in an auction advertisement appearing in the January 3, 1863, issue of the *Baltimore American*.

22 *Baltimore Sun*, October 12, 1866; *Baltimore County Union*, October 20, 1866.

23. *Baltimore Sun*, October 12, 1866.

24. Townsend, Diary, 2:1057, July 1868. Mrs. L. F. Ryan to John [M. Gordon], July 27, 1868, Gordon-Blackford Papers, Ms 398, John M. Gordon Family Correspondence, MdHS.

25. In their initial reports of the flood on Saturday, July 25, both the *Sun* and the *Baltimore American* stated that rainfall was quite heavy without giving a precise location for the downpour. The *Sun* repeated this assertion on the morning of Monday, July 27. On the afternoon of the twenty-seventh, however, the *Baltimore American* issued a story based on the testimony of identified witnesses in Ellicott City who indicated that the rainfall there was moderate. The *American* published additional stories on July 28, 29 and 30, the latter two reprinted respectively from the *Howard County Record* and the *Ellicott City Common Sense*, which corroborated the moderate rainfall story at Ellicott City. Certainly a tremendously heavy rainfall occurred, but all indications are that the flood reached Ellicott City first, before the drenching rains, which moved east into Baltimore County later in the morning, as the *Baltimore County Union* reported on August 1.

26. "The Flood at Ellicott City," *Baltimore American*, July 27, 1868, pp. 1, 4; "The Great Flood," *Baltimore County Union*, August 1, 1868, p. 2, identifies the *American* reporter by name. "Another Account of the Disaster at Ellicott City," *Baltimore American*, July 29, 1868, p. 4, quotes the shopkeeper story from the *Howard County Record*.

27. "Description of the Storm on the Baltimore and Ohio Railroad," and James M. Dalsell, "A Description of the Tornado of 24th of July, 1868," *Baltimore Weekly American*, August 8, 1868, p. 4. Dalsell's account places the storm's duration at six hours, the other at eight. After agreeing on most salient points, the accounts' differences here suggest exaggeration, though one may be sure that however long the passengers actually were trapped by the deluge, it no doubt was several hours.

28. *Baltimore Weekly American*, August 8, 1868, p. 4.

29. Ibid.; P. Unger, "The Great Flood," *Ellicott City Common Sense*, July 29, 1868.

30. "The Flood at Ellicott City," *Baltimore Sun*, July 27, 1868, p. 1; "The Damage at Ellicott City and Vicinity," *Baltimore Sun*, July 30, 1868, p. 1.

31. Townsend, Diary, 2:1058–62, July–October 1868. Paradoxically, Richard Townsend calls the injured mill at Union "the upper mill." Townsend also states that of two functioning mills at Union, only one was damaged, making it hard to believe that the possibly corresponding "lower" mill was the one uninjured. However, "upper," in this case may refer to the

factory building at the very end of the millrace; it was sited perpendicular to the river, and its lowest stories were probably close enough to the water to have been the ones flooded. Townsend says that water "came into the Card Room, in the Second story of the upper Mill," Diary, 2:1058, July 1868. *The Ellicott City Common Sense*, July 29, 1868, states that because of its relatively high elevation the Union complex "suffered but little damage." The *Sun*, July 27, 1868, suggests that the Granite complex "resisted the torrent for a while."

32. "The Flood at Ellicott City," *Baltimore Sun*, July 25, 1868, p. 1, gives the thickness of the Granite Factory wall. A lease of William W. Spence to George W. Sands, October 26, 1864, Howard 23/582, suggests that the pre-1866 Granite dam was a wooden frame containing fill material. Presumably the post-1866 dam was of similar construction. *Baltimore American*, July 27, 1868, p. 1; this story also states that the spray rose twenty feet. *Baltimore American*, January 3, 1863, gives the building description.

33. P. Unger, "The Great Flood," *Ellicott City Common Sense*, July 29, 1868.

34. Dr. Owings's first name is given in "County Items, Destructive Rain Storm," *Baltimore County Union*, October 20, 1866, p. 2, in relation to losses he suffered in the 1866 flood. P. Unger, of the *Common Sense*, July 29, 1868, spells Mrs. Owings' name alternatively as "Margaretha."

35. "Further Particulars of the Melancholy Disaster at Ellicott City," *Baltimore Sun*, July 28, 1868, p. 1. "Further Particulars of the Destruction of Ellicott City," *Baltimore American*, July 28, 1868, p. 4. *Ellicott City Common Sense*, July 29, 1868. Lishear's store, the brick building injured here in the 1866 flood, had been reconstructed by July 1868.

36. *Ellicott City Common Sense*, July 29, 1868.

37. Ibid.

38. Ibid.; *Baltimore American*, July 27, 1868, pp. 1, 4.

39. *Baltimore Sun*, July 28, 1868, p. 1, repeated in the *American*, July 28, 1868, p. 4.

40. *Ellicott City Common Sense*, July 29, 1868. I have relied most heavily here on Unger's story, with elaborations from the *Sun* and *American*. It is unfortunate that later issues of the *Common Sense* appear not to have survived.

41. *Ellicott City Common Sense*, July 29, 1868; *Baltimore American*, July 27, 1868, pp. 1, 4.

42. *Baltimore American*, July 27, 1868, pp. 1, 4. The *Howard County Record* story, reprinted in the *Baltimore American* of July 29, 1868, gives Koehl's rank as captain. Since this report includes numerous errors, the identification of rank is not reliable. The same story gives Parrish's name as Edwin.

43. "The Flood Beyond the City," *Baltimore American*, July 25, 1868, p. 4.

44. *Baltimore Sun*, July 28, 1868, p. 1. Robert Tyson did not own the Ilchester Mill, as the *Sun* reporter stated; see the lease of George Ellicott to Robert Tyson, June 27, 1864, Baltimore County 42/41, also recorded in the Howard 23/247.

45. *Ellicott City Common Sense*, July 29, 1868; *Baltimore American*, July 25, 1868, p. 4; *Baltimore Sun*, July 28, 1868, p. 1.

46. Mrs. L. F. Ryan to John [M. Gordon], July 27, 1868, Gordon-Blackford Papers, John M. Gordon Family Correspondence, MS 398, MdHS.

47. Dawson Lawrence, "Historical Sketch of Howard County, Md.," in G. M. Hopkins, *Atlas of Howard County Maryland*, (Philadelphia: F. Bourquin's Steam Lithographic Press, 1878), [no page numbers]. For literary effect, Lawrence referred to himself in the third person.

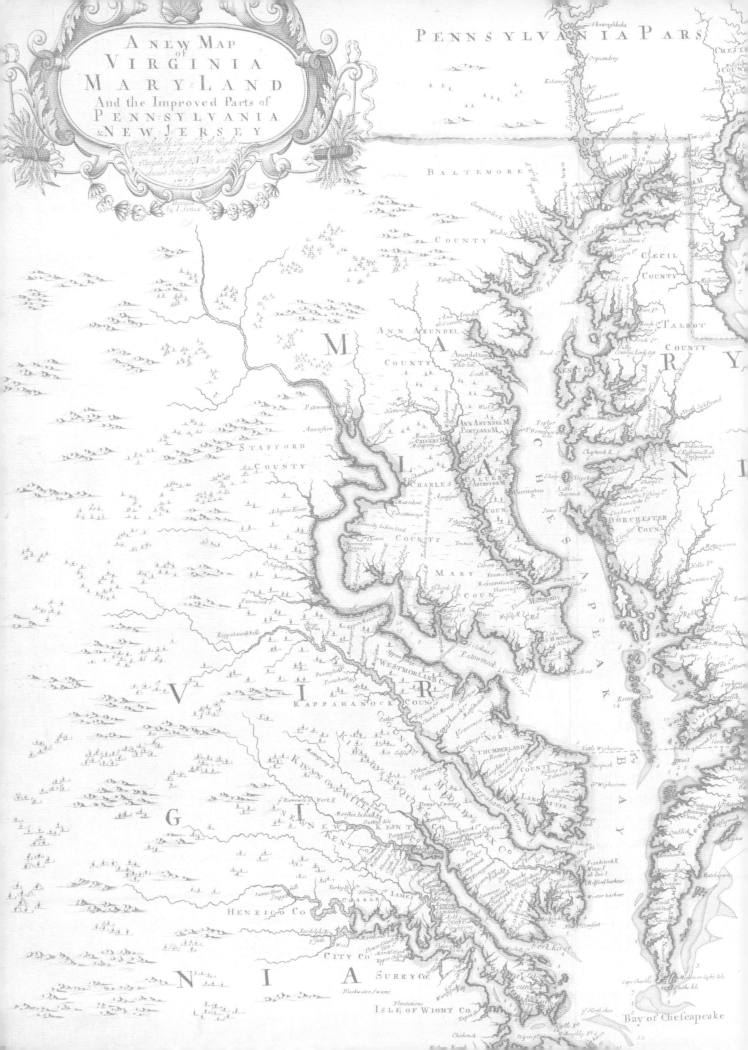